THE UNDYING FLAME

Judaic Traditions in Literature, Music, and Art

Ken Frieden and Harold Bloom, Series Editors

The Undying Flame
BALLADS AND SONGS OF THE HOLOCAUST

Jerry Silverman

110 Songs in 16 Languages with Extensive Historical Notes,
Illustrations, Piano Arrangements, Guitar Chords,
and Singable English Translations

Syracuse University Press

Copyright © 2002 by Jerry Silverman
All Rights Reserved

New Edition 2020
(Does not include CD)

20 21 22 23 24 25   6 5 4 3 2 1

For a listing of books published and distributed by Syracuse University Press, visit https://press.syr.edu.

ISBN: 978-0-8156-0709-0 (Paperback)

The many facets of Jerry Silverman's background and experience combine to make him one of this country's most prolific authors of music books as well as a teacher, guitarist, and folksinger. He has a bachelor's degree in music from the City College of New York and a master's degree in musicology from New York University. For his master's thesis he chose a unique subject: blues guitar technique. He has authored or edited some two hundred books with such wide-ranging titles as *Folk Blues, How to Play the Guitar, The Immigrant Song Book, The Liberated Woman's Song Book, The Yiddish Song Book, Ballads and Songs of the Civil War, The Complete Chorales of J. S. Bach,* to name but a few.

The Undying Flame is a logical and natural extension of his life's work, the appreciation and preservation of the musical and lyrical expression of "real people" who have had something important to say.

Contents

Illustrations — xi

On Translations, Musical Arrangements, and Copyrights — xiii

Introduction — xv

Acknowledgments — xxvii

The Gathering Storm, 1933–1939

Germany First, 1933

1. Die Moorsoldaten
   The Peat-Bog Soldiers — 3

2. Das Einheitsfrontlied
   The United Front Song — 6

3. Mein Vater wird Gesucht
   My Father, He Was Tracked — 9

4. Das jüdische Kind
   The Jewish Child — 11

5. Ich hab' kein Heimatland
   I Have No Native Land — 13

6. Buchenwald-Lied
   Buchenwald Song — 15

7. Dachau-Lied (a)
   Dachau Song (a) — 18

8. Dachau-Lied (b)
   Dachau Song (b) — 21

9. Ballade von der Judenhure Marie Sanders
   Ballad of the Jews'-Whore Marie Sanders — 23

From Spanish Trenches, 1936-1939

10. Hans Beimler — 26

11. Lied der Internationalen Brigaden
    Song of the International Brigades — 28

12. Die Thälmann-Kolonne
    The Thaelmann Column — 30

13. Jarama Valley — 32

14. Viva la Quince Brigada
    Long Live the Fifteenth Brigade — 34

15. Si Me Quieres Escribir
    If You Want to Write to Me — 36

16. Venga Jaleo
    Join in the Struggle — 39

17. Los Cuatro Generales
    The Four Insurgent Generals — 41

Shoah, 1940–1945

18. Gehat Hob Ikh A Heym
    Oh, Once I Had a Home — 44

19. Vu Ahin Zoll Ikh Geyn?
    Where, O Where Shall I Go? — 46

20. Gib A Brokhe Tsu Dayn Kind
    Bless the Child That Cries to Thee — 48

21. Mayn Mame Hot Gevolt Zayn Af Mayn Khasene
    My Mother Wanted So to See My Wedding Day — 50

22. Lid Fun Bug
    Song of the River Bug — 52

23. Makh Tsu Di Eygelekh
    Now Close Your Little Eyes — 54

24. Nit Keyn Rozhinkes, Nit Keyn Mandlen
    Neither Raisins Nor Almonds — 56

25. Tsi Darf Es Azoy Zayn?
    And Must It Be This Way? — 59

26. Tsu Eyns, Tsvey, Dray!
    So, One, Two, Three! — 62

27. Tsigaynerlid
    Gypsy Song — 65

#	Title	Translation	Page
28.	Far Vos Iz Der Himl?	Say, Why Was the Sky?	68
29.	Shlof, Mayn Kind	Sleep, My Child	70
30.	Motele Fun Varshaver Geto	Motele from the Warsaw Ghetto	71
31.	Der Hof-Zinger Fun Varshaver Geto	The Street Singer of the Warsaw Ghetto	74
32.	Varshe	Warsaw	76
33.	Minutn Fun Bitokhn	Moments of Confidence	78
34.	Treblinke	Treblinka	80
35.	Rivkele, Di Shabesdike	Rivkele, the Sabbath-Widow	83
36.	In Kriuvke	In the Dugout	86
37.	Unter Di Khurves Fun Poyln	Under the Ruins of Poland	88
38.	Aroys Iz In Vilne A Nayer Bafel	In Vilna Was Issued a Brand-New Decree	90
39.	Vilner Geto Lid	Song of the Vilna Ghetto	93
40.	Shtil, Di Nakht	Still, the Night	96
41.	Itsik Vitenberg		98
42.	Yeder Ruft Mikh Ziamele	People Call Me Ziamele	100
43.	S'Dremlin Feygl	Birds Are Dozing	102
44.	Yugnt-Himn	Youth Hymn	104
45.	Neyn, Neyn, Neyn	No, No, No	106
46.	Zog Nit Keynmol	Never Say	108
47.	Undzer Mut Vet Nit Gebrokhn	Our Courage Is Unbroken / Le Chant de Pithiviers — The Song of Pithiviers	111
48.	Mir Lebn Ebig	We Live Forever	114
49.	Ani Ma-amin	I Believe	116
50.	Parpar	Butterfly	118
51.	Skharkhoret	Dizzy	120
52.	M'khol Masada	Oh, Masada	122
53.	Mah Ko Mashma Lon?	What Is the Meaning?	125
54.	Le Chant des Partisans	The Song of the Partisans	128
55.	Le Maquisard	The Resistance Fighter	131
56.	Das Ende	The End	132
57.	Auschwitz-Lied	Auschwitz Song	133
58.	Żywe kamienie/Die lebenden Steine	The Living Stones	136
59.	Frauenlager	Women's Camp	139
60.	Wir Singen Ein Schlager/We Zingen Een Lied	We're Singing a Song	140
61.	Die Westerbork-Serenade	The Westerbork Serenade	142
62.	Wenn Ein Paketchen Kommt	When a Small Package Comes	146
63.	Det Har Vi	This Have We	148
64.	Przed Ostatnią Podróżą	Before the Last Journey	152

65. Warszawo Ma
    My Warsaw *156*

66. Pesnia Belostokskikh Partizanov
    Song of the Bialystok Partisans *158*

67. Katiusha *160*

68. Svyashchennaya Voina
    The Sacred War *162*

69. Kak U Duba Starovo
    Standing near the Old Oak Tree *164*

70. Oi, Tumany Moyi
    Oh, the Fog *166*

71. Ásó Kapa Vállamon
    On My Shoulder, Spade and Hoe *168*

72. Partigiani In Montagna
    Partisans in the Mountain *170*

73. Bella Ciao
    So Long, Dear *172*

74. Scarpe Rotte
    Worn-Out Shoes *176*

75. Domovina
    Homeland *178*

76. Embross, ELAS
    Forward, ELAS *179*

Theresienstadt and the Emigrant Cabarets

77. Theresienstadt *182*

78. Theresienstadt, die schönste Stadt der Welt
    Theresienstadt, the Best Town in the World *184*

79. Bad Blockhaus
    Blockhouse Resort *187*

80. Theresienstädter Fragen
    Theresienstadt Questions *190*

81. Als Ob
    As If *194*

82. Der Reisepaß Erzählt
    The Passport Relates *196*

83. Die Novaks aus Prag
    The Novaks from Prague *200*

84. Die Kosmopolitin
    The Cosmopolitain *204*

85. Transport *207*

86. Diese Emigranten!
    These Emigrants! *210*

87. Und die Musik spielt dazu
    And the Music Just Plays On *212*

88. Doch auch für uns kommt mal die Zeit
    Yet Soon for Us Will Come the Time *216*

89. Dopis
    The Letter *220*

90. Motýl
    Butterfly *222*

91. Máj 1945
    May 1945 *224*

Kaddish: A Post-War Retrospective

92. A Mol Iz Geven A Mayse
    I'll Tell to You All a Story *228*

93. Én Még Most Kicsi Vagyok
    I Am Still a Little Child *230*

94. Waterlooplein
    Waterloo Square *232*

95. O Mis Hermanos
    O My Brothers *238*

96. Asma Asmaton
    Song of Songs *245*

97. Bukhenval'dskii Nabat
    Buchenwald Alarm *249*

98. Lady of the Harbor *252*

99. Children of Poland *256*

100. Unter Der Gelber Late
     Under the Yellow Patch *258*

101. Denmark 1943	260	109. We Are Here	288
102. Tattoo	266	110. Kaddish	292
103. Last Train to Nuremberg	270	In Memoriam—Warsaw Ghetto	293
104. My Name Is Lisa Kalvelage	272	Notes	295
105. Anton Schmidt	275	Bibliography	299
106. We Didn't Know	277	Index of Song Titles	301
107. Auschwitz	280	Index of First Lines	303
108. Rain Falls Down in Amsterdam	282		

Illustrations

American soldiers of the 12th Armored Division	xv
Program cover of *Abschiedsvorstellung*	xx
Program of the *Bunter Abend* in the Westerbork Cabaret	xxii
Volume of antifascist poetry by Bill Silverman	xxiv
Pete Seeger, Jerry Silverman, and family	xxvii
Paul Robeson visits Camp Wo-Chi-Ca, with Silverman and campers	xxvii
French stamps	5
Jerry Silverman on Jüdenstraße, [East] Berlin, 1959	12
"Der Appellplatz" (The Roll-Call Yard)	20
En el frente de Gandesa	38
"Nazi Physical Culture"	57
Drawing by the artist Yakob Nafarstek	58
"Geto-Lider"	64
Photographs secretly taken during the *aktion* and smuggled out of Vilna	92
"Le Roi du Schnorer"	113
Program in Yiddish and Polish of a concert of choral music	124
Oradour-sur-Glane, "Cité Martyre"	130
Memorial du Martyr Juif Inconnu stationery inscription	135
"The Living Stones"	138
Monument in Tromsö with names of those murdered at Auschwitz	151
"The Beast of Berlin"	167
Memorial plaques and courtyard scenes from the San Sabba Concentration Camp	175
Scrip from Theresienstadt	199
Greta Elbogen with her family in Budapest	231
A precious document	237
Drawn in Buchenwald—"Hear their voices grow, hear their voices grow"	251
"The New Colossus"	255

About the Translations, Musical Arrangements, and Copyrights

Translating and, where necessary, transliterating poetry and songs is fraught with all sorts of dangers. Where different alphabets, such as Hebrew/Yiddish, Greek and Cyrillic are concerned, there is often a difference of opinion and an ambiguity as to the Roman alphabet equivalent of certain letters representing sounds which are not present in English. And even with so-called standard transliteration symbols and letter combinations it may not always be clear just exactly what is called for, even if we have some idea of the sounds in the language under consideration.

In typesetting, the Hebrew alphabet does not distinguish between upper- and lower-case letters. But writing out text in transliterated Yiddish or Hebrew without utilizing English capital letters at the beginning of sentences and for certain proper nouns would look awkward. On the other hand, there is a seeming inconsistency in poetry in many languages regarding the use of capital letters at the beginning of successive lines of verse. Some editors and writers use capitals, some don't. In general, I have respected the format found in my sources. I have been consistent in my inconsistency.

In fashioning the translations another series of problems arise. The *sine qua non* of a singable translation is that it must be singable. However, the other *sine qua non* (if there may be two) is that the English text be faithful to the original. "Singable" means following the curve of the melody with the stressed and unstressed syllables falling comfortably on accented and unaccented notes, respectively. In addition, the rhyme scheme of the original should be adhered to—if possible. But in order for accents to fall in logical places musically and for rhymes to delight the ear, often the precise meaning of the lyrics in the original language must be slightly "bent." In other words, as they say, "something gets lost in translation."

However, if skillfully done, something may also "get found" in translation. What is found, primarily, is an opportunity for a person not familiar with the original language to have the possibility of experiencing the pleasure of singing a song that would otherwise have been inaccessible. I firmly believe that this benefit far outweighs the risk... provided that the translation does not stray *too* far from the original and that the English vocabulary and rhyming words do not sound stilted and unnatural. In other words: *caveat traductor* and *caveat cantor!*

The musical arrangements have been kept relatively simple and straightforward. Attention has been paid to the stylistic traditions of the songs. We have songs here representing quite a number of countries, from Spain to Russia, from Norway to Greece. This ethnic mix includes the characteristic eastern European Jewish harmonic and melodic style, the German *Lied* and marching song, the flamenco-like *canción* and points in between. The contemporary American songs add their own flavor to the stew. While all the arrangements are are my own, whenever there existed a prior harmonization by the composer I made every effort to follow his or her intentions.

The keys of the piano arrangements have been carefully selected from those generally thought of as "guitar friendly." Guitarists will know what is meant by this.

Finally, comes the all-important question of when, where and how to sing these songs. Perhaps, more fundamentally: Can we bring ourselves to sing them at all? The answer to this last question should be a resounding YES! For even though they represent "history"—and a particularly tragic history at that—the songs themselves should always remain what they were intended to be by their composers: songs to be sung, not merely considered as museum pieces to be studied quietly. The word "Ballads" in the title of this book was chosen advisedly. A ballad is a sung narrative; a twice- and thrice-told tale. It tells a story that the singer wants his audience to listen to attentively. It is full of details: names, places, events, emotions, life and death. The ballads and songs in this collection more than amply fulfill those requirements. Each one is a precious gem, a link to a certain time, a certain place and a certain person that must never be forgotten.

Every effort has been made to contact the composers and/or the copyright holders of the songs and to obtain permission for their inclusion in this collection. In every instance where contact has been made, the request for permission has been graciously accorded. For this consideration I sincerely thank all concerned. However, in view of the provenance of many of the songs it has not always been possible to determine authorship or to obtain formal permission for their use. If, however, at some future date a substantiated claim of authorship or copyright is presented for a composition, proper recognition will be credited in subsequent editions.

Jerry Silverman

Introduction

די גאַנצע וועלט איז אַ חלום–נאָר בעסער אַ גוטער חלום איידער אַ שלעכטער.

Di gantse velt iz a kholem— nor beser a guter kholem eyder a shlekhter.
The whole world is a dream— only better a good dream than a bad one.

Questions

How could a period in history as incomprehensibly evil and inhuman as the Holocaust have given rise to such a great number of remarkable songs? What was there to sing about? Who composed the songs? Who sang? Who listened? On first glance there would seem to be no satisfying answers to these questions, just as there is no answer to the ultimate question of the WHY of the Holocaust itself. But the songs do exist. People did compose them, sing them, and listen to them. Perhaps the songs themselves will supply the answers to the questions.

> Dei campi del dolore
> rinascera l'amore ... domani.
>
> From these fields of pain,
> Love will be born again ... tomorrow.

An unknown Italian woman prisoner wrote these simple, heartfelt words in the Ravensbrück concentration camp in Germany. If we would understand how in the face of the ultimate horror people could still compose poetry and songs we must gaze deep into the human soul.

Two words stand out in this woman's verse: *l'amore* and *domani*, "love" and "tomorrow." We hear these words repeated and sung over and over again in many languages, in the ghettos and concentration camps, on the battlefields and in exile: *libe, morgn; Liebe, morgen; amour, demain; amor, mañana; liubov, zavtra.*

Despite persecution and brutalization, two fundamental human qualities were never extinguished: sentiment and hope. It is these qualities that have always given rise to great works of art, literature, and music. There is a long history of singing in the face of adversity. Wars, hard times, natural disasters, slavery, pogroms, discrimination have always inspired the victims or the witnesses to chronicle those events. The Holocaust pushed this need for love and hope (and witness) to a degree never before imagined or experienced.

Gleichschaltung

We have heard the cry "Let my people go,"[1] sung by slaves in our own country. Immigrants to these shores have sung of a potato famine in Ireland[2] and pogroms in Russia[3], of poverty and political repression in countless lands. However, nothing in this long litany of sorrows can equal the sheer intensity of the outpouring of emotion that began with that most terrible Nazi institution in March 1933: the concentration camp.[4] Referring to this vicious instrument of terror and repression innocuously enough as *Gleichschaltung* (coordination), some fifty concentration camps, including the very first one at Dachau in Bavaria, were created between March and December 1933 alone.

By April 22, 1933, the *New York Times* could already report from Dachau that four thousand new inmates would soon join the five hundred starving, shaven-headed prisoners who were already slaving away in the camp. (Dachau was liberated by U.S. troops almost exactly twelve years later, on April 25, 1945.)

American soldiers of the 12th Armored Division, 7th U. S. Army in Kaufering IV (Hurlach), a sub-camp of Dachau. The apparently well-fed prisoner was the camp cook. However, the G. I.s also found the remains of some two hundred prisoners who had been either beaten, shot, burned, or starved to death. Photo by Robert J. Hartwig, from the collection of Debbie Gaynes, whose husband, Lt. Al Gaynes, was among the liberating troops.

The German political prisoners—the "peat-bog soldiers" *(die Moorsoldaten)* who marched out to work every morning from the Börgermoor concentration camp near the Dutch border that year—had the dubious "distinction" of creating, perhaps, the very first song in what would develop into a musical repertoire unparalleled in human history. Others soon followed their example. A new musical genre was born: *Lager-Lieder,* concentration camp songs. These songs circulated by word of mouth, often as prisoners were transferred from one camp to another. However, not all of these *Lieder* came out of the camps themselves. Sophisticated professionals, such as composer Hanns Eisler and poet-playwright Berthold Brecht, exiled in England, collaborated in the creation of powerful and dramatic anti-Nazi songs. Music as a political weapon was their forte. Their stage at first was the "exile-cabaret" that opened wherever significant numbers of refugees settled. But as their songs began to be translated into English, French, and other languages, their messages reached a wider audience.[5]

As the repression under the Nazis worsened during the 1930s, more and more voices began to be heard in Germany itself. Not all of the composers' names are known. The songs took on darker and darker overtones. Their very titles lead us along the downward spiral to hell, *My Father He Was Tracked, I Have No Homeland, The Jewish Child,* and others, until the horrors of the *Buchenwald Song* and the *Dachau Song* are attained.

Perhaps even more chilling than these songs from the Germany of the 1930s was the song composed by the Nazi street thug Horst Wessel, who was murdered in 1930. *Das Horst Wessel Lied,* which soon became the official song of the Nazi Party, second only to *Deutschland Über Alles* in popularity among the faithful, contains the memorable line: *Wenn das Judenblut vom Messer spritzt, dann geht's nochmal so gut* ("When Jewish blood spurts from the knife, then we'll have a much better life").

The harmonies echoed, but the world was not listening.

Or not wanting to hear for fear of getting "involved." On February 23, 1940, U. S. Secretary of State Cordell Hull received a memorandum from Assistant Secretary Adlof A, Berle Jr. stating that the U. S. embassy in Berlin had gotten reports that Jews were being sent to "unnamed concentration camps in Poland." Berle had the right reaction: "I see no reason why we should not make our feelings known regarding a policy of seemingly calculated cruelty which is beginning to be apparent now." But there *was* a reason, as succinctly expressed by another assistant secretary, Breckenridge Long, who, while "thoroughly in sympathy in with the sentiment" in Berle's memorandum, nevertheless felt that "this is a question entirely within the power of Germany." Any overt action, he warned, might involve the United States in a war in Europe.

No Pasarán

> Our war is not a Spanish civil war, it is a war of western civilization against the Jews of the entire world.
> —General Queipo de Llano,[6] October 10, 1936

> Can you imagine not having to go through World War II? Unfortunately, we were not listened to and the holocaust of World War II ensued.
> —Moe Fishman, National Treasurer of the Veterans of the Abraham Lincoln Brigade.[7]

> The moon shines ghostly white
> In Spain tonight.
> A million dead sleep well
> Beneath its light.
> Defenders of their freedom,
> Their task done,
> Sank earthward and became
> With it as one.
> The dead sleep well,
> But we must carry on.
> Pick up the torch and swear—
> NO PASARÁN![8]
> —*Lest We Forget,* Bill Silverman, 1940

On July 22, 1936 Hitler received a request for military aid to support the fascist rebellion in Spain. He had just attended a performance of *Die Walküre* at the annual Wagner Festival at Bayreuth, when he was handed a letter from Franco, outlining the insurgents' needs, particularly air support. As it turned out, fellow music lovers Hermann Goering and General Werner von Blomberg (commander-in-chief of the *Wehrmacht*) were also in Bayreuth and were summoned to an urgent meeting with Hitler. That very night, with the opera's "Magic Fire Music" still ringing in his ears and visions of Valhalla dancing in his brain, der Führer launched Unternehmen Zauberfeuer, Operation Magic Fire, in support of Franco's rebels. Although the world did not realize it at the time, World War II had begun.

The involvement of Germany a mere four days after the outbreak of the conflict in Spain inspired a counterreaction among progressive forces throughout Europe and America. There *were* those who recognized the nature of the fascist and Nazi threat in Spain . . . and beyond. International Brigades were recruited and organized by the Comintern, though not all those who joined in the struggle were Communists.

In light of post-Holocaust questions about the "passivity" of Jews facing extermination, it is important to mention that Jews made up a disproportionately large percentage of combatants in the International Brigades. According to Albert Prago, a veteran of the Abraham Lincoln Brigade, "estimates of the total number of volunteers vary from 40,000 to 50,000 men and women from 53 countries. Estimates of the number of Jews range from 7,000 to 10,000; not less than 15.5% and perhaps as much as 17.5% of the Brigades were Jewish. (Alberto Fernandez, a Spanish Catholic, in *Judíos en la Guerra de España*[9] asserts that 22 to 25% of the Brigadiers were Jews!)"[10] Fernandez offers the following breakdown of Jewish participants by country of origin: Poland, 2,250; U.S.A., 1,250; France, 1,043; Great Britain (including Ireland), 214; Palestine, 267. In addition there were some 1,095 coming from Hungary, Austria, Czechoslovakia, Yugoslavia, Canada, Italy (including Vittorio Vidali, alias "Commandante Carlos," the political commissar of the 5th Regiment, celebrated in the song *Venga Jaleo*, page 39), Scandinavia and Germany; 1,062 from 40 other countries and 53 from the Soviet Union. The contingent from Palestine included *khalutzim* (pioneers) organized by the Socialist-Zionist organization, Hashomer Hatzair.[11]

By the end of November 1936 the first International Brigade had taken up position in the defense of Madrid. The following February the American Abraham Lincoln Brigade arrived in Spain. They were immediately thrown into action in the battle of the Jarama Valley (see the song, *Jarama Valley,* page 32) south of Madrid (Feb. 23, 1937), where the fighting was so intense it was referred to as "the Marne of Madrid."[12] According to war correspondent Ernest Hemingway, these hastily trained, poorly equipped young men "fought as well as American fighting men have fought anywhere."

Hemingway's appreciation was more than seconded in the report written on May 9, 1938, by Vladimir Copic, the Croatian commander of the 15th International Brigade (see the song, *Viva La Quince Brigada,* page 34), referring to operations in the sector of Batea-Calaceite-Gandesa (see the song, *Si Me Quieres Escribir,* page 36) between March 30 and April 2, 1938: "On the night of March 30–31, I received an order . . . to deploy the 58th Battalion . . . to establish contact with . . . the 11th Brigade. . . . The Lincoln Battalion carried out this task with great success. . . . Political Commissar Blank of the 11th Brigade . . . said that the Lincoln Battalion was better than some of his own units . . . The Lincoln Battalion remained at this position the entire day of March 31 . . . until . . . we were ordered . . . to retreat . . . As we were starting our retreat movement . . . (t)he Lincoln Battalion was surrounded and sustained an enemy attack. As a result of this attack, we lost about 450 of our personnel . . . there were many soldiers and officers who performed exceptionally well. Among the best I would name . . . Captain [Milton; subsequently promoted to Lt. Col.] Wolff,[13] commander of the Lincoln Battalion, and his political commissar, [John] Gates [*nom de guerre* of Sol Regenstreif]; commanding officer Dunbar and several others."[14]

More than a third of the 2,900 American volunteers died fighting Franco. Upon their return home, the survivors encountered the suspicion and hostility of the U. S. government because of the Soviet backing of the international brigades. They were labeled "premature anti-fascists" [!], but they bore that ridiculous appellation proudly through years of political activism and blacklisting at home. Finally, on October 14, 1998, over 60 years after they put their "premature antifascism" to the test on the battlefields of Spain, a modest granite memorial to their struggles and sacrifices was unveiled on the campus of the University of Washington in Seattle. A year later, on October 31, 1999, the nation's second memorial to the Abraham Lincoln Brigade was dedicated in Madison, Wisconsin.[15] Lincoln vet Clarence Kailin was quoted in the *Wisconsin State Journal:* "I was a member of the Communist Party here, as many were at the time. We understood the implications of the war in Spain. We knew who Hitler was, we knew what fascism was. We knew what antisemitism was. I'm Jewish. Here was a chance to go over there and fight back."[16]

Another *antifascisto prematuro,* Pablo Picasso, had to wait (posthumously) to be "vindicated," when on June 25, 1999 the Spanish Cortes officially blamed Franco for ordering Nazi planes to carry out the bombing of the village of Guernica on April 26, 1937, the atrocity that inspired Picasso's masterpiece *Guernica.* Franco had attributed the attack to "Communist separatists."

The Spanish, German, and English songs that were born, sung, and recorded, literally under fire, in those heroic and tragic days, stand as musical monuments to a time when something still could have been done to prevent the carnage that was to come.[17]

They may shoot thousands of men and throw many more into concentration-camps, the songs live on. In spite of Franco's brutal terror, the Spanish peasants and the Spanish workers will continue to sing their songs of struggle and those of the International Brigades, although they are now all forbidden. French workers . . . start to sing the ballad of the Czech Eleventh Brigade. In German concentration camps Czech vets from the Spanish war sing the Dombros hymn of their Polish comrades right under the eyes of their unsuspecting jailers. Could the international songs of the Spanish war of liberation, which had so wonderfully united the fighters and established contact and understanding between them, ever be forgotten? Soldiers would sit together who did not know each other. Sometimes they were all new recruits, other times wounded soldiers directly from the front, a third time soldiers from a passing truck who had to wait for a shattered bridge to be built again, and finally men, already tried in battle, ready for new action. A question was being asked. The answer was a shrug, meaning "I don't understand." Calls were drowned out in the general hubbub. Then someone put a mouth organ to his lips. After the first notes a variety of voices and languages is carried by the same rhythm, and soon a single melody is heard. They do not only sing; they also listen. From one corner there comes the song of the Serbian Partisans—and at once a Serbian trio distinguishes itself from the general chaos of languages. And then you can hear a Polish quartet near by—there is not one knapsack without the *Canciones de la Guerra,* the book in which there are so many songs and still more languages. These *canciones* link as in a ring: the song of one nation's people together with the songs of all the nations' people, telling the story of one individual or the story of all time; stories about the sufferings of slaves and their longing for freedom. When Paul Robeson,[18] the American Negro singer, when Ernst Busch,[19] his white brother, sang at the front or in an army hospital, the chorus was sung by all voices in many languages. The Brigade of the Twenty Nations, when they met the Spanish Fascists, would roar out to them in twenty languages, the *Riego Marching Song* [the official hymn of the Spanish Republic] or the playful *Mamita Mia.* And before Guadalajara, Mussolini's drafted soldiers could hear the *Bandiera Rossa* or the *Garibaldi Song,* both of which were forbidden at home. And against Franco's German Nazis roared the songs of the batallions which carried the names of Ernst Thaelmann,[20] wasting away in prison, and Hans Beimler,[21] killed in battle, and of the executed Edgar André.[22] Freedom is their battle companion, and their battalion, well-tried in battle, fights in her name. The Germans of the International Brigades also knew a song that came from home, the only beautiful song from Nazi Germany, the only true German folksong: *The Peat [Bog] Soldiers*. In the camps below the Pyrenees the chorus of this song about the Germans in concentration camps is now repeated by many hundreds of Spanish combattants. Winter is not over yet, but the harder time moves on, the nearer the last verse of the Peat Soldiers comes to its fulfillment.

Egon Erwin Kisch (Paris, 1939.)[23]

Hitler made his triumphant entry into Prague on March 15, 1939. Two weeks later Franco declared himself dictator of Spain. Many of the German and Italian antifascists who were still fighting in Spain when the Republic finally fell fled across the Pyrenees into France, where they were interned by French authorities in camps such as Gurs,[24] in the southwestern department of *Basses Pyrénées*. Under Nazi occupation the Vichy collaborationist government turned these men *("des juifs* [Jews] *et des anti-Nazis")* over to the S.S., who transported them to the internment-staging area at Drancy, near Paris,[25] and thence east to the concentration camps, and soon to be constructed gas chambers.[26] The fatal link between "stages" of the Holocaust was thus forged.

By 1940 Gurs had been "cleansed" of its Spanish Civil War refugees. It was now ready to receive Jews from France, as well as other Jews who had been expelled from Germany and Bohemia-Moravia (including young children) on the first stage of their journey to Drancy and ultimately Auschwitz. It was said that these unfortunates had been arrested by the Gestapo (for their race), by the Third *République* (for their nationality) and by Vichy (for their religion).

There was, however, a reverse flow of Jewish refugees after the fall of France who passed through Spain and Portugal on their way to exile. By the summer of 1942, over 20,000 Jews had managed to escape Nazi and Vichy roundups. Many were able to book ocean passage to safety through Lisbon, assisted by the HICEM[27] office there. On September 24, 1941, for example, the Portuguese liner *Serpa Pinta* docked in New York with fifty-six children who had evacuated from Gurs. Their parents did not make the trip.

Witness

Link by link the chain stretched ever eastward and ever tighter around the necks of the Jews, following close behind the advancing *Wehrmacht*. Jewish urban neighborhoods were transformed into ghettos; Jews from the outlying *shtetlakh* were rounded up and herded into these ghettos. The diabolical web of work camps and death camps was expanded and perfected.

The songs of this period chronicle the destruction of European Jewry in merciless detail. Orphaned children, widows, dead mothers, murdered fathers, sealed box cars, destroyed homes, uprooted lives — the very gas chambers themselves — all found their way into song. Resistance also found a voice, and with resistance the will to live, to survive. *Libe . . . morgn.*

And to bear witness.

After the Bergen-Belsen concentration camp was liberated by the British army on April 15, 1945, the site was transformed into a displaced persons camp. Since there was no immediate place for most of the former prisoners to go (returning to eastern Europe was not an attractive option, visas to western European countries and America were slow in coming, getting to Palestine posed other problems), some semblance of "normal life" was organized around the Tsentraln Yidishn Komitet in Bergen-Belsen (Central Jewish Committee in Bergen-Belsen). The Committee represented all Jews in the displaced persons camps and all the Jewish-German community of the British occupation zone. One of the first things that it did was to publish a song book [!] in 1946, entitled *Katset un Geto-Lider* (Concentration Camp and Ghetto Songs).[28] In the introduction to the book, the editor Zami Feder writes:

> While still in the concentration camp I began collecting concentration camp and ghetto songs by known and unknown poets. . . . After the liberation I recommenced the same task. I prepared a brochure of some of the songs from the Cultural Division of the Jewish Central Committee, as a sample of this collection, which will enable future historians to illustrate this tragic period in our lives. I considered the songs' historical character. Thus had "someone" written, and thus had it been sung. Unfortunately it is not possible for me to present the names of all the composers.

Kabarett

Others have also attempted to preserve this priceless record with varying degrees of success. The *Stiftung Deutsches Kabarettarchiv* (German Cabaret-Archive Foundation) in Mainz, responding to a letter of inquiry, offered the following [English unedited]:

> therefore the music of the songs, created in the various "Konzentrationslagern" between 1939 and 1945, has never been written down or even published at that time, only a few of them is known in our days. Usually first noted after 1945, more or less only the music of the so called "Lager-Lieder," 'cause of there relative popularity under the prisoners, has had a chance to get edited. The "Stiftung Deutsches Kabarettarchiv" is, in respect of these remarks, only able to send you the music of two songs from your list ("Dachau-Lied" and "Buchenwald Lied"); the music of the other demanded songs is lost, if ever noted.

The reader may be wondering what a "German Cabaret-Archive Foundation" has to do with songs of the Holocaust. The fact is, that in addition to the songs in Yiddish, with their graphic descriptions of horror and death, there are a great many songs in German (and other languages), composed in exile and in a number of camps, including notably Westerbork in Holland and Theresienstadt (Terezín) in Czechoslovakia.

The first deportees to Theresienstadt were Jews from Prague who arrived in November 1941. They were the *Aufbaukommandos*, the construction teams whose task was to set up a model, showcase camp for so-called older prominent and privileged Jews from Germany and other west European countries. Included among these "prominent and privileged" Jews were Czech, German, and Austrian Jews, some of whom had been active as composers, librettists, and performers in the vibrant cabarets and theaters of pre-war Prague, Berlin, and Vienna.[29] Their language was German[30] (many spoke French and English as well) and their musical and literary style reflected more of Franz Lehár *(The Merry Widow)* and Oscar Strauss *(The Chocolate Soldier)* than Mark Warshawsky *(Oyfn Pripetchik)*[31] and Abraham Goldfadden *(Rozhinkes Mit Mandlen,* see page 56). The shtetl world of Sholem Aleichem was utterly foreign to them. They wrote catchy, witty songs, full of sophisticated tunes and clever rhymes, sprinkled here and there with French and English expressions.

Founded in 1927, the Viennese "Jewish Political Cabaret" presented topical productions that took pointed aim at contemporary life. Their initial reactions to the rise of Nazi power were equally sharp and incisive. As in all other areas of life in Austria and Germany in the 1930s, it became increasingly dangerous for these political satirists to express themselves. Nazi Propaganda Minister Joseph Goebbels summed it all up in a speech in early 1938 on what he perceived as the sad state of the cabaret in Germany: "One should not come to us with criticism. It is only through positive humor that our policies should be supported. We do not need such support from *conférenciers* [pointedly employing the commonly used French, but nevertheless, "foreign-sounding"[32] word for masters of ceremonies in lieu of the German equivalent, *Zeremonienmeister*] and so-called comics."[33]

Of course, it was impossible to exorcise all "foreignisms" from the German language. In a post-Kristallnacht meeting (November 12, 1938), which included Goering, Goebbels, Heydrich and other Nazi luminaries, the question of payment of insurance to Jews who had suffered losses during the rampage was raised. Goering proposed to a representative of the insurance companies that only certain damages be covered, thereby assuring the companies a large *rebbes*—using the Berlin slang term for "profit," derived from the Hebrew [!], *ribbith*.

Goebbels' pointed message to the cabarettists could not have been any clearer. Many of them chose exile. Sunday, March 13, 1938, marked the final hour *(die Todesstunde)* of the cabaret in Vienna with the departure for America of Jimmy Berg, Anton Kuh, Alfred Polgar, and Oskar Teller, all prominent figures in the cabaret, the "small art stage" *(die Kleinkunstbühne)* that had existed in that city since 1890. They were the fortunate ones. Exile-cabarets opened wherever a sufficient number of these displaced artists wound up: New York (Die Arche [The Ark][34], Kadeko[35]), London (Four-And-Twenty Black Sheep), Zurich (Cornichon), Amsterdam (Ping Pong,[36] Nelson-Kabarett), to name but a few. For those who remained behind, an altogether different stage was prepared in Theresienstadt. When these people found themselves confined in a camp where theatrical performances were permitted, and even encouraged, they quickly adapted themselves to their new environment. Satire and gallows humor were their stock-in-trade. Although they were certainly prisoners whose lives hung by a thread (in all, some 150,000 Jews were transported from Theresienstadt to Auschwitz and other extermination camps; more than 30,000 died in Theresienstadt itself), their songs, for the most part, reflect a different version of reality: a drop of champagne mixed into the bitter wormwood.

A notable collection of these songs entitled *Kabarett unterm Hakenkreuz* (Cabaret under the Swastika), edited by Volker Kühn, was published in Germany in 1989. The word *cabaret* in this context refers to those pre-war establishments in Germany and Austria that Goebbels found so objectionable, the wartime exile-cabarets in other countries, as well as the compositions that came out of Theresienstadt itself. However, Kühn's sources concerned themselves more with collecting the lyrics to these gems than transcribing the music (which, as has been noted, was often not preserved).[37] As a result, I was confronted with a dilemma: How to include these "songs without music" in an anthology of songs.

After considering, and rejecting, the option of not including them at all, I decided to set a number of the texts to my own original music in, more or less, the style of the period. Composing new melodies to an existing text does not do any more violence to its spirit than the related practice of borrowing a well-known tune to carry a new lyric. This time-honored technique was employed by the composers of such songs in this collection as *Und die Musik spielt dazu; Scarpe Rotte; Tsu Eyns, Tsvey, Dray; Jarama Valley* and most of the Spanish Civil War songs, which are based upon traditional Spanish melodies.

Adieu, Westerbork

> One of the first newspapers to appear in any language was the Yiddish-language *Dinstagishi* (Tuesday) *Courantin* and *Fraytagishi* (Friday) *Courantin,* which appeared twice a week in Amsterdam from August, 1686 to December, 1687.

> Friday, 9 October 1942
>
> Dear Kitty: I've only got dismal and depressing news for you today. Our many Jewish friends are being . . . loaded into cattle trucks and sent to Westerbork.
>
> (Anne Frank: The Diary Of A Young Girl)

Westerbork was originally set up before the war [1939] by the Dutch government as a camp for German Jewish refugees who came to Holland without money or Dutch relatives or friends to sponsor them and to vouch to the government that they would not become a burden to the state. The establishment of the camp angered the German Jews, making them feel unwelcome, and confining them in the dreary northeast of Holland [near the hamlet of Hooghalen in the province of Drenthe, not far from the Börgermoor concentration camp in Germany, the birthplace of the first concentration camp song in 1933, *Die Moorsoldaten,* The Peat-Bog Soldiers]. When the Nazis invaded Holland [May 1940], barbed wire was placed around Westerbork, and the Nazis designated this village as the eventual detention center for all Jews in the

Netherlands; from there they would be sent off to concentration camps in the East.[38]

Despite the ominous foreshadowing in that last phrase ("in the East"), the rhythm of daily life in Westerbork mirrored, to some extent, life on the outside, if one didn't ponder the future. Inmates Jaap (Jakob) Polak and Ina Soep, for example, carried on an interbarracks correspondance that evinces a semblance of "normalcy," touching on their personal relationship, everyday family affairs, and extending even to musical presentations in the camp. A letter of Jaap's dated January 15, 1944, describes "a classical program with dances by Brahms and Schubert . . . a Bach Violin Concerto . . . [pianist, vocalist] Martin Roman singing different clever pieces, such as *Tea For Two*." On January 23, "there was a Russian singer with his own guitar and songs." The program of February 8 included Cantor Moskowitz who sang Yiddish songs. On another occasion, a survivor recalled, a "famous" cantor sang the tragically appropriate aria *Vesti la giubba,* from Pagliacci ("Laugh, clown, although your heart is breaking").

The Westerbork Cabaret featured some of the leading lights of the Berlin and Viennese stage. In fact, there were so many well-known "artists in residence"[39] in Westerbork that it was referred to sardonically as the "Stronghold *(Festung)* of European Cabarets." It was directed by Willy Rosen (Wilhelm Julius Rosenberg) and Max Ehrlich. Both Rosen and Ehrlich had been well-known figures in the Berlin Jewish cabaret scene during the 1920s and '30s. Ehrlich was the director of the cabaret theater of the Jewish Culture Association in the German capital, which he founded in 1935 upon his return from self-imposed exile in Holland. It was on this stage that Rosen often performed his satirical and humorous numbers. Rosen's radio broadcasts, films, and recordings were very popular throughout Europe, and particularly in Holland, where he often performed with his emigrant cabaret company, *Kabarett der Prominenten* (Cabaret of the Prominent People) in the mid 1930s. Now in Berlin, for almost five years, beginning in 1935, in the face of the ever-increasing anti-Semitic repression around them, Rosen and Ehrlich collaborated in the production of topical revues with titles like "Contraband," "Curtain Up," and "Mixed Compote." It obviously couldn't last, and in March 1939, compelled to identify themselves in the program as Willy *Israel*[40] Rosen and Max *Israel* Ehrlich, they gave their farewell performance in Berlin in *"Revue der Revuen"* (Revue of Revues).

Es war mal eine Pointe,
Sie war so schön und gut,
Aus allerbester Familie,
Von allerbestem Blut.

Doch eines schönes Tages,
Geschah die Schweinerei:
Man zog die arme Pointe
An ihren Haaren herbei.

Ein wilder Pointemörder
Der hat sie umgebracht.
Da lag sie unterm Tische.
Kein Mensch hat mehr gelacht.

Once there was a punch-line,
It was so fine and good,
From the very best family,
From the very best blood.

But then upon a fine day,
A dirty joke was said:
They dragged the poor punch-line
By the hair of its head.

A savage punch-line killer
Then slew it with a roar.
It lay under the table.
No one laughed anymore.

They then established themselves in Holland at the seaside resort of Scheveningen, near the Hague. Their cabaret was called the Lutine Palace and was decorated with an "underwater" motif. However, events soon overtook them there. After the German invasion of Holland in May 1940, they were compelled to

The program cover of the *Abschiedsvorstellung* (Farewell Performance) of Max Erlich and Willy Rosen. Berlin, March 1939.

relocate to Amsterdam, where they merged (in December) with another German emigrant cabaret group directed by Rudolf Nelson (Lewysohn) at the popular club, La Gaîté. That interlude lasted until June 1942. Then Nelson, Rosen, and Ehrlich, along with many of their colleagues, were interned in Westerbork, where they continued their theatrical collaboration under "somewhat different" circumstances from those they had previously enjoyed.[41] Nevertheless, they strove to maintain the "lighthearted" tone of their productions in the Westerbork cabaret, with such revues as *Humor und Melodie, Bravo! Da Capo* and *Total verrückt* (Completely Crazy). In all, six cabaret productions were performed between July 1943 and June 1944.

On September 3, 1943, the news arrived that Himmler wanted western Europe to be made *judenfrei* as quickly as possible. As chance would have it, the next day was the premiere of *Humor und Melodie*, which had as its motto: *"Wenn man bis zum Halse im Dreck sitzt, hat man nicht zu zwitschern,"* that is, "When you are sitting up to your neck in shit you'd better not chirp"—in other words, "Don't make waves." Erlich, however, commented ruefully: *"Ich zwitschere trotzdem!"* ("I chirp nevertheless!").

A typical program, Program No. 4 of March 1944, was entitled *Bunter Abend* (Colorful Evening). Directed by Ehrlich and with music by Rosen and Erich Ziegler, there were 16 scenes, an evening of variety sketches and songs. Among the perfomers was the Dutch singing duo "Johnny and Jones," (Max Kannenwasser and Arnold van Wesel) whose *Westerbork Serenade* is included in this collection.

This "Colorful Evening," like all the other "colorful evenings" in the camp was merely a camouflage designed by the commandant, *Oberstürmführer* Konrad Gemmeker[42] to distract the captive audience (in the literal sense of the term) from the real "business at hand." Opening night at each cabaret production always took place the evening after a transport had departed for Auschwitz. It was cabaret-as-tranquilizer, designed to calm the next trainload of doomed humanity.

Nobody was fooled.[43] *"Mein Gott,"* one inmate noted in his diary, "the hall is filled to bursting. And we laugh tears. Yes, tears!" Just like the audience, the performers understood their position all too well. As long as they continued appearing on stage they reckoned that they had a chance to survive. However, reality, terrible reality could not ultimately be avoided. The Allied invasion of Normandy on June 6, 1944, abruptly shattered any illusions the artists may have held about their future. The cabaret was shut down after the June performance of the diabolically appropriately named revue, "Completely Crazy." In August 1944, along with their fellow artists, Willy Rosen and Max Ehrlich were deported to Theresienstadt and thence to Auschwitz, where, linked in death as they had been in life, they shared the same fate on September 29, 1944. A few days before the train took them "to the east," Willy wrote a long, simple, almost banal poem entitled *Abschied von Westerbork* (Parting from Westerbork). It was never set to music.

Mein liebes Westerbork, ich muß nun von Dir scheiden,
'ne kleine Träne läßt sich dabei nicht vermeiden.
Warst Du auch öfters hart und ungemütlich,
Du bliebst doch letzten Endes immer friedlich.
Mein Westerbork, Du plagtest mich sehr viel,
Und trotzdem hattest Du so'n eigenes Sex-Appeal.
Nun sag ich leise Servus, liebes Kesselhaus,
Ein letzter Flötenton, und dann ist's aus.
Leb wohl, mein Hinterzimmer mit dem kleinen Teppich,
Ich flüstre heute selber zu mir leise: nebbich.
Leb wohl, Du kleine Küche, leb wohl. W. C.
Daß ich den Kocher lassen mußte, das tut mir weh.
Du machtest öfters Kurzschluß, ach, das war nicht schön,
Dann konnte man den guten Türkel immer wütend sehn.
Adieu, mein Schrank, adieu, mein Bücherbrett,
Es hat mich sehr gefreut, es war sehr nett.
Adieu, mein lieber Stamppot und mein Vuilnisbak,
Ich gehe auf die Wanderschaft mit Sack und Pack.
Ich drücke Dir zum letzten Mal die Hände, E. H. B. U.
Noch ein Driepoeder, und dann fällt die Vorhang zu.
Lebt wohl, Ihr vielen lieben Dienstbereiche,
Ich bin nun nicht mehr eingeteilt, ich mache Platz, ich weiche.

Manchen Transport sah ich von hier verreisen,
Und jetzt, jetzt wirft man selber mich zum alten Eisen.
Jetzt steig ich selber mit dem Rucksack in den Zug.
Ganz unter uns gesagt, ich find es schlimm genug.
Doch Mitleid will ich nicht und keinen guten Rat,
Ich werd's schon schaffen, ich bin alter Frontsoldat.
In Westerbork kann mir nichts mehr passieren,
Ich geh wo anders Zores organisieren.
Gebt mir zum letzten Mal noch meine Zusatznahrung,
Ich geh mit Butter weg, und mit sehr viel Erfahrung.
Ich packe alles ein, ich lasse nichts zurück,
Sogar mein Frauchen nehm ich mit, mein bestes Stück.
Adieu, FK. und V., adieu auch Wäscherei,
Es wird heut meine Wäschenummer wieder frei.
Auch liebe Ipa, lebe wohl, ich muß jetzt wandern,
Erzähle deine Schmonzes nun den andern.
Lebt wohl, Ihr alten Kampinsassen, liebe Brüder,
Vielleicht sehen wir uns im Leben nochmals wieder.
'ne Ansichtskarte darf ich Euch nicht schreiben,
Vielleicht kann ich bei Euch so im Gedächtnis bleiben.
Nun sitz ich im Coupé, gleich wird es pfeifen.
Noch einmal laß ich meinem Blick über die Gegend schweifen.
Nun weiß ich doch—ich leide Qualen.
Adieu, mein Westerbork, Post Hooghalen.

My dear Westerbork, I must now be leaving,
I just can't avoid a little tear of grieving.
Though you were often hard and stressful,
In the end you always remained peaceful.
My Westerbork, you tormented me a great deal,
And yet, you have your own sex appeal.
Now I say softly, so long, my dear boiler house,
A last flute-tone, and then then lights I'll douse.
Be well, my back room[44] with the little carpet,

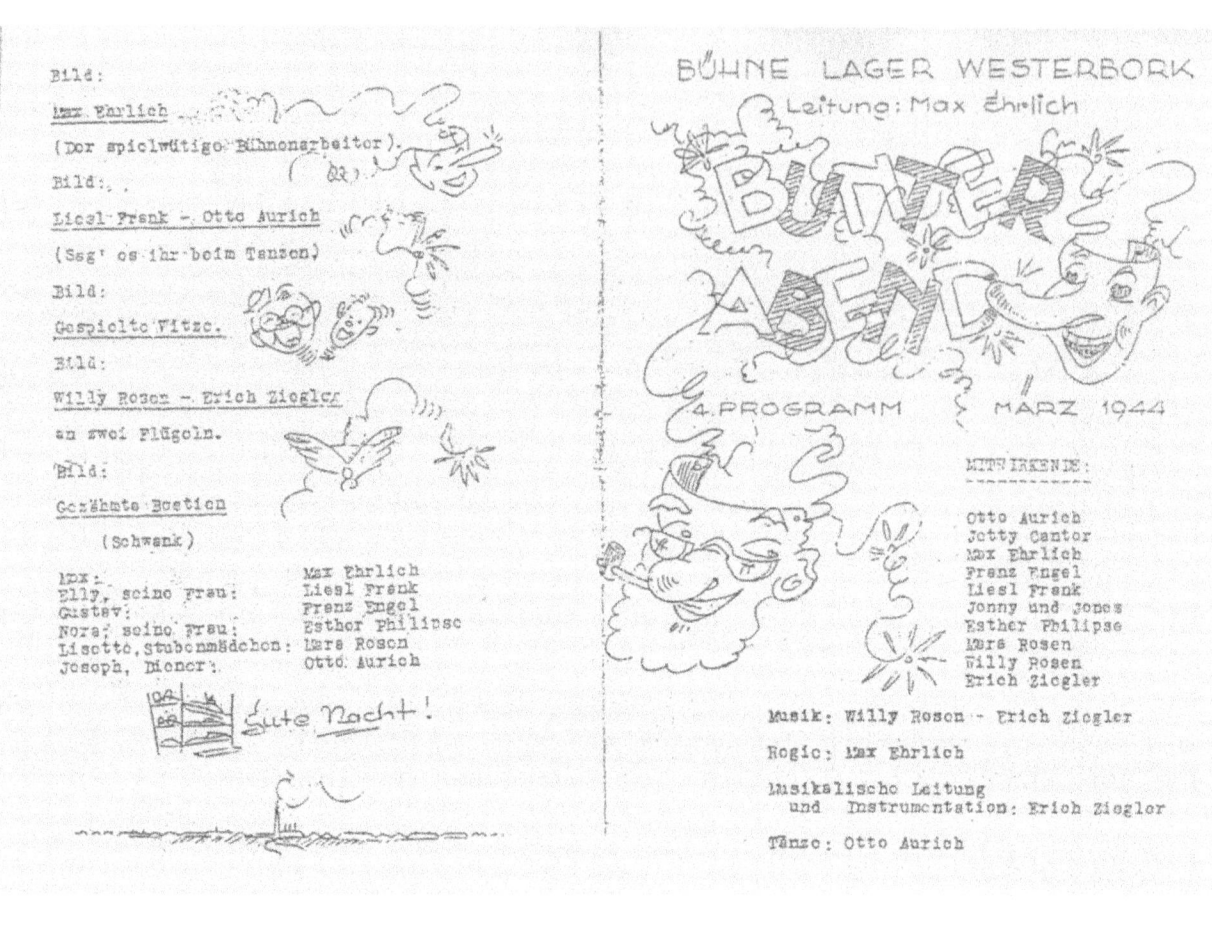

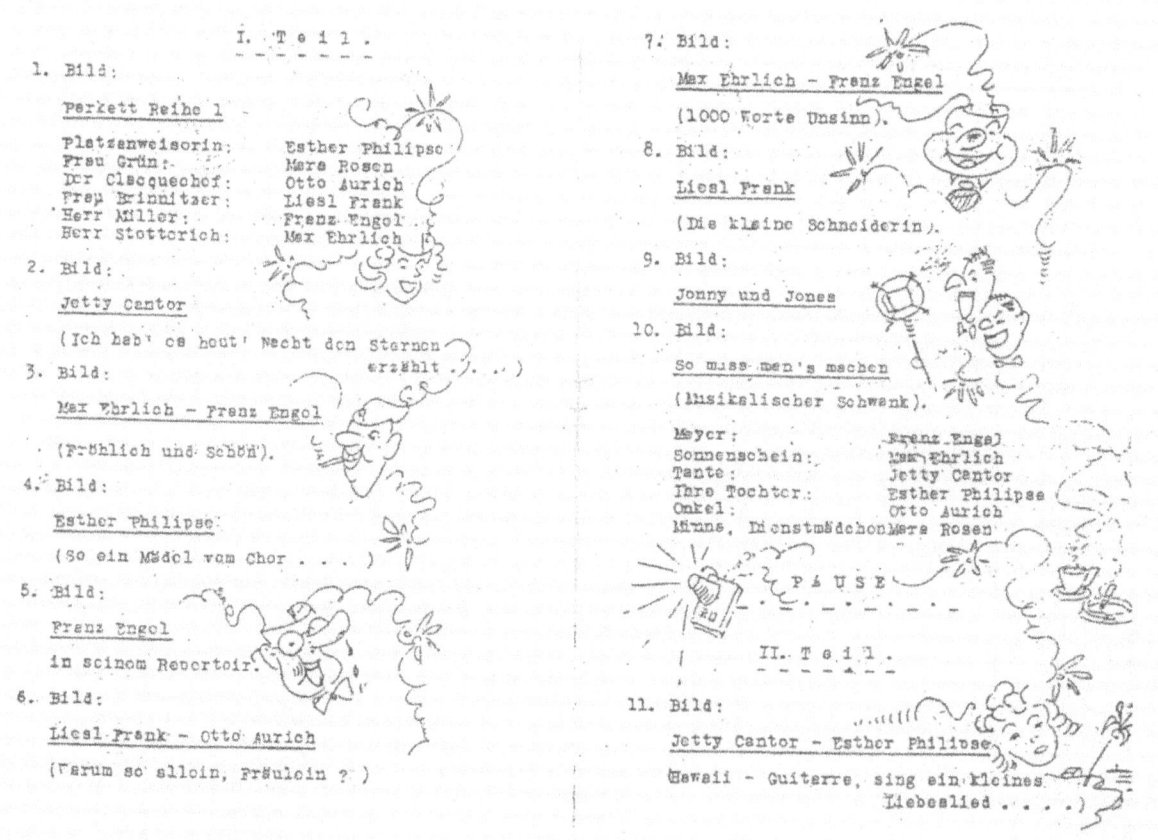

The program of the *Bunter Abend* (Colorful Evening) in the Westerbork Cabaret under the direction of Max Ehrlich.

I whisper to myself today: *nebbich*,[45] so be it.
Be well, you tiny kitchen, be well, W. C.
That I must leave my electric cooker, does pain me.
You often shorted out, ah, now that was bad,
Then one could see good Mr. Türkel[46] always getting mad.
Adieu, my closet, adieu, my bookshelf, too,
It made me very happy to have the two of you.
Adieu, my dear Dutch stew[47] and my garbage can,[48]
I'm setting out on the road, sack and pack in hand.
I shake you hands for the last time. *E. H. B. U.*[49]
Just one more pill, then pull the curtain to.
Be well, you well-beloved service zone,
I am no longer on the list, I make room, I move on.
Many transports I have seen pulling out of here,
And now—now they're throwing me on the scrap iron heap, I fear.
Now I climb myself, with knapsack, on the train.
And just between us let me say, I find this is a pain.
But sympathy I do not want—advise me, do not try.
Somehow I'll make it, an old front-line soldier am I.
Nothing more can happen in Westerbork to me,
I'm going where other *tsores*[50] are in store, you see,
Give me my extra rations for the last time,
I go with butter on my way, with experience sublime.
I pack it all together, I leave nothing behind,
I even take my dear wife[51] with me, the best that man can find.
Adieu FK[52] and *V*,[53] *adieu* to the laundry,
Today my laundry number will once again be free.
Also dear IPA,[54] live well, I'm on my way today,
Now tell all your nonsense to someone else, I say.
Live well, you old camp inmates, my dear brothers,
Perhaps another time in life we'll see one another.
A picture postcard to you I don't have to send,
Perhaps I will remain in your memory till the end.
Now I'm sitting in the compartment, soon the whistle will be blowing.
My gaze wanders over the neighborhood—now we're going.
Now I know already—I suffer torments in anticipation.
Adieu, my Westerbork, Hooghalen Station.

In that same fatal month of August, 1944 another train transported Anne Frank from Westerbork directly to Auschwitz.[55]

Shtetl Bronx

Growing up during the war in an east Bronx neighborhood populated almost entirely by eastern-European Jewish immigrant families, we followed the curving lines on the war maps in the newspapers that traced the ebb and flow of the Allied forces with great interest. Little pins on maps at home marked Stalingrad, El Alemein, Anzio, Monte Casino, Normandy, Bastogne, and finally, Berlin. Pearl Harbor, Bataan, Iwo Jima, Guadalcanal, and Midway had their pins too. So did Hiroshima and Nagasaki.

But the pins that pierced our flesh the deepest were stuck into the towns and cities of eastern Europe from which our friends' and neighbors' families (mine included) migrated. The accents heard on Allerton Avenue and Bronx Park East were those of Bialystok, Grodno, Minsk, Mogiliev, Vilna, and the countless *shtetlakh* that did not show up on the battle maps. There were endless, and sometimes heated, street-corner discussions about the wisdom, or lack thereof, of military tactics. The Red Army, the *mighty* Red Army, could do no wrong! But what was with Roosevelt and Churchill? Where was the long-awaited Second Front[56]?!

I never had the slightest bit of trouble
With algebra or trigonometry.
At chemistry the profs all called me wizard,
For I "discovered" H_2S, you see.
The Greeks, I know, wrote odes and metaphysics,
I know what causes tides to ebb and flow.
But there's something puzzling me,
And it's got me up a tree—
WHERE IS THAT SECOND FRONT, I'D LIKE TO KNOW?

Spinoza was no mystery to me.
The theory of Einstein was quite simple,
In very little time I mastered Hegel,
I know the cube of twelve times ninety-three.
Egyptian hieroglyphics were mere child's play,
I know the miles from here to Kokomo.
But there's something on my mind,
And it has me down, I find—
WHERE IS THAT SECOND FRONT, I'D LIKE TO KNOW?

Bill Silverman, 1943

Recordings of the Red Army Chorus were best sellers in our part of town. Who can forget their stirring rendition of "Meadowlands" *(Poliushko-Pole),* with their voices singing softly in the distance, gradually growing into a mighty crescendo, then fading away once again? Paul Robeson inspired and moved us with his antifascist freedom songs in Spanish, Russian, German, Yiddish, and a dozen other languages. We sang along with the Almanac Singers (Pete Seeger, Woody Guthrie, Lee Hays, and Millard Lampell) as they belted out to the tune of *Old Joe Clark:*

'Round and around Hitler's grave,
'Round and around we go.
We're gonna lay that poor boy down—
He won't get up no more.[57]

We gathered scrap metal, bought war bonds, contributed to Russian War Relief, and dimmed our lights. My hard-working father, Bill Silverman, found time to write poetry. In his way he was mirroring the efforts of the song writers "known and unknown" across the sea who were also trying to come to terms with the madness that was engulfing them. In the introduction to the slim volume of my father's poems published in 1946, entitled *Rhymes for Our Times,* author Mike Gold *(Jews Without Money)* wrote: "When Bill gets mad at fascism or other evils with which mankind is afflicted, he writes blistering verse. . . . I like Bill's spontaneity and genuine rage. Nobody has brooded longer over the evil incarnated in the figure of Hitler. Half a dozen verses cast sufficient light on every evil phase of the Nazi."

From 1940 to 1945 Bill Silverman chronicled the tides of the war in this slim volume of antifascist poems.

Have you heard of Maidenek...
Just outside of Lublin town;
Have you seen a bent, old Jew,
By a savage brute struck down?
Have you seen an open grave
Filled with bodies young and old;
Have you seen a little child,
Lying frozen in the cold?

Have you seen a group of girls,
Terror-stricken, led away;
Have you heard their anguished cries,
Have you seen young hair turn gray?
Have you seen a town destroyed,
Where free men were wont to tread:
Have you seen the Nazi beasts
Burn and loot, while death they spread?

Have you seen a torture rack;
Have you seen a man gouged blind?
Have you seen a prison camp,
Where all hope was left behind?

Have you felt the hopelessness
Of the ones who sit and wait...
Do you wonder why I hate...
DO YOU WONDER WHY I HATE!

    Bill Silverman, "Do You Wonder?" (1945)

Man, Beasts, And Music

In his book *Among Man and Beasts,* published by the Bergen Belsen Memorial Press in 1978, Paul Trepman (who survived *six* concentration camps, including Bergen Belsen and Maidanek, thanks in part to false "Polish-Aryan" identification papers[58]) quotes a fragment of a Maidanek Song composed by an unknown Polish prisoner:

There never has been,
Nor will there ever be,
Anywhere on earth,
A sun like that which shines
Upon our Maidanek.[59]

Trepman goes on to say:

We sang it everywhere we went, all day long: at work, at mealtime, before going to sleep, and even when we were kicked and beaten by our jailers. At night, as we lay on our bunks, our stomachs hollow, our spirits despairing, we would hum the *Maidanek Song* and see visions of fields and forests, towns and villages, visions of peace and contentment. And for a little while the heavy burden pressing on our hearts dissolved into healing tears of hope and yearning.

Such was the power of music.

Later a prison guard casually tells Trepman: "You know, when we took them [groups of Jewish women] out to be shot, they were singing! I don't get it."

And such was the power of music.[60]

Another powerful testimonial was offered by former Buchenwald inmate Walter Wolf as recorded by the Archive of the National Buchenwald Memorial, February 4, 1946:

I remember: In the hungry winter [*Hungerwinter*] of the first war year: Water and kohlrabi, kohlrabi and water. Typhus in the camp.... One night I return to the damp, stuffy air of the overcrowded dormitory. In the day room the loudspeaker is still sounding: Music, the second movement of Schubert's "Unfinished." I slip down on to a bench and listen. What unending longing for happiness [*Glückssehnsucht*] of suffering, oppressed man sings in this music. The work remained unfinished. Schubert died too young. But his music gives us the strength that we may live, in spite of everything. And then other times, on short, bearable days in Buchenwald: A double quartet—Beethoven and once again Mozart's *Kleine Nachtmusik.* They inspired us more than once, letting an enthusiastic vitality [*Lebenskraft*] grow in us.... Mozart's *Kleine Nachtmusik* will ever be bound up with our need, with our battle, with our triumph in *Konzentrationslager Buchenwald.*

This almost idyllic interlude stands in stark counterpoint to other utilizations of music as sadistic torture. Another former prisoner in Buchenwald, Julius Freund, recalled[61] an evening of Strauss waltzes in the infamous roll-call yard *(der Appellplatz)*. The prisoners were forced to spin in place in time to the music until they collapsed from dizzyness. Then they were dragged up and, once again to the lilting strains of their beloved Viennese waltzes, they had to crouch and hop around like frogs, *eins, zwei, drei . . . eins, zwei, drei*. The nightmarish *"Strauß Abend"* ("Strauss Evening") did not end there. As the *pièce de résistance,* two prisoners were tied to wooden planks and whipped by the guards in time to the music, *eins, zwei, drei* while the prison orchestra played on, and the grotesque *danse macabre* of the "frogs" continued on the other side of the yard.

Coming to Terms

Wotan's Spawn

> "We will be here for a thousand years."
> Hitler, before his defeat at Stalingrad

> No power on earth can move us.
> For a thousand years or more,
> We are taking root to stay here
> Upon the Volga shore.
>
> We are the sons of Wotan,
> His fire is in our blood,
> And woe betide our enemies—
> We'll engulf them like a flood.
>
> From the Baltic to Crimea,
> Within the broad Ukraine,
> We Supermen will flourish
> And grow strong on Russian grain.
>
> The world is ours to conquer,
> From Albion to Cathay;
> Our word is law—our law is might,
> That is the only way.
>
> But a thousand million people
> Together rose as one,
> And into dust ground Wotan's spawn—
> A tyrant's day was done.
>
> Bill Silverman (1944)

Musical reactions to, and reflections on the Holocaust did not end with the end of the war in Europe and the liberation of the camps in 1945. Although there was the understandable desire on the part of many survivors to "put it all behind them," others sought to come to terms with the events and try to give them some meaning. While there are far fewer post-war songs dealing with the Holocaust than those composed between 1933 and 1945 (new problems quickly replaced the old), the Holocaust as "history" has attracted a number of contemporary composers. While some chronicle specific wartime incidents or look back nostalgically upon the "good old days," and how they are gone forever, others, seizing upon the theme of "Never Again," use the Holocaust as a metaphor for current social and political issues. Collective guilt and innocence, denial of responsibility, the woes of immigrants, racism, genocide (chillingly renamed "ethnic cleansing" in the Balkans in the 1990s), the Vietnam war, the rise of neo-Nazi organizations—all have inspired song writers to view these and other topics in relation to the Holocaust.

For the first time in this tragic chronicle since the Lincoln Brigaders sang of the Jarama Valley the voices of Americans are heard. Long-time advocates of social justice through their music, such as Pete Seeger, Tom Paxton, Janis Ian, and Si Kahn, among others, have made powerful contributions to the repertoire of Holocaust-inspired songs. These songs continued to be written into the 2000s, over seventy years after *die Moorsoldaten* first sang of hope and freedom behind the barbed wire of the Börgermoor concentration camp.

Answers

So, to come back to our original *kashes*, the eternal "questions" . . .

How could a period in history as incomprehensibly evil and inhuman as the Holocaust have given rise to such a great number of remarkable songs?

I have attempted to bring forth in this Introduction some of the deeply personal and emotional reasons that inspired people on the very brink of the abyss to express themselves in poetry and song. The songs speak—sing—for themselves: Each song in this collection carries its own message.

What was there to sing about?

Simply put, everything: life, death, sentiment, hope . . . *amore . . . domani . . . libe . . . morgn.*

Who composed the songs? Ordinary folk and professional composers, ghetto poets and resistance fighters.

Who sang? The people who lived and died through those terrible years, responding to the primal urge to have their voices heard.

Who listened? There were no *listeners*. Everybody was a *singer*.

Testament

On the very first page of the song book published in Bergen-Belsen in 1946 is a poem entitled *Tsevuah* (The Will) by Yasha Rabinovitch. He had been interned in the Kaiserwald concentration camp near Riga, in Latvia, but in the waning days of the war, ahead of the advancing Red Army, he was transported west to another camp in Neustadt (in Schleswig-Holstein), where he was shot on May 3, 1945, five days before the Nazi surrender. His prescient poem sets the tone, not only for the Bergen-Belsen collection, but is the *raison d'être* for this present one as well:

Ikh vil azoy leben,	I so want to live,
Ikh kan nokh nisht shtarbn.	I'm not ready to die.
Men zol mir oyf oygn nisht legn keyn sharbn.	I do not want stones to be placed on my eyes.
Ikh vil nokh derlebn di gliklekhe tsayt,	The happier times I would live to see,
Un zeyen di brider fun leydn bafrayt.	To see all my suffering brothers be free
Di tsayt iz nisht vayt,	The time's not far off— it must soon arrive,
Dos muz bald gesheyn,	But if it should happen that I'm not alive,
Ikh ober muz faln el kidush hashem.	I leave in my will all these songs that are ringing:
Ikh loz mayn tsevuah in klingende lider,	O, my poor tired sisters and brothers—keep singing!
Far mayne gemateter shvester un brider:	

Acknowledgments

In undertaking a project as vast as represented by this anthology it was impossible to imagine in advance where the road would lead. Libraries, museums, and archives yielded positive results time and again. Survivors with songs to share and memories to recount have made many pages of this book come alive. In this regard, I would like to offer my deeply felt thanks the following people:

PETE SEEGER of Beacon, New York. Friend, colleague, and lifetime inspiration. It was his singing that first introduced me to the beautiful songs of the Spanish Civil War and so many other musical gems of peace, brotherhood, and the struggle for human dignity. Two of his composition, *Lisa Kalvelege* and *Last Train to Nuremberg* help round out the section of post-war songs.

PAUL ROBESON, citizen of the world. My earliest recollections of this great singer and humanitarian date from an outdoor rally in Pelham Bay Park in the Bronx, early in the war (1940?) in support of "Russian War Relief." I particularly remember his singing of the Spanish Civil War song *Los Cuatro Generales* (The Four Insurgent Generals), and the special emphasis he placed on the line: *"Para la Nochebuena seran ahorcados"*—"By Christmas holy evening they'll all be hanging."

The next time I saw Robeson it was in 1943 from the balcony of the Broadway theater where he was giving his memorable performances of *Othello*. Then over several summers between 1945 and 1948 on his regular visits to a summer camp, Camp Wo-Chi-Ca, where I was first a camper and then a counselor he sang to us in many languages and inspired us with tales of the battles for freedom waged throughout the world, including the Spanish, Jewish, German, Chinese, and Russian people during the war and the Negro people right here at home.

Pete Seeger, Antoine Silverman, David Silverman and Jerry Silverman performing at the annual sloop *Clearwater* annual "Pumpkin Sail," October 1979. Photo by Tania Silverman.

Paul Robeson visiting Camp Wo-Chi-Ca in 1947. Jerry Silverman with his arms around the shoulders of two young campers.

ANNA CHRISTAKE CORNWELL of Hastings on Hudson, New York, for introducing me to the extraordinarily moving song *Asma Asmaton* by Mikis Theodorakis and Iakovos Kambanellis. Anna was born in the United States of Greek immigrant parents who returned to Greece with her and her younger brother in 1937, just before the outbreak of the war. Warned by the U.S. consul in 1940 that it would be unwise to remain in Greece in view of the precarious military situation, her father returned to the United States in order to prepare for the eventual return of the family, but the German invasion slammed the door shut before Anna and her mother and brother could escape. They spent the war years running from mountain village to mountain village, always one step ahead of the Germans who were pursuing the Resistance Fighters. After the war, in 1946, the Christake family was reunited in the United States. Anna, whose love of books and learning had sustained her during those terrible years, entered the City College of New York in 1948 and graduated in 1952. I spent those same four years at CCNY, but it was only while working on this book, forty-five years later, that I got to know her as a friend and neighbor.

LEAH GOLAN-PINKHOF of Kibbutz Sa'ad, Israel, survivor of Bergen-Belsen, for two songs composed by her father JOSEPH ZVI PINKHOF during their incarceration in that concentration camp. And to RABBI EDWARD SCHECHTER of Hastings on Hudson and DAVID SEGAL of Yonkers for translating these songs.

HANS SCHAPER of Hastings on Hudson, escaped from Germany in 1935 to avoid military service in the *Wehrmacht*. He had been a member of the militant anti-Nazi *Reichsbanner* Social Democratic movement. For carefully proofreading the German lyrics, as well as his helpful insights into political conditions in Germany in the 1930s and his infallible good humor.

TAMAS MOLNAR of Scarborough, New York, for his skillful help with Hungarian translations.

AVRUM KUSHNER of Stockholm. Avrum is a childhood friend of mine from the "Shtetl Bronx" days. He has been living in Sweden for over forty years, and I contacted him with hopes that he might be able to come up with some songs from the Swedish Jewish community. He put me in touch with LENNART KERBEL of Bromma, who is a teacher of Yiddish and director of a small Yiddish-language publishing house, Megilla-Förlaget. It was Kerbel that sent me a copy of the collection of concentration camp songs that was published by the Central Jewish Committee in Bergen-Belsen (discussed in the Introduction). Quite by chance, I mentioned this collection to a friend who informed me that the parents of a teacher-colleague of my wife were Bergen-Belsen survivors. Imagine my astonishment, upon showing the book to that colleague, to learn that her own parents had assisted in its publication—and that their names are cited as contributors in the introduction!

After the liberation they, BABEY and PAUL TREPMAN, emigrated to Montreal, always taking an active part in Holocaust-memorial related activities. Paul is the author of the memoir, "Among Men and Beasts" (also herein cited). I had the pleasure of meeting Babey when she visited her daughter in Scarsdale, New York, in December 1997. She had brought with her, for my benefit, a number of ghetto songs *(Unter Der Gelber Late, Motele Fun Varshaver Geto, Di Hoyf-Lid Fun Varshaver Geto)* which have made a significant contribution to this collection.

In December, 1997 Avrum took a trip from Sweden to New Jersey to visit his cousins. We had dinner together one evening during which time I told them all the story of the Trepmans. No sooner had I finished the tale of the amazing series of coincidences that had put me face to face with Babey Trepman, than Avrum's cousin Alex announced that he too had something to show me. With that, he produced an envelope containing mint-condition Theresienstadt bills *(Theresienstadt Gelt)*, scrip used as currency in the camp bearing the signature of Jacob Edelstein, *der Älteste der Juden* (the elder, or leader of the Jews). He had come upon them by chance while cleaning out his affairs prior to retiring from his company. They belong to the family of his late employer and, with the permission of William and Edward Nelkin they are included as illustrations on page 199.

Upon his return to Stockholm, Avrum, ever in pursuit of the elusive Swedish-Jewish song for this collection, finally made contact with the right person, DOCTOR SALOMON SCHULMAN, who had written a song on an unusual subject—the rescue of some of the last Jews alive in German concentration camps by the Swedish Red Cross in the spring of 1945. That song, *A Mol Iz Geven A Mayse (I'll Tell to You All a Story)*, tells this little-known story from a particularly ironic and bitter point of view.

On January 11, 1998 I attended an art exhibition and concert in Teaneck, New Jersey, entitled "Children of the Holocaust and the Third Reich Create Art and Music Together." This remarkable affair was sponsored by an organization called One By One, which seeks to effect reconciliation and understanding between these two seemingly irreconcilable groups. (For more on One By One, see the background for the song *We Are Here.*) One of the performers at this affair told me that his mother was a concentration camp survivor who knew, and had herself composed some songs that, except for her own singing, had never been heard in this country. So it was that I met IRENE HAAS SHAPIRO, a survivor of the Bialystok ghetto, its uprising and liquidation (August 1943), now living in Scarsdale, New York.

She was shipped off to Maidanek after the liquidation of the ghetto, where she remained until September 1943. From there she was moved to a camp at Blizhyn until her transfer to Auschwitz in May 1944. She survived the Auschwitz uprising of October 1944, only to be transported in November to a *Munitionswerke* in Westphalen-Liebstadt (Germany), making hand grenades for the by now retreating *Wehrmacht*. In March 1945, with the war nearing its conclusion, weakened by typhus, she was once again moved, this time to Bergen-Belsen. Liberation by the U.S. Army took place on April 15. A year later, in May 1946, she arrived in New York aboard the *Marine Perch*.

The songs that Irene sang for me in Yiddish, Polish, and Russian (*Vilner Geto Lid/Song of the Vilna Ghetto, Przed Ostatnią Podróżą /Before the Final Journey, Warszawo Ma /My Warsaw. Pesnia Bialystokskikh Partizanov/Song of the Bialystok Partisans*) were deeply moving, all the more so since the Polish and Russian ones are her own compositions. They are the personal statements of a survivor and a *fighter.*

Then came the greatest surprise of all. She told me that in 1956, while she was living on Gun Hill Road in the Bronx, she took guitar lessons from a certain Jerry Silverman! It was I who taught her to play the chords for the very songs that forty-two years later she would be singing for me. Our interview had been transformed into a reunion of the class of 1956!

JAAP (JAKOB) POLAK and CATHARINA (INA) SOEP POLAK, of Eastchester, New York, survivors of Westerbork and Bergen-Belsen. Since their arrival in New York in 1951 Jaap has devoted much of his energy to documenting and preserving the record of the Dutch Jews in the Holocaust. On the occasion of his eightieth birthday on December 31, 1992, and in recognition of his contributions in the field of Dutch Holocaust studies in general, and in particular, for his service as president of the Anne Frank Center, U.S.A., he was knighted by Queen Beatrix of the Netherlands. Ina and Jaap's contribution to this collection include a hitherto unpublished German-Dutch song from Bergen-Belsen *(Wir Singen Ein Schlager/We Zingen Een Lied/We're Singing A Song)*, priceless personal concentration camp documents from their collections, as well as offering invaluable first-hand insights into daily life in Westerbork and Bergen-Belsen. They also led me to DAVID NATALE, of New York City, an actor whose one-man show "The Westerbork Serenade" was staged in August 1997 as part of the New York International Fringe Festival. David supplied me with a recording of the song, *The Westerbork Serenade,* which was made in Amsterdam in 1944 by its composers, "Johnny and Jones." The extraordinary story behind that recording appears with the song in this collection.

My search for clarification of the meaning of some obscure terms in Willy Rosen's poem, *Adieu, Westerbork* led me to Amsterdam radio host and author JACQUES KLÖTERS. Jacques, who was for many years librarian at the Theater Institute of Amsterdam, was able to clear up a number of mysteries, as well as supply me with a wealth of information regarding pre-war and wartime musical cabaret activities in Holland.

ANTON KRAS of the Joods Historisch Museum (Jewish Historical Museum), Amsterdam. The song he contributed, *Waterlooplein,* offers a rare insight into Dutch-Jewish reactions to the Holocaust in Holland. Also the text to the Anne Frank Cantata, *A Child Of Light* by Hans Kox provided some invaluable citations from the archives of the SS.

SARA HALPERYN of the Memorial Du Martyr Juif Inconnu (Memorial of the Unknown Jewish Martyr), Paris. The crumbling, yellowed pages of their files yielded a small treasure of manuscripts of songs written by "martyrs," known and unknown, in French, Yiddish, and German.

JÜRGEN KESSLER of the Stiftung Deutsches Kabarettarchiv (German Cabaret-Archive Foundation), Mainz. He came up with the music for *Dachau-Lied* and *Buchenwald-Lied* as well as invaluable documentation on the background of those songs.

EILEEN GRIMES of the University of Manchester. Helped fill in some of the gaps in the life of Talmudic scholar and Theresienstadt survivor Dr. Berthold Jeitteles, descendant of an illustrious Jewish Czech family.

DIANE R. SPIELMAN of the Leo Baeck Institute, New York. Documentation on the wartime "emigrant cabarets" in New York and other cities was especially valuable.

LIV DAHL of the Sons of Norway Foundation, Minneapolis, for supplying a rare Norwegian concentration camp song, and to RANDI DALAGAR for translating it.

VOLKER KÜHN of Berlin. He compiled and edited the priceless collection *Kabarett unterm Hakenkreuz* (Cabaret under the Swastika) and generously shared some of the previously unpublished music with me.

Greek composer and patriot MIKIS THEODORAKIS, whom I had the good fortune to meet in June 2000, when he came to New York for the Carnegie Hall performance of his opera *Elektra*. When I requested permission to include his song *Asma Asmaton* (Song of Songs, page 245) in this collection, he graciously and enthusiastically gave me his blessing. My thanks go to him for composing it and allowing me to use it.

EDMOND AND CLAUDE KAHN of Paris, who supplied the Russian, French and German translations of the Vilno Ghetto partisan song, *Zog Nit Keynmol*.

The YIVO INSTITUTE FOR JEWISH RESEARCH in New York, in whose library were found precious historical items in German, Czech, Polish, French, and English that made significant contributions to this volume.

Other songwriters, friends and colleagues, have generously and graciously contributed their songs to this collection: TOM PAXTON, JANIS IAN, JUDY FRANKEL, ERIC ANDERSON, FRED SMALL, ROSALIE GERUT and SI KAHN. Thanks to you all.

I would be seriously remiss in acknowledging assistance and contributions to this book if I did not mention the most important source of all: The countless people who documented their hopes and despair, triumphs and defeats, cries and shouts in their songs through some of the darkest days that humanity has ever known.

The human spirit is truly AN UNDYING FLAME.

The Gathering Storm, 1933–1939

Germany First, 1933

1. Die Moorsoldaten (The Peat-Bog Soldiers)

The Börgermoor concentration camp was located in the northwest corner of Germany, near the Dutch frontier. In August 1933, in a *Zirkus Konzentrazoni,* a cabaret presentation in the camp, sixteen prisoners with spades on their shoulders marched onto the stage singing this song. The composer, Rudi Goguel, conducted the *Chorus* with a broken spade handle. Two days after its debut the song was *verboten.* Nevertheless, it was smuggled out to other camps and also published in exile newspapers. In 1935 it came to the attention of singer Ernst Busch, who recorded it with a musical arrangement by composer Hanns Eisler in Spain during the Civil War in 1938. It was largely due to this recording, and subsequent performances by Busch, and later by Paul Robeson, that this song became widely known throughout the world.

Words by Johann Esser and Wolfgang Langhoff

Music by Rudi Goguel

Hier in dieser öden Heide
ist das Lager aufgebaut,
wo wir fern von jeder Freude
hinter Stacheldraht verstaut. *Refrain*

Morgens ziehen die Kolonnen
in das Moor zur Arbeit hin.
Graben bei dem Brand der Sonnen,
doch zur Heimat steht der Sinn. *Refrain*

Heimwärts, heimwärts jeder sehnet
sich zu Eltern, Weib und Kind.
Manche Brust ein Seufzer dehnet,
weil wir hier gefangen sind. *Refrain*

Auf und nieder gehen die Posten,
Keiner, keiner kann hindurch.
Flucht wird nur das Leben kosten!
Vierfach ist umzäunt die Burg. *Refrain*

Doch für uns gibt es kein Klagen,
ewig kann's nicht Winter sein.
Einmal werden froh wir sagen:
Heimat, du bist wieder mein. *Refrain*

    Letze mal
‖:Dann ziehn die Moorsoldaten
nicht mehr mit dem Spaten ins Moor.:‖

Here in dreary desolation,
We're behind the prison wall.
Far from every consolation,
Barbed wire does surround us all. *Chorus*

Mornings we're marched out in one line,
On the moorland to our toil.
Digging in the burning sunshine,
Thinking of our native soil. *Chorus*

Homeward, homeward, each is yearning
For his parents, child and wife.
In each breast a sigh is burning—
We're imprisoned here for life. *Chorus*

Up and down the guards are pacing,
No one can escape this place.
Flight would mean a sure death facing,
Four-fold 'round the guards do pace. *Chorus*

But for us there is no complaining,
Winter will in time be past.
One day, free, we'll be exclaiming:
Homeland, you are mine at last. *Chorus*

    Last time
‖:Then no more will peat-bog soldiers
March with spades on shoulders to the bog.:‖

On April 24, 1990, the international day of commemoration of the deportees, this French version of *Die Moorsoldaten* (the first and last two verses) was sung at Yad Vashem in Jerusalem by a group of survivors who had gathered there to plant trees in memoriam.

Chant des Déportés—Song of the Deportees

Loin dans l'infini s'étendent
Les grands prés marécageux.
Pas un seul oiseau ne chante
Dans les arbres secs et creux.

Refrain
Ô terre de détresse,
Où nous devons sans cesse piocher.

Dans ce camp morne et sauvage,
Entouré de murs de fer,
Il nous semble vivre en cage,
Au milieu d'un grand désert. *Refrain*

Bruit de chaînes et bruit des armes,
Sentinelle jour et nuit;
Des pleurs, des cris et des larmes,
La mort pour celui qui fuit. *Refrain*

Mais un jour dans notre vie
Le printemps refleurira.
Libre alors, ô ma patrie,
Je dirai: "Tu est à moi."

Refrain Final
Ô terre enfin libre,
Où nous pourrons revivre, aimer.

French stamps commemorating the fiftieth anniversary of Franco-Israeli diplomatic relations.

Recommended Listening

Busch, Ernst. *Songs of the Spanish Civil War.* Vol. 1. Folkways/Smithsonian FH 5436 (cassette).

2. Das Einheitsfrontlied (The United Front Song)

Composed in 1936 in London, this song was popularized by German antifascist singer Ernst Busch, particularly through his recording "Six Songs for Democracy," which was made under fire in Barcelona during the Spanish Civil War in 1938. Hanns Eisler composed the music as a result of a direct request by Berthold Brecht, who had emphasized the need for a powerful song to be sung at the Popular Front Congress, then taking place in London. "Brecht phoned me," recalled Eisler, "and said the question of the unity of the workers was again important, and a song must be written about this. The next day already Ernst Busch was singing it in English." The song has been translated into many languages. A sampling of a few of them is given here.

Words by Berthold Brecht

Music by Hanns Eisler

Copyright © Deutscher Verlag für Muskik, Leipzig

Und weil der Mensch ein Mensch ist,
Drum braucht er Kleider und Schuh',
Und macht ihn kein Geschwätz nicht warm,
Und auch kein Trommeln dazu. *Refrain*

Und weil ein Mensch ein Mensch ist,
Drum hat er Stiefel im Gesicht nicht gern.
Er will unter sich keinen Sklaven sehn,
Und über sich keinen Herrn. *Refrain*

Und weil der Prolet ein Prolet ist,
Drum kann ihn kein anderer befreien,
Es kann die Befreiung der Arbeiter nur
Das Werk der Arbeiter sein. *Refrain*

Because a man is human,
He also needs clothing and shoes.
He won't get warm on idle talk,
And drum beats are just bad news. *Chorus*

Because a man is human,
He doesn't want a boot right in his face.
He neither wants slaves under him,
Nor lords from the "master race." *Chorus*

Because he's a proletarian,
No one else can ever set him free.
The liberation of the working class
Is the job of the worker, you see. *Chorus*

Spanish

Y como ser humano,
El hombre lo que quiere es su pan.
Las habladurias le baston ya,
Porque éstas nada le dan.
    Pues: un, dos, tres; Pues: un, dos, tres,
    Compañero, en tu lugar!
    Porque eres del pueblo afiliate ya
    En el frente popular.

French

Tu es un ouvrier—oui!
Viens avec nous, ami, n'ai pas peur!
Nous allons vers la grande union
De tous les vrais travailleurs.
    Marchons au pas, marchons au pas,
    Camarades, vers notre front!
    Range-toi dans le front de tous les ouvriers,
    Avec tous les frères étrangers.

Russian

I tak kak vsye my liudi,
To dolzhnyi my, izvinite, chto-to est'.
Khotyat nakormit' nas pustoi boltovnei—
K chortyam! Spasibo za chest'!
    Marsh levoi! Dva! Tri! Marsh levoi! Dva! Tri!
    Vstan' v ryadi, tovarishch, k nam!
    Tyi voidyosh' v nash edinyi rabochii front,
    Pochemu chto rabochii ty sam!

For the Yiddish version of this song see "Tsu, Eyns, Tsvey, Dray," page 62

Recommended Listening

Busch, Ernst. *Songs of the Spanish Civil War.* Vol. 1. Folkways/Smithsonian FH 5436 (cassette).
Haden, Charlie. *Liberation Music Orchestra.* Impulse 188 (CD).

3. Mein Vater wird Gesucht (My Father, He Was Tracked)

The first appearance of this song in Germany dates from that fatal year: 1933. There wasn't much singing possible in the *Illegal* (with the stress on the last syllable—the German word for the anti-Nazi movement) for obvious reasons, but the first waves of emigrants fleeing the rising oppression brought this song with them.

Words by Hans Drach

Music by Gerda Kohlmey

Die Mutter aber weint.
Wir lesen in Bericht,
der Vater sei gefangen
und hätt sich aufgehangen;
das glaub ich aber nicht.

Er hat uns doch gesagt,
so etwas tut er nicht.
Es sagen die Genossen,
SA hätt ihn erschossen
ganz ohne ein Gericht.

Heut weiß ich ganz genau,
warum sie das getan.
Wir werden doch vollenden,
was er nicht konnt beenden!
Und Vater geht voran!

My mother she does cry.
We read it in the news,
That father was arrested—
Hung himself—I contest it;
I don't believe it's true.

For he did tell us so,
That this was not his style.
Our comrades they all say,
He was shot by the S. A.,
Without even a trial.

Today I understand
The thing that they have done.
We'll end the work he started,
Since he is now departed;
And father will live on!

4. Das jüdische Kind (The Jewish Child)

I feel that is impossible that my son should sit alongside a Jew in a German high school and be taught German history. It is absolutely indispensable that Jews be expelled from German schools.
  Joseph Goebbels, November 12, 1938

Until the pogroms of *Kristallnacht* in November 1938, Jewish children were permitted to attend German public schools, although a majority were enrolled in Jewish schools. These Jewish schools bore a role of ever-increasing difficulty, doubling as educational institutions and safe havens for their students. They taught the general curriculum, as well as Jewish subjects and Hebrew. Beyond that, the teachers had to try to make sense to the children out of what was happening all around them. After *Kristallnacht* the influx of new students who had been expelled from the public schools made this task all the more onerous due to the shortage of teachers.

The moving text to this song was found, without music, in the archives of the *Memorial du Martyr Juif Inconnu* (Memorial to the Unknown Jewish Martyr) in Paris.

Music by Jerry Silverman

Ich spielte nie im Sonnenshein,
Und spielte nie im Blumenhain,
Und spielte nie im Sande.

Und als den Spielplatz ich durchging,
Ein Schreien und Rufen mich empfing:
Geh'weg, du feiger Jude.

Da weinte ich bitter und mit Schmach,
Da warfen sie mir Steine nach:
Geh' weg, du schmuts'ger Jude.

Da packte mich ein wilder Zorn,
Ich riß den Steck'n von dem Dorn,
Und wollte den Kerlen zeigen.

Da rief die Mutter, "Gott bewahr!
Mein Kind du bringst uns in Gefahr.
Mein Kind, der Jude muß schweigen."

I didn't play in bright sunshine,
Nor in woods where flowers twine,
Not even in the sandbox.

And when I walked through the playground,
I heard screams and cries all around:
Go 'way, you rotten Jew-boy.

So bitterly I cried in disgrace,
As they all threw stones in my face:
Go 'way, you dirty Jew-boy.

Into a great rage flew I.
I seized a thorny stick nearby,
To show those boys—I swear it.

My mother called out, "For God's sake,
There's danger here, make no mistake.
My child, a Jew must bear it.

Jerry Silverman on Jüdenstraße (Jews Street), [East] Berlin, 1959.
Photo by George Ohye.

5. Ich hab' kein Heimatland (I Have No Native Land)

Another of the songs found without music or background information in the Paris *Memorial du Martyr Juif Inconnu*.

Music by Jerry Silverman

Ich hab' kein Heimatland!
Ich habe nichts auf dieser Welt.
Ich zieh' von Land zu Land,
Und bleibe dort wo man mich hält.
Und als ich endlich dacht'
Daß ich den Frieden fand,
Doch muß ich weiter ziehn —
Ich hab' kein Heimatland.

I have no native Land,
I've not a thing in this wide world.
I roam from land to land,
And I remain where I am held.
And when at last I think
That peace is here at hand,
Then I must wander on —
I have no native land.

6. Buchenwald-Lied (Buchenwald Song)

It was as yet before the war, when the camp commandant announced a prize-competition: 10 marks and 100 cigarettes for a camp song. As a pocket-size "Führer," he wanted his camp to have its own camp song. We discussed it in our circle of comrades. It should be our song, in the prisoners' language [Sklavensprache] — of those of us who were under the authority of the SS. It should speak of our hope and unbroken faith. As our spokesman, an Austrian comrade composed it. He himself was later one of those who could no longer stand on his feet. In the Auschwitz camp he, along with many others, went to his death. But we are certain that in his last hour he bore in his heart the belief in the victory of freedom.

The SS had some idea of what this song meant to us. On a number of occasions they tried to introduce other songs composed by eager lackeys. But we clung to our song. We sang it in the mornings when we marched through the camp gate to our daily slave labor assignments; when, in the evenings, tired and bruised, we carried in our sick and dead. Often, after the hard day's labor, we stood, hungry and freezing in the roll-call until late at night, because, once more we were punished for something or other. Often because one of us had tried to escape; sometimes only because the report of a new military setback spoiled the mood of our torturers. When the order came to sing, our eyes sought out the crematorium, from whose chimney the flames rose to the sky. We put all our hatred into the song. As the hot coals burned we shouted the "Free" of the Chorus so that the forest resounded with it.

Robert Liebbrand, Prisoner No. 6613

Writing in the *Thüringer Zeitung* on July 23, 1945, Stefan Heymann added a wealth of detail to the fascinating story of this song:

Toward the end of 1938, the then Lagerführer Rödl announced: "All other camps have a song. We must get a Buchenwald song. Whoever writes one will get ten marks." Many outlines were submitted by the "poets" and "composers," but either they were not suitable or they did not meet with the approval of the SS command. Only the aforementioned song, the one then declared the official "Buchenwald Hymn," was successful, because the existing kapo of the sub-post office had the necessary connections with the SS. That kapo identified himself as the composer of the words and music of the song. In reality, the song was composed by two Austrian prisoners: the text by Beda-Löhner, Lehár's librettist, the music by Leopoldi, a Viennese cabaret singer. Beda-Löhner died in a sub-camp of Auschwitz. Leopoldi was able to emigrate to the United States of America just in time. Needless to say, the camp directors never found out who the real composers of the song were.

The [prisoners'] blocks had to rehearse the text and melody of the song in their free time, until one day, during evening roll call — it was late December 1938, bitter cold and with deep snow — came the order: Sing the Buchenwald Song! Naturally, the first time (11,000 people were standing in the roll-call yard) it did not sound well. Enraged, the stinking-drunk Rödl stopped it and gave the order that each block should practice it in the yard as long as it would take to get the song right. One can imagine what an infernal concert took place in the yard. When Rödl realized that it was not going to work out this way, he had them sing it verse by verse, over and over again. Only after the whole camp stood in this manner for about four hours in the bitterest cold, did he give the order to fall out. But even though each block generally made an about-face and returned to the camp, this time it was different. Lined up in rows of ten, each block had to march smartly by the gate past Rödl and other drunken SS officers singing the "Buchenwald Song." Woe to the block that did not line up properly enough, or whose singing did not satisfy Rödl's desires. Mercilessly, it was ordered to go back and march by once again. Finally, about ten o'clock at night we returned, starving and frozen stiff to our blocks. This scene in deepest winter, with the hungry and freezing people singing while standing in the glare of the spotlights in the garishly illuminated snow, has irrevocably engraved itself in the memory of each participant.

Composer Hermann Leopoldi added his recollections to those of Stefan Heymann:

This Buchenwald march extremely pleased the Lagerführer [Rödl]. In his weakness of intellect he absolutely did not see how revolutionary the song actually was. From that day on we had to sing the song morning, noon, and night. As the columns marched to work, they struck up the song after a few paces. Rödl enjoyed dancing to the melody, as on one side the camp orchestra played, and on the on the other side the people were whipped.

Buchenwald prisoner Robert Siewert recalled:
When we sang it we always put all our hatred and conviction into it.

The "Buchenwald Song," whose true authorship in the camp was concealed for fear of reprisals by the SS, was widely circulated. It was sung in other concentration camps and was even broadcast by foreign radio stations.

Fritz Beda-Löhner, who wrote the lyrics to "Buchenwald Song" was a well-known popular song lyricist, librettist and satirist for the thriving world of the Viennese cabaret in the post World War I years. His Doctor of Laws degree did not preclude his becoming one of the most popular "hit makers" of the 1920s. He wrote theatrical pieces, reviews, and cabaret numbers, as well as the librettos for Franz Lehár's operettas, "The Land of Smiles" and "Frederike," which contains the well-known aria, "Thine Is My Heart Alone" *(Dein ist mein ganzes Herz)*. He was arrested in 1938 by the Nazis and brought first to Dachau, then to Buchenwald, and finally to Auschwitz, where he died of exhaustion in December 1942.

On August 30, 1999 conductor Zubin Mehta directed a performance of Gustav Mahler's Symphony No. 2 ("The Resurrection") at the site of the Buchenwald camp. The orchestra was composed of musicians from the Bavarian State Symphony and the Israeli Philharmonic. "This concert," said Bernd Kauffmann, director of the festival which included the Mahler work, "was about showing that even the past symbolized by Buchenwald can be overcome, and the Germans whose forebears murdered Jews can sit now with Israelis and play the music of a Bohemian-Jewish-Austrian-German composer."

Words by Fritz Beda-Löhner Music by Hermann Leopoldi

Und das Blut ist heiß und das Mädel fern,
Und der Wind singt leis, und ich hab sie so gern,
Wenn treu sie, wenn treu sie mir bleibe!
Und die Steine sind hart, aber fest unser Schritt,
Und wir tragen die Pickel und Spaten mit,
Und im Herzen, im Herzen die Liebe. *Refrain*

Und die Nacht ist kurz und der Tag so lang,
Doch ein Lied erklingt, das die Heimat sang:
Und wir lassen den Mut uns nicht rauben!
Halte Schritt, Kamerad, und verlier nicht den Mut,
Denn wir tragen den Willen zum Leben im Blut,
Und im Herzen, im Herzen den Glauben. *Refrain*

And my blood is hot, and my girl's not here,
And the wind sings soft, and she is my dear.
If only, if only she stays true!
And the stones they are hard, but our step it is strong,
And we carry our picks and shovels along.
In my heart I love her — yes, I do! *Chorus*

And the night is short, and the day so long,
Yet the tune rings out — our homeland's song,
And our courage they'll never steal from us.
Keep it up, *Kamerad* — to your courage hold fast,
For our strong will to live will keep to the last,
In our hearts, in our hearts, we promise. *Chorus*

7. Dachau-Lied [a] (Dachau-Song [a])

Jura Soyfer was a well-known lyricist in the cabaret world of pre-war Vienna. He also wrote topical poetry for the *Arbeiterzeitung* ("Worker's Newspaper"). When the Germans marched into Vienna in March 1938 he attempted to escape to Switzerland but was captured and transported to the Dachau concentration camp that very same month. It was there he met the composer Herbert Zipper, and by that August the "Dachau Song" was born. The cynical inscription over the gate to the camp, *Arbeit macht frei* (Work Liberates), takes on new meaning in the chorus of this song. On his release from Dachau, Zipper brought the song to France, where it was sung in the internment camps. In March 1940 it was performed in the London exile cabaret *Laterndl* in the program "From Adam To Adolf."

Jura Soyfer was eventually transferred to Buchenwald where he died of typhus.

Words by Jura Soyfer

Music by Herbert Zipper

Vor der Mündung der Gewehre
leben wir bei Tag und Nacht.
Leben wird uns hier zur Lehre,
schwerer, als wir je gedacht.
Keiner mehr zählt Tag' und Wochen,
mancher schon die Jahre nicht,
Und so viele sind zerbrochen
und verloren ihr Gesicht. *Refrain*

Heb den Stein und zieh den Wagen,
keine Last sei dir zu schwer.
Der du warst in jüngsten Tagen,
bist du heute schon nicht mehr.
Stich den Spaten in die Erde,
grab dein Mitleid tief hinein,
und im eigenen Schweiße werde
selber du zu Stahl und Stein. *Refrain*

Einst wird die Sirene künden:
Auf, zum lezten Zählappell!
Draußen dann, wo wir uns finden,
bist du, Kamerad, zur Stell'.
Hell wird uns die Freiheit lachen,
schaffen heißt's mit großem Mut.
Und die Arbeit, die wir machen,
diese Arbeit, sie wird gut. *Refrain*

With the muzzles of their rifles
Pointed at us night and day,
We live here under a system
Harder than a man can say.
Days and weeks—nobody counts them;
Many do not count the years.
And so many men are broken—
Faces that are wet with tears. *Chorus*

Drag the stone and pull the wagon,
There's no task that you can't do.
Who, in bygone days you once were,
That man is no longer you.
Stick your shovel in the soil,
Bury deep just how you feel,
For in your own sweat you'll soon be
Like a stone and hard as steel. *Chorus*

One day when the sirens call us:
Out! This roll-call is the last!
Then, out there, where we'll be standing,
Comrade, we'll forget the past.
Brightly, Freedom will smile on us,
With fresh courage we'll advance.
For the work that we are doing,
Yes, this work's our only chance. *Chorus*

"Der Appellplatz" (The Roll-Call Yard). From *Concentration Camp and Ghetto Songs*, Bergen-Belsen, 1946. Artist, Rubin Koltar.

8. Dachau-Lied [b] (Dachau Song [b])

In 1940, in the French internment camp at Damigni (near Alençon), a second setting of Soyfer's lyrics was composed for chorus and piano by Marcel Rubin. A fellow prisoner had memorized the words and brought them to Rubin's attention. During the war this version of the song was sung by political emigrés in Mexico.

Words by Jura Soyfer

Music by Marcel Rubin

9. Ballade von der Judenhure Marie Sanders
(Ballad of the Jews'-Whore Marie Sanders)

On September 15, 1935, the so-called Nuremberg Laws were adopted. They effectively deprived German Jews of their citizenship; they were henceforth to be considered "subjects." Among other indignities inflicted upon them, Jews were forbidden to marry "Aryans" or to have sexual relations with them. Jumping on the anti-Semitic wagon with a vengeance was the unsavory Julius Streicher, a sadist and pornographer, who was the *Gauleiter* (administrative director) of Franconia. He published a crudely obscene weekly "newspaper" in Nuremberg entitled *Der Stürmer*, ("The Forward," or "Striker," a term borrowed from soccer) which was filled with lurid and inflammatory ravings about so-called Jewish sexual crimes and other imaginary depravities, such as "ritual murders." In reality, Streicher was expressing his own sick sexual fantasies in his articles. William L. Shirer recounted his impression of Streicher in his *Rise and Fall of the Third Reich*: "Until I faced him slumped in the dock in Nuremberg, on trial for his life as war criminal, I never saw him without a whip in his hand or in his belt, as he laughingly boasted of the countless lashings he had meted out." Streicher went to the gallows on October 16, 1946. It was in reaction to the Nuremberg Laws, Streicher, and the pogroms that they inspired that the incomparable Brecht-Eisler duo composed this song. It was widely performed in many exile cabarets. In 1939, with another musical setting by Fred Manfeld, Brecht's lyrics were sung in a program entitled "Going, Going—Gong!" in the London cabaret *Four-and-Twenty Black Sheep*.

Words by Berthold Brecht

Music by Hanns Eisler

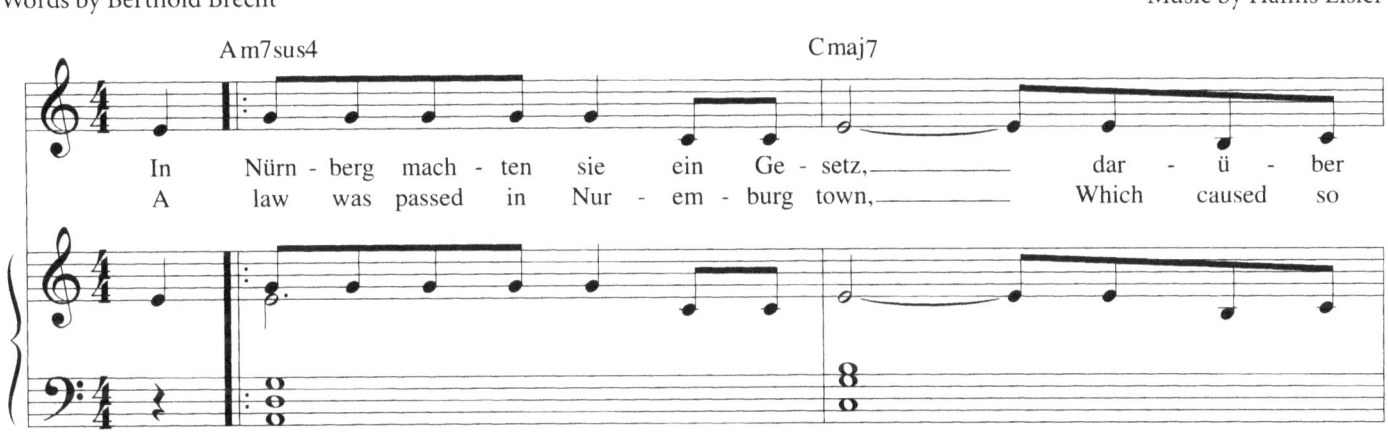

Copyright © by Deutscher Verlag für Musik, Leipzig

Marie Sanders, dein Geliebter hat zu schwarzes Haar,
Besser du bist heut' zu ihm nicht mehr
wie du ihm gestern warst. *Refrain*

Mutter, gib mir den Schlüssel,
Es ist alles halb so schlimm,
der Mond schaut aus wie immer. *Refrain*

Marie Sanders, your sweetheart's hair is a shade too black,
Today you'd better not go back,
As you did yesterday. *Chorus*

Mother, give me the key, please.
It is not so bad I'm sure—
The moon shines with the same allure. *Chorus*

From Spanish Trenches, 1936-1939

10. Hans Beimler

In 1809 German poet Johann Ludwig Uhland wrote a sentimental poem entitled *Ich hatt' ein Kameraden,* which described a soldier's reaction to the death in combat of his comrade-in-arms during the Napoleonic Wars. Friedrich Silcher set the poem to music in 1827, and since that date every German schoolchild has sung it. It was in the spirit of that song that Ernst Busch wrote *Hans Beimler.*

Hans Beimler, a deputy in the Bavarian Diet, was imprisoned in the concentration camp in Dachau early in 1933. He was one of the very few prisoners ever to escape from Dachau. He fought in the Spanish Civil War as Chief Political Commissar of the first contingent of International Brigade volunteers who helped save Madrid from fascist troops in November, 1936. ("*¡No pasarán!*" —"They shall not pass!" was their cry.) He was killed in action in Madrid in December 1936. This song was recorded by German singer Ernst Busch during an air raid on Barcelona in June 1938. He was backed by a chorus of members of the Thälmann Battalion (the 11th International Brigade). The original disc bore a sticker reading: "The defective impression of this recording is due to the interruptions of electric current during an air raid."

Music by Friedrich Silcher (1789–1860)
Words by Ernst Busch

Seine Heimat musst er lassen,	He was forced to leave his homeland,
Weil er Freiheitskämpfer war.	And to fight in freedom's war;
Auf Spaniens blut'gen Straßen,	On Spain's bloody streets it came to pass,
Für das Recht der armen Klassen,	For the rights of the poor working class,
Stand Hans, der Kommissar,	Died Hans, the commissar,
Stand Hans, der Kommissar.	Died Hans, the commissar.
Eine Kugel kam geflogen	A bullet came a-flying
Aus der «Heimat» für ihn her.	From his "homeland" it did come.
Der Schuss war gut erwogen,	The shot it struck him in the breast,
Der Lauf war gut gezogen—	The rifle barrel was the best—
Ein deutsches Schiessgewehr,	A German army gun,
Ein deutsches Schiessgewehr.	A German army gun.
Kann dir die Hand drauf geben,	I reach my hand out to you,
Derweil ich eben lad'—	As I load, I swear to God,
Du bleibst in unserm Leben,	That within our hearts you'll always live,
Dem Feind wird nicht vergeben,	The enemy we'll not forgive,
Hans Beimler, Kamerad,	Hans Beimler, *Kamerad*,
Hans Beimler, Kamerad.	Hans Beimler, *Kamerad*.

Recommended Listening

Busch, Ernst. *Songs of the Spanish Civil War.* Vol. 1. Folkways/Smithsonian FH5436 (cassette).

11. Lied der Internationalen Brigaden (Song of the International Brigades)

The International Brigades were formed of men who came from many countries and came to Spain to defend Spanish democracy against German, Italian, and Spanish fascism. A number of the songs sung by these fighters were issued by Keynote Records in 1940, under the title "Six Songs For Democracy." In the album notes singer Paul Robeson wrote: "Here are the songs recorded during heavy bombardment by men who were themselves fighting for the 'Rights of Man.' Valiant and heroic was the part played by the International Brigade in the glorious struggle of the Spanish Republic. I was there in the course of that struggle and my faith in man—in the eventual attaining of his freedom—was strengthened a thousand fold."

Words by Erich Weinert

Music by Espinosa-Palacio

Spaniens Brüder steh'n auf der Barrikade,
Unser Brüder sind Bauer und Prolet.
||:Vorwärts, Internationale Brigade!
Hoch die Fahne der Solidarität!:||

Spaniens Freiheit heißt jetzt unser Ehre.
Unser Herz ist international.
||:Jagt zum Teufel die Fremdenlegionäre,
Jagt ins Meer den Banditengeneral.:||

Träumte schon in Madrid sich zur Parade,
Doch wir waren schon da, er kam zu spät.
||:Vorwarts, Internationale Brigade!
Hoch die Fahne der Solidarität!:||

Mit Gewehren, Bomben und Granaten,
Wird das Ungeziefer ausgebrannt.
||:Freit das Land von Banditen und Piraten,
Brüder Spaniens, denn euch gehört das Land.:||

Dem Faschistengesindel keine Gnade,
Keine Gnade dem Hund, der uns verrät!
||:Vorwärts, Internationale Brigade,
Hoch die Fahne der Solidarität!:||

On the barricades, our Spanish brothers—
Workers fighting for their liberty.
||:Forward march, the International Brigade troops!
Raise the banner of solidarity!:||

Spanish freedom now is our honor,
Our heart is international.
||:And to hell with the hated Foreign Legion;*
To the sea with the bandit general.†:||

Dreamt that in Madrid he'd be parading,
We were there first—he was late, you see.
||:Forward march, the International Brigade troops!
Raise the banner of solidarity!:||

With our rifles, bombs and hand grenades, now,
Fascist vermin will be burned away.
||:All the bandits and pirates will be gone soon,
Spanish brothers, the land is yours today.:||

Show no mercy to the fascist lackeys,
To the dog guilty of such treachery!
||: Forward march, the Intenational Brigade troops!
Raise the banner of solidarity!:||

Recommended Listening

Busch, Ernst. Songs of the Spanish Civil War. Vol. 1. Folkways/Smithsonian FH 5436 (cassette).

* Moorish (North African) fascist soldiers.
† Franco.

12. Die Thälmann-Kolonne (The Thaelmann Column)

Named after after Ernst Thaelmann (Thälmann), the Communist candidate who placed third behind Hindenburg and Hitler in the presidential election of 1932, the Thaelmann Column (or Batallion) was the first unit of the International Brigades to arrive in Spain. It was commanded by author Ludwig Renn, and was composed mainly of German, and some British, Communists. At dawn on the morning of November 7, 1936, the beleaguered inhabitants of Madrid were awakened by the firm tramp of disciplined troops marching through the city. They rushed to their windows thinking that Franco's army had captured the city. What they saw was the first body of highly trained troops marching behind the purple, gold and red banner of Republican Spain. It was the Thaelmann Batallion marching out to the Manzanares River west of the city to do battle with the advancing fascists. It was largely the heroism of the Thaelmann Batallion, together with the French 14th Brigade, that saved Madrid then, when Franco was at the city gates. Only a handful of the original 500 men in the batallion survived the Civil War. Thaelmann himself never set foot in Spain. He was imprisoned in Buchenwald, where he died in August 1944. The Germans announced that he had been killed by American bombs, but the U. S. Air Force stated that there had not been an air raid at or near the camp during that period. In all probability he was murdered on Himmler's orders, as part of a purge to eliminate all possible leaders of any post-Hitler government. German composer Paul Dessau, using the *nom de plume* Peter Daniel, wrote the music for this song (which is also known as *Freiheit*—"Freedom") in exile in Paris in 1936.

Words by Karl Ernst

Music by Peter Daniel

Dem Faschisten werden wir nicht weichen,
Schickt er auch die Kugeln hageldicht.
Mit uns steh'n Kameraden ohne gleichen,
Und ein Rückwärts gibt es für uns nicht. *Refrain*

Rührt die Trommel! Fällt die Bajonette!
Vorwärts marsch! Der Sieg ist unser Lohn!
Mit der roten Fahne brecht die Kette!
Auf zum Kampf das Thälmann-Bataillon! *Refrain*

We'll not yield a foot to Franco's fascists,
Even though the bullets fall like sleet.
With us stand those peerless men, our comrades,
And for us there can be no retreat. *Chorus*

Beat the drums and get the bayonets ready.
Forward march! For vict'ry's our reward.
With the scarlet banner smash the shackles.
Into battle with Thaelmann's mighty sword. *Chorus*

Recommended Listening

Busch, Ernst. *Songs of the Spanish Civil War.* Vol. 1. Folkways/Smithsonian FH 5436 (cassette).

13. Jarama Valley

You came to us from all peoples, from all races. You came like brothers of ours, like sons of undying Spain; and in the hardest days of the war, when the capital of the Spanish Republic was threatened, it was you, gallant comrades of the International Brigades, who helped save the city with your fighting enthusiasm, your heroism and your spirit of sacrifice. In deathless verses of Jarama and Guadalajara, Brunete and Belchite, Levante and the Ebro, sing the courage, the sacrifice, the daring, the discipline of the men of the International Brigades . . . LONG LIVE THE HEROES OF THE INTERNATIONAL BRIGADES!

Dolores Ibarruri (*La Passionaria*). Farewell speech to the International Brigades, Barcelona, September, 1938.

The first Americans to fight in World War II saw action in the Jarama Valley on February 23, 1937. They had arrived in Spain one month earlier—3200 strong, as members of the Lincoln Brigade (the 15th Battalion of the International Brigade). It was the first time in American history that there was a mass volunteering for service in a foreign war. During the second attack, on February 27, out of a front-line force of 500 men, 127 were killed and 200 wounded. The Lincoln Battalion fought as shock troops in every major battle from then on until the battle of the Ebro River in September 1938 when all the International Brigades were dissolved. About half of the "Lincolns" never returned from Spain. Of the survivors, almost all who were able donned uniforms again when the United States entered the war on December 7, 1941. Of these, four hundred more perished fighting fascism on far-flung battlefields in North Africa, Europe, and the Pacific. During the McCarthy witchhunts of the 1950s, these brave men were labled "subversives" and, incredibly, "premature anti-fascists." Time and reason have vindicated them.

Tune: Red River Valley

There's a val-ley in Spain called Ja-ra-ma, It's a place that we all know so well.

We are proud of the Lincoln Battalion,
And the fight for Madrid that it made;
There we fought like true sons of the people,
As part of the Fifteenth Brigade.

Now we're far from that valley of sorrow,
But its memory we ne'er will forget—
So, before we conclude this reunion,
Let us stand to our glorious dead.

British troops who fought alongside the Lincolns added:

We are proud of our British Battalion,
And the stand for Madrid that they made,
For they fought like true sons of the soil,
As part of the Fifteenth Brigade.

With the rest of the international column,
In the fight for the freedom of Spain,
They swore on the Valley of Jarama
That fascism never should reign.

Recommended Listening

Guthrie, Woody. In *Songs of the Spanish Civil War*. Vol. 2. Folways/Smithsonian FH 5437 (cassette)

Guthrie, Woody. *This Land Is Your Land.* Folkways/Smithsonian 40100 (CD).

Seeger, Pete. In *Songs of the Spanish Civil War*. Vol. 1. Folkways/Smithsonian FH5436 (cassette).

Glazer, Tom. In *Songs of the Spanish Civil War*. Vol. 1 Folkways/Smithsonian FH5436.

14. Viva la Quince Brigada (Long Live the Fifteenth Brigade)

The album *Songs of the Lincoln Brigade* was recorded in New York in 1940 by Asch Records. Pete Seeger was the soloist, backed up by Bess Lomax, Baldwin Hawes, Tom Glazer and a Chorus of Lincoln Brigade veterans. In the booklet accompanying the album, Norman Corwin wrote: "These are the songs of men who left home and safety behind them in 1937 to fight fascism four years before it was fashionable. Against the majority of that time, they insisted that America's emblem was indeed an eagle and not an ostrich. It may be a long time before popular history gives them due and proper honor; but free men everywhere who recognized them and judge them now, will welcome these tangible memoranda of their brave struggle." This song (with different lyrics) was sung by Spanish partisans fighting Napoleon's armies in 1808.

||:Luchamos contra los moros,
Rumbala, rumbala, rumbala.:||
||:Mercenarios y fascistas,
¡Ay, Manuela! ¡Ay Manuela!:||

||:We are fighting 'gainst the Moors now,
Rumbala, rumbala, rumbala.||
||:They are mercenary fascists,
¡Ay, Manuela! ¡Ay Manuela!:||

Similarly

||:Solo es nuestro deseo . . . :||
||:Acabar con el fascismo . . . :||

||:En el frente de Jarama . . . :||
||:No tenemos ni aviones,
Ni tanques, ni canones,!Ay, Manuela!:||

||:Ya salimos de España . . . :||
||:Por luchar en otros frentes . . . :||

||:We have only one desire . . . :||
||: That's to put and end to fascism . . . :||

||: In the front lines of Jarama . . . :||
||:We do not have any airplanes,
Or tanks or any cannons.:||

||:Now from Spain we are departing . . . :||
||:For to fight in other battles.:||

Recommended Listening

Haden, Charlie. *Liberation Music Orchestra.* Impulse 188 (CD).
Seeger, Pete. *The Essential Pete Seeger.* Vanguard 97/98 (CD & cassette).
———. *Songs of the Spanish Civil War.* Vol. 1. Folkways/ Smithsonian 5436 (cassette).

15. Si Me Quieres Escribir (If You Want to Write to Me)

On July 17, 1936, an army mutiny broke out in Spanish Morocco. Within forty-eight hours the fighting had moved to the mainland, and all of Spain was soon involved in a bloody civil war. On October 1, Franco assumed the leadership of nationalist Spain, outlining his proposed governmental policies, which included the chilling concept of preferential treatment for "nations of related race, language or ideology." His racist policies notwithstanding, Franco relied heavily on the use of Moroccan troops (obliquely referred to in the song as *"un moro Mojame"* — "a Moor that's called Mohammed"). Gandesa, near the Ebro River, was the scene of bitter fighting in the spring and summer of 1938. By August, Franco's troops, armed with the latest German equipment, succeeded in decimating the Republican army. On October 1, the League of Nations supervised the repatriation of the International Brigadiers from Barcelona.

||:Si tu quieres comer bien,
Barato y de buena forma,:||
||:En el frente de Gandesa
Allí tiene una fonda.:||

||:En la entrada de la fonda
Hay un moro Mojame,:||
||:Que te dice, "Pasa, pasa.
¿Que quieres para comer?":||

||:El primero plato que dan
Son grenadas rompedoras,:||
||:El segundo de metralla,
Para recordar memorias.:||

||:If you want to dine quite well,
Cheaply, yet in proper manner,:||
||:In the front lines near Gandesa,
There they have a little tavern.:||

||: At the entrance to the tavern,
There's a Moor who's called Mohammed,:||
||:Who says to you, "Enter, enter.
What would you like for your dinner?":||

||:Well, the first course that they serve
Is made up of hand grenades,:||
||:And the second is machine guns,
So you won't forget this day.:||

Repeat verse one

Recommended Listening

Seeger, Pete. *Songs of the Spanish Civil War.* Vol. 1. Folkways/Smithsonian FH5436 (cassette).

En el frente de Gandesa.

16. Venga Jaleo (Join in the Struggle)

In immediate response to the Franco rebellion, the Fifth Regiment was formed by the Spanish Communist Party in July 1936. By December of that year, this group of 70,000 strong was the backbone of the defense of Madrid. Other Loyalist political parties (Socialist, Anarchist, Republican) also recruited their own military units, but these splinter groups were soon broken up, reorganized, and put under unified command in early 1937.

The expression *venga jaleo* is a hunter's rallying cry, similar to the British "view halloo."

Con el Quinto, Quinto, Quinto,	With the Fifth, the Fifth, the Fifth,
Con el Quinto Regimiento,	With the Fifth Regiment I'm leaving.
Tengo que marchar al frente,	I must march up to the front line,
Porque quiero entrar en fuego. *Estribillo*	For I want to join the battle. *Chorus*

Con los cuatro batallones
Que están Madrid defendiendo,
Va toda la flor de España,
La flor mas roja del pueblo. *Estribillo*

With the noble four batallions
That Madrid has to defend her,
Goes the flower of the people,
Yes, the reddest Spanish flower. *Chorus*

Con Lister y Campesino,
Con Galán y con Modesto,
Con el commandante Carlos,
No hay miliciano con miedo. *Estribillo*

With Lister* and Campesino,*
With Galan* and with Modesto,*
With the commandante Carlos,*
There is none who fears the battle. *Chorus*

Madre, madre, madre,
Vaya usted mirando,
Nuestro regimiento
Se aleja cantando. *Estrebillo*

Mother, mother, mother,
Won't you come and look and wonder,
Our regiment is leaving,
With our voices loud as thunder. *Chorus*

Recommended Listening

Seeger, Pete. *Songs of the Spanish Civil War.* Vol. 1. Folkways/Smithsonian FH5436 (cassette).

*Gen. Enrique Lister, Cmdr. Valentín Gonzales ("El Campesino"), Maj. Francisco Galán, Gen. Juan Modesto, Carlos J. Contreras (*nom de guerre* of Jewish Italian journalist Vittorio Vidali).

17. Los Cuatro Generales (The Four Insurgent Generals)

The "four insurgent generals" were Francisco Franco, Emilio Mola, Gonzalo Queipo de Llano and José Enrique Varelo. Each one was in command of one of the four columns advancing on Madrid in 1936. The term "fifth column" was coined by Franco at this time describing the traitors operating on his behalf within the gates of the city. Defending Madrid were the International Brigades led by General Miaja.

Madrid, qué bien resistes, (3)
Mamita mía,
Los bombardeos, los bombardeos.

De las bombas se rien, (3)
Mamita mía,
Los madrileños, los madrileños.

Para la Nochenbuena, (3)
Mamita mía,
Seran ahorcados, seran ahorcados.

Madrid, how well you stand up, (3)
Mamita mía,
To the bombardments, to the bombardments.

At the bombs they are laughing, (3)
Mamita mía,
The *madrileños*, the *madrileños*.*

By Christmas holy evening, (3)
Mamita mía,
They'll all be hanging, they'll all be hanging.

Recommended Listening

Busch, Ernst. *Songs of the Spanish Civil War.* Vol. 1. Folkways/Smithsonian FH 5436 (cassette).
Haden, Charlie. *Liberation Music Orchestra.* Impulse 188 (CD).
Robeson, Paul. *Songs for Free Men 1940-1945.* Pearl/9264 (CD).

*Citizens of Madrid.

Shoah, 1940–1945

18. Gehat Hob Ikh A Heym (Oh, Once I Had a Home)

Born in Krakow, Poland, in 1877, Mordekhai Gebirtig wrote poems and songs mirroring the life of the Jewish people around him. With the German invasion of Poland in 1939, that life turned into a horrible nightmare. This song was written in 1941, one year before he fell victim to the Gestapo round-up of Jews in Krakow. Emil Gorovets, Russian-Yiddish singer and composer, emigrated to the United States in 1974.

Words by Mordekhai Gebirtig

Music by Emil Gorovets

Used with the kind permission of The Workman's Circle

Gehat hob ikh a heym, a shtibl un a kikh
Un shtil gelebt azoy zikh yorn lang.
Gehat fil gute fraynd, khaveyrim arum zikh,
A shtibl ful mit lider un gezang.
    Gekumen zey, vi kumen volt a pest,
    Aroysgeyogt fun shtot mit vayb un kind.
    Geblibn on a heym vi feygl on a nest,
    Nisht-visndik far vos, far velkhe zind?

Yes, once I had a home, a kitchen, room and all,
And lived there peacefully—who knows how long.
I had so many friends that often came to call.
The house was filled with singing and with song.
    And then, just like the plague, they did arrive.
    Exiled with wife and child we did submit.
    Like homeless birds, how could we then survive,
    Not knowing why—what sin did we commit?

Sung to last 8 measures

Gehat hob ikh a heym, itst hob ikh zi nisht mer,
A shpil geven far zey mayn untergang—
Ikh zukh itst a naye heym, nor shver—oy zeyer shver,
Un kh'veys nisht vu—un kh'veys nisht af vi lang

O, once I had a home—but now I have no more.
For them my degradation was child's play.
I seek another place—I go from door to door;
But where? How long? Impossible to say.

19. Vu Ahin Zol Ikh Geyn? (Where, O Where Shall I Go?)

A pre-war song of uncertain origin, whose prophetic words took on bitter meaning in the grim years of the war. Korntayer, an actor in the Polish-Yiddish theater, perished in the Warsaw ghetto in 1942.

Words by S. Korntayer (?) Words by Oscar Strock (?)

20. Gib A Brokhe Tsu Dayn Kind (Bless the Child That Cries to Thee)

Ikh gedenk vos iz demolt geven,
Eyn tog der vayser, herlekh un sheyn.
Un mayn mame iz bay der kikh farnumen,
Di shvester, di kleyne, iz arayngekumen.
Zi hot gehert a nayes haynt af der gas,
Az morgn fri vet a registratsye zayn,
Az yunge mener biz finf un draysik yor,
Muzn morgn baym arbetsamt shteyn.
    Mame, mame, blayb gezund,
    Avek fun dir muz ikh atsind.
    Az got vet gebn gezunt un lebn,
    Veln mir zikh zen gezunt.

I do remember how it all occurred
That pleasant day — I still hear every word.
My mother, occupied with kitchen chores,
My sister, coming in from out of doors.
Out on the street that day the news she heard,
"Registration" — that doubly hated word;
That all young men up to age thirty-five,
Must report to work or lose their lives.
    Mother, for your health I pray.
    I must leave — I'm on my way.
    If God will give now good health, we'll live now.
    We will meet again some day.

21. Mayn Mame Hot Gevolt Zayn Af Mayn Khasene (My Mother Wanted So to See My Wedding Day)

Shtarker, beser! Di rod, di rod makht greser!
Groys hot mich Got gemakht,
Glik hot er mir gebrakht.
Hulyet, kinder, a gantse nakht!
Di mezinke oysgegebn!
Di mezinke oysgegebn!

Better, stronger! Let's dance a little longer!
God has exalted me,
He has made me happy.
Let the party just be carefree!
For my youngest daughter's married!
For my youngest daughter's married

Di Mezinke Oysgegebn (My Youngest Daughter's Married), a wedding song from a happier time

Words by David Bromberg

Music by Emil Gorovets

Mayn mame hot gevolt zayn af mayn khasene.
To vos zhe shlingstu, narele, a trer?
Me zogt, az me darf veynen af a khasene,
Iz veyn zhe, az du zolst nit veynen mer.

Mayn mame hot gevolt zayn af mayn khasene.
A gliklekhe, zi kumt tsu mir aher.
Klezmorim, shpilt, klezmorim shpilt gelasener,
Mayn mame geyt mit alemen a sher.

My mama wanted so to see my wedding day,
Then tell me why a tear is in your eye.
They say one has to cry upon a wedding day
So cry today, and nevermore you'll cry.

My mama wanted so to see my wedding day.
A happy one—I see her standing there.
Musicians, play—musicians, o, why don't you play?
See mama dance with everyone *a sher.**

*A lively Russian folk dance.

22. Lid Fun Bug (Song of the River Bug)

The River Bug defines the border between Poland and its neighbors Belarus and the Ukraine. Further south, in the Ukraine, west of the Bug, flows the Dniester. The land between the Bug and the Dniester is known as Transniestria. Rumanian and Moldavian Jews were transported to camps in this region, located in Lvov and Stryzh. Before the German invasion of the USSR in June 1940, Jews in Nazi-occupied Poland were sometimes driven by the Gestapo to River Bug frontier crossing points, where they were permitted entry by sympathetic Red Army border guards. However, in mid-October 1939 the border was suddenly sealed. That did not deter the Gestapo from continuing to transport Jews to the no-man's land, where they often were literally chased back and forth in a grotesque "dance of death." Uncounted numbers perished in the open fields.

Fun der heymat undz fartribn
In a fremdn land.
‖:Gornisht iz undz mer farblibn,
Mir zaynen farbant.:‖

Dort vu s'flist der breyter Dnyester,
Shikt a grus dir tsu,
‖:Fun dayn mame, fun dayn shvester,
Vos zey zaynen do.:‖

Keyn grub un keyn matseyve
Zaynen far undz do.
‖:In a masngrub a groysn,
Legt men undz tsu ru.:‖

Eybik vet der tsorn nit doyern,
Endikn vet zikh der krig.
‖:Un di zun vet vider shaynen,
Undzerer iz der zig.:‖

We've been driven from our homeland,
To a foreign land.
‖:We will never see our own land,
For we all are banned.:‖

There, where flows the River Dniester,
Greetings come to you.
‖:From your mother and your sister.
They are captives, too.:‖

No grave and not a tombstone
Do await us here.
‖:In a huge and unmarked mass grave
We will disappear.:‖

Our suffering's not endless,
One day the war's end we'll see.
‖:Once again there'll be bright sunshine;
Ours will be the victory.:‖

I also crossed the River Bug but under vastly different conditions than those described in this song. It was July 1959. My friend George Ohye and I were on a six-month jaunt through Europe, driving a Ford station wagon loaded with guitars, banjos, recording equipment, music books, and other odds and ends from London to Moscow— "from Soho to Red Square"— and back. We had built into the rear of the wagon three large "coffins"— complete with brass handles— to hold all our belongings. These coffins occupied the space all the way from the tailgate right up to the backs of the front seats. The only way their hinged lids could be opened was by dragging them out of the car and laying them flat on the ground. They were designed this way in order to foil the attempts of any would-be thieves. Our design worked perfectly. Of course, it caused much curiosity in the minds of customs inspectors as we crossed border after border. When we left Western Europe and traveled further east through Czechoslovakia and Poland the car itself contributed to the general wonderment. In those years American visitors were somewhat of a rarity in those parts, and American cars were virtually never seen at all. Leaving Warsaw, we approached the Polish-Soviet border with rising anticipation and a little apprehension. As we neared our destination the country grew more and more desolate. Flat fields and a few farm houses. No real signs of life. We could not help thinking about the mighty armies that surged over these very plains not so long before. This road carried Hitler's Panzer Divisions eastward in 1940 and the Red Army westward in 1944. The River Bug, the border between Poland and what then was the Soviet Union, is spanned by a narrow wooden bridge. As we dragged our "coffins" out for the Polish guards to inspect we saw a Red Army soldier with a machine slung over his shoulder watching us curiously from the other side of the bridge. Having satisfied the Polish inspectors, we reloaded the car and proceeded slowly across the bridge toward the closed railroad-crossing type gate on the other side and the young soldier with the machine gun. We had crossed the Bug.

23. Makh Tsu Di Eygelekh (Now Close Your Little Eyes)

In spite of the overwhelming odds against surviving, some *did* come out of the camps alive. Poet Isaiah Shpigl lived through the Lodz ghetto and Auschwitz to resume his writing career in Israel. David Beyglman wrote music for the vibrant pre-war Yiddish theater. He perished in Treblinka's gas chambers.

Words by Isaiah Shpigl

Music by David Beyglman (1887–1944)

Di velt hot got farmakht,
Un umetum is nakht.
Zi vart af undz
Mit shoyder un mit shrek.
Mir shteyn beyde do,
In shverer, shverer sho,
Un veysn nit vuhin
S'firt der veg.

Men hot undz naket, bloyz,
Faryogt fun undzer hoyz.
In finsternish
Getribn undz in feld.
Un shturem, hogl vint,
Hot undz bagleyt, mayn kind,
Bagleyt undz inem opgrunt
Fun der velt.

God has forsaken all,
The world is in a pall.
It waits for us
With terrifying deeds.
We both are standing here,
And we are gripped by fear,
For we cannot say where
The highway leads.

They chased us naked, bare —
Our home they did not spare.
In dark of night
They drove us out as well.
The hail and wind blew wild,
As you and I, my child,
Were chased into the very
Depths of hell.

Recommended Listening

Gorby, Sara. *Unforgettable Songs of the Ghetto.* Arion 64081 (CD).

Rubin, Ruth. *Yiddish Songs of the Holocaust.* Global Village 150 (CD).

24. Nit Keyn Rozhinkes, Nit Keyn Mandlen (Neither Raisins Nor Almonds)

Unterm yidele's vigele,
Shteyt a klor vays tsigele.
Dos tsigele iz geforn handlen,
Dos vet zayn dayn baruf.
Rozhinkes mit mandlen—
Shlof-zhe, yidele, shlof,
Shlof-zhe, yidele, shlof.

'Neath the cradle of my young son,
Stands a goat, yes, a pure white one.
The little goat has been fated to wander.
That will be your fate, too.
Raisins, sweet, and almonds—
Sleep then, my little Jew,
Sleep then, my little Jew.

Rozhinkes Mit Mandlen (Raisins and Almonds), by Abraham Goldfadden, 1840–1906.

Words by Yeshaye Shpigl

Music by David Beyglman

Shrayen soves, s'voyen velf,
Got, derbarem zikh un helf,
    Lyulinke, mayn zun.
Ergets shteyt er un er vakht,
Mandlen, rozhinkes a zakh,
    Lyulinke, mayn zun.

Owls do screech and wolves do yelp,
Pity us, dear God, and help,
    Hush-a-bye, my son.
He is keeping watch somewhere,
Almonds, raisins will be there,
    Hush-a-bye, my son.

Sung to last 6 measures

Kumen r'vet af zikher shoyn,
Zen dikh, kind, mayn eynstik kroyn,
    Lyulinke, mayn kind

Surely, he'll come back to town,
To see you, my precious crown.
    Hush-a-bye, my son.

"Nazi Physical Culture." From *Concentration Camp and Ghetto Songs*, Bergen-Belsen, 1946. Artist, Rubin Koltar.

From *Concentration Camp and Ghetto Songs*, Bergen-Belsen, 1946. Artist, Yakob Nafarstek.

25. Tsi Darf Es Azoy Zayn?(And Must It Be This Way?)

In an effort to maintain some sense of "normalcy" in the Vilna ghetto, theatrical perfomances and concerts continued, despite ever-worsening conditions. Kasriel Broydo directed many of these productions until his arrest by the Gestapo. He was first sent to the Stutthof concentration camp near Gdansk. With the Red Army drawing ever nearer, on January 25, 1945, the 20,000 (some estimates put the number as 50,000) inmates of the camp were cleared out of the camp and forced to march through a bitterly cold snowstorm. Some were sent westward toward Germany. Another contingent of about 7,000 was directed east. It was literally a death march, with their SS escorts shooting stragglers, while other exhausted prisoners simply froze to death along the way. When the ragged eastbound column reached Palmnicken (now called Yantarny), near Königsberg (Kaliningrad), on the frozen Baltic Sea, they were imprisoned for a few days in the Palmnicken locksmith's factory. Then they were marched *zu Fünfen*—five abreast, the standard concentration camp formation—to the water's edge, where the Nazis began pushing them into the frigid waters through holes they had blasted in the ice. Anyone attempting to scramble out of the water was either shot or pushed back. Broydo was one of those who drowned.

On January 30, 2000, on the 55th anniversary of the all-but-forgotten Palmnicken massacre, about 200 mourners gathered on the freezing, wind-whipped beach at the very place where the innocents had been murdered to dedicate a small pyramid of stones and a plaque to their memory. It was the first "official recognition" of the atrocity that had taken place there. Rabbi David Shvedik of the Jewish Community of Kaliningrad who spoke at the ceremony said, "For the authorities in Yantarny and in the region, it was not at all interesting to them to remember the 7,000 dead Jews."

By Kasriel Broydo

Far zey di skvern un bulvarn,
Far mir aza kvartal.
Far vos zol yener mikh alts narn?
Far vos far mir a trern-kval?
Far vos der oyfshrift afn bretl:
"Farvert iz nit vayter geyn"?
Far vos far zey mayn heym, mayn betl,
Un mayn geleger hart vi shteyn? *Tsuzung*

For them the boulevards and squares,
While I live in a slum.
Why should I suffer mocking stares?
I weep hot tears till I grow numb.
Why this inscription on the wall:
"You cannot go past here"?
Why do they take my home, my all?
At night I lay me down in fear. *Chorus*

26. Tsu Eyns, Tsvey, Dray! (So, One, Two, Three!)

The Brecht-Eisler *United Front Song* was known and sung throughout pre-war Europe. Its militant anti-fascist lyrics and stirring melody inspired Republican soldiers in the trenches of the Spanish Civil War, underground resistance fighters and concentration camp prisoners. Leyb Rozental borrowed Eisler's tune, while reworking the lyrics to fit the ever-worsening conditions of the Vilna ghetto where he lived and died.

Words by Leyb Rozental (1916–1941)

Music by Hanns Eisler (adapted)

Itst iz far undz farvert trotuaren,
Khotsh andere geyen dort fray.
Un mir, tut a kuk afn sheynernem bruk,
Und ayzerne klep fun nagay.
    Tsu, eyns, tsvey, dray; tsu, eyns, tsvey dray,
    Dem bruk hot men undz nor gelozt.
    Hot der trot aza klang, gor an ander gezang,
    Ven du geyst un du veyst nit far vos.

Es hobn alte un yunge
Dos lebn geboyt un gehoft,
Biz es hot aza shverd, alts farvisht fun der erd,
Und gefirt hot men undz vi di shof.
    Tsu, eyns, tsvey, dray; tsu, eyns, tsvey, dray,
    Azoy vi di shof zikh gelozt.
    Vu dayn vayb, vu dayn kind, vu dos ganze gezind?
    Keyner veys nit vuhin un far vos.

Nor, bruder, an anderer ritm
Vet bald tsu dayn oyer dergeyn.
Un di, vos far shrek, geven ersht farshtekt,
Shpanen mit undz nit aleyn.
    Tsu, eyns, tsvey, dray; tsu, eyns, tsvey, dray,
    Di geslekh, dem toyer farlozt.
    S'hot der trot aza klang, gor an ander gezang,
    Ven du geyst, un du veyst shoyn far vos.

Now forbidden to us are the sidewalks,
While others do freely walk past.
And we, down below, on the roadway do go,
'Neath merciless blows of the lash.
    So, one, two, three; so, one, two, three,
    The roadway's for us, and no more
    Every step has its ring—changed the song we do sing,
    When you go, but don't know what it's for.

The old and the young worked together;
A life they did build and did keep.
Til a sword swept away all we'd built—in a day,
And we were led away like some sheep.
    So, one to, three; so, one, two, three,
    Yes, just like some sheep, and no more.
    Where's your child, where's your wife, where's your health,
        where's your life?
    No one knows where we're bound, and what for.

But, brother, another rhythm
Will soon be picked up by your ear,
And those who from fright did not venture to fight,
Will march next to us, never fear.
    So, one, two, three; so, one, two, three,
    The back alleys and gates nevermore.
    Every step now does ring with a new song we sing,
    When you go and you know just what for.

Recommended Listening

Songs of WWII Jewish Resistance, The. Flying Fish 450 (CD).

"Geto-Lider" (ghetto songs) from *Concentration Camp and Ghetto Songs,* Bergen-Belson, 1946. Artist, Yakob Nafarstek.

27. Tsigaynerlid (Gypsy Song)

Zhizn' prokhodit streloi,
Unosia za soboi
Pesni goria, liubvi, pesni radosti—
O privol'nykh tekh dniakh,
O bessonykh nochakh,
O vesel'e, o schaste, o mladosti.
    Ekh, poteriali voliu,
    Zaglushili serdtsa ston.
    Pozabili pesn' tsyganskuiu,
    I gitary perezvon

Like an arrow, life flies,
Taking with it our lives.
Songs of sorrow, of love, songs of happiness.
All our former delights,
And those wild sleepless nights;
Songs of joy and of gladness of our youth.
    O, we have lost our freedom.
    Stifled are our heartfelt cries.
    Gypsy songs are all forgotten now;
    And the sound of our guitars.

Traditional Russian Gypsy song: *Ekh, Poteriali Voliu* (Oh, We Have Lost Our Freedom)

David Beyglman, himself trapped in the Lodz ghetto along with his fellow Jews, was nevertheless moved by the plight of the thousands of Austrian Gypsies who were transported there by the Germans in 1941. He had been a concert violinst before the war, touring Europe and, as a member of a theater orchestra, played in the United States. The musical center of his life, however, remained Lodz, where he actively took part in that city's cultural and literary life. He continued his activities as best he could in the ghetto until he was transported to Auschwitz in May 1944. It was there he perished in February 1945.

500,000 Gypsies were murdered in the Holocaust.

By David Beyglman

Nit vu men togt, nit vu men nakht;
A yeder sikh plogt, nor kh'trakht un trakht.
Mir tsigayner lebn vi keyner,
Mir laydn noyt, genug koym oyf broyt. *Tsuzung*

Nowhere to stay—daytime or night,
Others resist—I think of my plight.
Gypsies suffer—live like no other.
Soon we'll be dead—we even lack bread. *Chorus*

Recommended Listening

Ganz, Isabelle and Robert Paul Abelson. *Composers of the Holocaust.* Leonarda LE 342 (CD)

28. Far Vos Iz Der Himl? (Say, Why Was the Sky?)

This song comes out of the struggles of the Vilna ghetto—that cauldron of oppression and inspiration. Leyb Opeskin helped organize the partisans in the Vilna region. As the Red Army battled westward, nearing Vilna in midsummer 1944, the partisans increased their harassment of the Germans. Opeskin was killed in one of the last battles before the liberation of the city.

Words by Leyb Opeskin (1908–1944)

Far vos iz der hi-ml ge-ven nekh-tn loy-ter, Fun freyd hot ge-shaynt ye-de gas? Far vos iz di zun a-za likh-ti-ke, roy-te, Far-khmu-ret haynt, beyz un in kas? Far vos iz di zun a-za

Say, why was the sky yes-ter-day so much light-er, And each street with joy did re-sound? And why is the sun, which has shone so much bright-er, So an-gry and not to be found? And why is the sun, which has

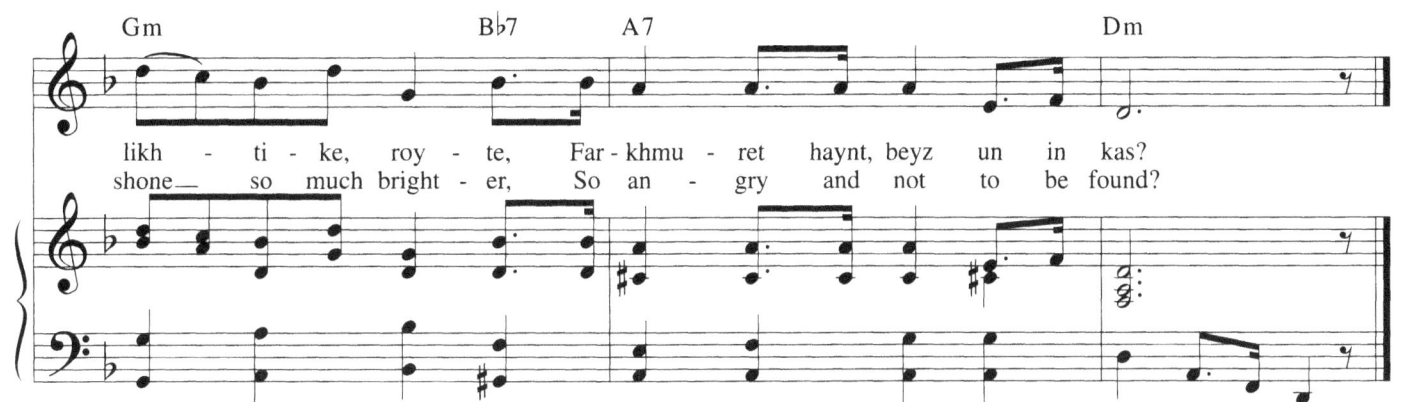

Es veynt haynt der himl, dos hoyz un dos gesl,
Es troyert dos harts shtilerheyt.
Tsi ken men fargesn, vi ken men fargesn
Fargangenen shoen fun freyd?

Vish oys dayne trern, farges dayne zorgn,
Tsu troyern iz nit keday.
S'ken zayn shoyn, az morgn, s'iz zikher, az morgn
Vet oyfshaynen zun af dos nay!

The heavens, the house and the street are all crying,
The heart mourns the past silently.
We cannot forget—there can be no denying,
The happy hours that used to be.

Away with your tears now, forget all your sorrow,
For mourning is not the right way.
It could be that soon—it's sure that tomorrow
The sunshine will brighten the day!

29. Shlof, Mayn Kind (Sleep, My Child)

Der tate vet shoyn mer nit kumen,
Men hot im fun undz genumen.
Iber gasn im geshlept,
In gazkamern im dershtikt.
Shlof, mayn kind, shlof vider ruiuk eyn.

Du zolst di fonen hoykh heybn,
Geyn foroys mit festn gloybn.
Az men muz bafrayen shklafn.
Firn tsu a nayem hafn.
Firn tsu a nayer, frayer velt.

Your father won't come home one day,
They came and took him far away.
Through the streets of town they passed him,
In the gas chambers they gassed him.
Sleep, my child, sleep calmly, child of mine.

You shall raise the banners flying,
And go forth with faith undying.
For the slaves must all be free
To live their lives peacefully.
Onward, to a new, to a free world.

Repeat first verse

30. Motele Fun Varshaver Geto (Motele from the Warsaw Ghetto)

The dedication page of Reuven Lipshitz's slim volume of poems and songs *Tsu Zingn Un Tsu Zogn* ("To Sing and to Say"), published in Munich in 1949, reads: "Dedicated to my murdered mother, Rokhl." Over the music to this song is written simply *Varshe* [Warsaw] 1943.

Munich—the city that witnessed the rise of Nazi power in the 1930s was the immediate post-war site of the Jewish Central Committee as well as a Displaced Persons Camp. The Committee maintained an information and publishing center. Lipshitz spent some time in the camp and his book is one of the JCC publications.

Words by Reuven Lipshitz

Music by Stelmakh

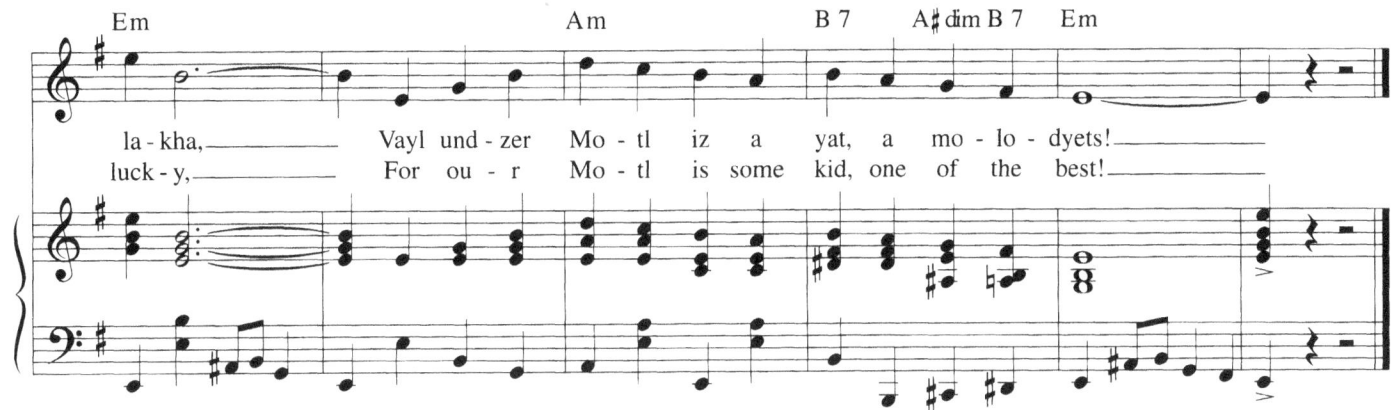

Yidn shteyn oyf kegn barbarn,
Taykhn blut in yede geto-gas.
Motele helft boyen barikadn,
Un dos puniml fun khes toyt blas.
In dem fayer finklen oygen bloye,
Dursht un hunger trikenen dos moyl.
S'klapt zayn heldish hertsele fun groyl,
Far zayn folk shikt er zey yede koyl. *Tsuzung*

Dzhike, Fave, Mile, Niske, Genshe—
Tsungen fayer flaken iber zey.
S'klapn dort harmatn, s'tsitert Varshe,
Gevalt! Hilkht op dos hilfloze geshrey.
In dem roysh fun bombes, kananadn,
Motls nomen hot arumgeshvebt.
Vi a held gefaln oyf barikadn,
Zayn eygene bar-mitzve nisht derlebt. *Tsuzung*

Jews are fighting back against barbarians,
Streams of blood the ghetto streets do trace.
Helping build the barricades is Motl,
Deathly pale with rage is his small face.
In the fire bright blue eyes are shining,
Thirst and hunger drying out his tongue.
His brave heart with horror it is beating:
For his people's sake he shoots his gun. *Chorus*

Dzhike, Fave, Mile, Niske, Genshe,*
Tongues of fire blazing all around.
Cannons roar and all of Warsaw trembles,
Save us! We hear the helpless cry resound.
In the smoke of bombs and cannonades then,
Motl's name did float above the fray.
Died a hero on the barricades then—
He didn't live till his bar-miztvah day. *Chorus*

*Warsaw streets.

31. Der Hoyf-Zinger Fun Varshaver Geto (The Street Singer of the Warsaw Ghetto)

In March 1943 Reuven Lipshitz composed this song. On April 19, the first day of Passover, German troops stormed the ghetto, to be met by unexpectedly fierce resistance by its desperate inhabitants. The last tragic verses of this song soon played themselves out into reality.

Words by Reuven Lipshitz

Music: Traditional.

| Gehat a tate-mame, | I had two loving parents, |

Gehat a tate-mame,
||:Un sheyninke shvesterlekh dray.:||
Avek mitn roykh in flamen,
Geblibn bin ikh itst aleyn.

Ikh drey di katerinke,
||:Un shpil haynt far oykh mit kurazh.:||
Vayl morgn kan zayn, in Treblinke
Vet vern fun undz a barg ash.

Der hunger iz a tsore,
||:Mit toyte farzeyt iz der bruk.:||
Oi, yidn, bney rakhmonim,
Es vilt zikh nokh lebn a tog.

Mayn kol di luft tseshtetert
||:Fun morgn biz shpet in der nakht.:||
Farshaltn zol zayn dos geto,
Un di, vos hobn es oysgetrakht.

Men roydeft undz vi khayod,
||:Dos lebn iz vi a tom.:||
Es vign zikh sharbns oyf tlie,
Tsum teyvl — es shaynt nokh di zun.

Fun hertser broyzt a fayer,
||:Genug undz gekoylet vi shof.:||
Oi Yidn, nemt di "shpeyers,"
Un kumt, lomir makhn a sof!

Drey ikh di katerinke,
||:Farshpil undzere laydn un noyt.:||
Vayl eyder tsu geyn in Treblinke,
Iz beser in kamf faln toyt.

I had two loving parents,
||:And beautiful sisters three.:||
They're gone in smoke and fire,
And all that is left now is me.

I spin the hurdy-gurdy,
||:And play today for you with dash.:||
Tomorrow, perhaps, in Treblinka,
We'll end in a mountain of ash.

O, hunger's an affliction,
||:How many dead — no one can say.:||
O Jews, just show some pity,
I want to live just one more day.

My voice it breaks the silence
||:From morning until late at night.:||
Accurséd shall be the ghetto,
And those who crush us with their might.

They persecute us like wild beasts,
||:In the abyss we all drown.:||
The skulls swing upon the gallows.
The devil! The sun still shines down.

In our hearts glows a fire.
||:No more to be slaughtered like sheep.||
O Jews, now take your weapons,
And end this — a promise we'll keep!

I spin the hurdy-gurdy,
||:And sing of our terrible plight.:||
Before we are sent to Treblinka,
It's better to die in the fight.

32. Varshe (Warsaw)

In July 1959 I presented a program of American folk music on Polish television in Warsaw. It was, perhaps, the first time that an American, folksinger or otherwise, had appeared before Polish television audiences. The Director of the Music Division of Polish Televison, Wladislaw Szpilman had a story to tell me. Before the war he had been a concert pianist who performed regularly on the radio and in clubs and theaters in Warsaw. When the German army entered Warsaw on September 27, 1939, he and his family were trapped there along with the rest of the population. He watched in ever-growing horror as friends, colleagues, and neighbors were systematically transported away in those sealed boxcars. As Jews, living in the Ghetto, the Szpilman family knew that their turn might come at any moment. When, in fact, the order came for them to assemble at the dreaded *Umschlagplatz* (the assembly point near the railroad station), they found themselves part of a mass of terrified, exhausted and weeping men, women, and children. As his parents, brothers, and two sisters were clambering onto the trucks that were to carry them to the train, someone shouted, "Szpilman, over here!" An unknown hand pulled him back out of the line and beyond the police perimeter. Too stunned to react, he watched as his family was driven away, never to return. It was August 16, 1942. Then began his three-year nightmare. In the Ghetto he worked on labor details, smuggling weapons in from the "Aryan" side for the eventual uprising. Moving from one burned out apartment to another, he managed to elude capture by the SS. When the Ghetto was destroyed he found himself for a time in the relative safety of the Aryan side of the city. By mid-1944, in the face of the oncoming Red Army, the Germans began to evacuate Warsaw, driving out the civilian population as well. Then they set about to level the city. Destroying a modern city does not consist merely of blowing up its buildings. Teams of demolition experts were left behind to do the job "properly." Some specialists were in charge of destroying the city's electrical system, with its power stations and underground cables. Others were detailed to take care of the sewage system, and still others, the water supply. So it went. It was not a haphazard affair. The net result was that roughly ninety percent of the city was leveled and all of its utilities were destroyed. Somehow Wladislaw Szpilman managed to survive in the rubble. As far as he knew, he was the *only person left alive in Warsaw*, not counting the remaining German units. He lived a solitary, desperate existence, scavenging in the ruins during the terrible winter of 1944–45. One day while foraging in an abandoned building, he was unexpectedly confronted by a German officer. Expecting to be shot on the spot, he was astounded to be asked, "What do you do for a living?" When he managed a reply, "I'm a pianist," the officer led him into another room and pointed to a piano, saying, "Play something!" It had been over three years since Szpilman had touched the keys of a piano. His hands were calloused and stiff, and they trembled as he approached the instrument. The sounds of the Chopin Nocturne in C-sharp minor echoed through the ruins. It was then that the officer asked, "You're Jewish?" Receiving an affirmative answer, the officer helped him find a more secure hiding place and brought him some food. Then it was Szpilman's turn to ask: "You're German?" The answer was even more surprising: "Yes I am! And ashamed of it." As the officer turned to leave, Szpilman took his hand and said: "I never told you my name; you didn't ask me, but I want you to remember it. Who knows what may happen? You have a long way to go home. If I survive, I'll certainly be working for Polish Radio again. If anything happens to you, if I can help you then in any way, remember my name: Szpilman, Polish Radio." But Szpilman was never able to return the gift of life to Captain Wilm Hosenfeld, who perished in a prisoner of war camp in Stalingrad.

In khurves dos geto, di yidn—in shlakht,
Der yid shprayzt durkh roykh un durkh flamen.
Nekome! Nekome!—es shturemt di nakht—
Far kinder, far tates, far mames!

Der shney shit un shit un di erd vert nit vays,
Es halt nokh dos blut in eyn zidn.
Es ruft nokh nekome af shneyikn ayz—
Dos blut fun di heldishe yidn.

Keyn tog vet nit zayn, ruft der yid, un keyn nakht.
Mir veln di velt nit fargebn!
Di velkhe zaynen gefaln in shlakht,
Eybik in undz veln lebn!

Mir veln gedenken dem vey un dem mut,
Es fibert in gli di neshome.
Krits oys zikh in hartsn dray verter fun blut:
Nekome! Nekome! Nekome!

The ghetto's in ruins—the Jews in despair;
Through fire and smoke march our brothers.
O, vengeance! O, vengeance!—cries out the night air,
For children, for fathers, for mothers.

The earth is not white, though the snow falls and falls,
The seething blood covers the cold snows.
The blood-covered ice for vengeance now calls,
For the blood of our brave Jewish heroes.

There will be no day, cries the Jew, and no night,
There will never be a forgiving.
Those who have fallen in unequal fight,
Forever in us will be living.

We'll always remember the bravery and pain,
Our souls keep the awful remembrance.
Etched deep in our hearts these three words remain:
Just vengeance! O, vengeance! Yes, vengeance!

33. Minutn Fun Bitokhn (Moments of Confidence)

In an attempt to disorient the Jewish population of Krakow and lull them into a false sense of security, the Germans first drove them out of the city into nearby villages in 1940, and back again into Krakow two years later. Poet Mordekhai Gebirtig and his family were caught up in these displacements. On June 4, 1943, after all the Jews had been relocated into the ghetto came the fatal order. The cattle cars were waiting and they were ordered to assemble at the station for the trip to the extermination camp at Belzets (Belzec). Gebirtig did not move fast enough for the SS. He was shot right there on the street.

In 1997 a collection of all previously published works by Gebirtig as well as a number of his hitherto unknown poems and songs was published in an Italian/Yiddish edition in Florence, Italy. The editor, Rudi Assuntino, noted: "If history had been different, if several million Jews had not been exterminated and their culture canceled from the face of the earth, Gebirtig clearly today would be as important as the Gershwin brothers."

By Mordekhai Gebirtig

Used with the kind permission of the Workman's Circle

Nor geduld, bitokhn,
Nit lozt aroys fun hant
Undzer alt kley-zayin.
Vos halt undz gor banand.
Hulyet, tantst, talyonim,
Shoyn nit lang, ikh hof.
Geven a mol a Hamen —
Es vart af im zayn sof.

Hulyet, tantst, talyonim,
Laydn ken a yid.
S'vet di shverste arbet
Undz keyn mol makhn mid.
Kern? Zol zayn kern!
Kol-zman ir vet zayn.
Iz umzist dos kern,
S'vet do nit vern reyn.

Vashn? Zol zayn vashn!
Kayins royter flek.
Hevls blut fun hartsn —
Dos vasht zikh nit avek.
Traybt undz fun di dires,
Shnaydt undz op di berd!
Yidn, zol zayn freylekh!
Mir hobn zey in d'rerd.

Only hope and patience,
But keep in your hand
Our old faithful weapons,
From our native land.
Sing and dance, you butchers,
Long, we will not wait.
Once there was a Hamen —
His will be your fate.

Sing and dance, you butchers,
Jews can bear the pain.
And the hardest labor —
We can stand the strain.
Sweeping? Let us sweep then!
We know what they mean.
But despite the sweeping,
Nothing will be clean.

Washing? Let us wash then!
The red mark of Cain.
But poor Abel's heart's blood
We will wash in vain.
Drive us from our homes now,
Cut our beards as well!
Jews, let us be happy!
They can go to hell.

34. Treblinke (Treblinka)

I visited Treblinka to find out how they carried out their extermination. The camp commandant at Treblinka told me that he had liquidated 80,000 in the course of half a year. He was principally concerned with liquidating all the Jews from the Warsaw ghetto. He used monoxide gas and I did not think that his methods were very efficient. So when I set up the extermination building at Auschwitz, I used Zyklon B . . . It took from three to fifteen minutes to kill the people in the death chamber, depending upon climatic conditions . . . Another improvement we made over Treblinka was that we built the gas chambers to accommodate 2,000 people at one time, whereas at Treblinka their ten gas chambers only accommodated 200 people each.

Rudolf Franz Ferdinand Hoess, Commandant at Auschwitz from May 1940 to December 1943 testifying at the Nuremberg War Crimes Trial in 1946

Continue after measure 8 to the end—do not repeat melody.

Undzere brider un shvester fun yener zayt yam,
Zey kenen nit filn undzer bitern tam.
Zey kenen nit visn undzer bitere noyt,
Az undz dervart yede minut der toyt.
Kvaln trern veln rinen,
Ven men vet a mol gefinen
Dem greysten keyver in der velt!
Dort ruen yidn milyonen fil:
    In Treblinke! In Treblinke!

Our brothers and sisters across the wide sea,
They just cannot feel our deep misery.
They cannot imagine the terrible fear,
As we are confronted by death over here.
Streams of tears from all their eyes
Will flow, when once they realize,
Here's the biggest graveyard in the world,
Where millions of Jews do rest:
    In Treblinka! In Treblinka!

35. Rivkele, Di Shabesdike (Rivkele, the Sabbath-Widow)

Shabesdike is the feminine adjectival form of the noun *shabes*—sabbath. In its masculine and feminine forms it modifies ordinary nouns, such as sabbath "prayers," "clothes," "meals," etc. In this song it is a substantive, describing Rivkele as a "sabbath..." A sabbath what? A "sabbath-widow." What is a sabbath-widow? The term, the very concept, did not exist before Saturday (*shabes*), July 5, 1941. That was the day the SS trucked three thousand Jewish men from the Bialystok ghetto to nearby Pietrasze. They and their families had been deceived into believing that for a payment of a considerable ransom in gold and other valuables, they would be returned to their homes. The ransom was raised and delivered, but it was a bargain with the devil; the men had all been shot down upon their arrival at the killing fields of Pietrasze. Even as the awful news filtered back to Bialystok, many could not, and would not believe it. Rivkele, in spite of everything, still has not given up the hope of seeing her husband again. She is more than a symbolic sabbath-widow. The real Rivkele worked in a factory, knitting socks for German soldiers. Irene Shapiro, whose "Song of the Bialystok Partisans" is to be found elsewhere in this book, worked in the same factory and remembers: "One of the weaver girls keeps on calling attention to herself, and I have a feeling that this is a very special girl.... I see her pensive sad face turn toward the windows as if she were expecting to see someone there.... Why is this girl so much sadder than the other girls?... I can't help noticing that the girl is crying. I quietly ask the inspector about the girl and she tells me that the girl is *'di Shabesdike'*.... And a few days later, I overhear one of the other weavers address the sad girl as Rivkele." Pesakh Kaplan himself died in the ghetto in March 1943. He did not live to see the uprising the following August in which the ghetto was totally destroyed, with its handful of survivors sent to the death camp at Maidanek.

By Pesakh Kaplan, 1870–1943

Ir getrayer Hershele
Iz avek, nito.
Zint fun yenem shabes on,
Zint fun yener sho.
Iz fartroyert Rivkele,
Yomert tog un nakht,
Un atsind bayn redele
Zitst zi un zi trakht:

Vu iz er mayn libinker,
Lebt er nokh khotsh vu?
Tsi in kontsentratsye lager,
Arbet shver on ru?
Oy, vi finster iz im dort,
Biter iz mir do —
Zint fun yenem shabes on,
Zint fun yener sho.

Her devoted Hershele,
He is gone — not here.
Since that awful Saturday,
Since that hour of fear,
Rivkele just sits and mourns,
Weeps both night and day.
Sitting by her spinning wheel,
Since he went away.

Where is he, my dearest one,
Is he living — where?
In a concentration camp,
Working slaving there?
Painful must it be for him,
Bitter for me here,
Since that awful Saturday,
Since that hour of fear.

Recommended Listening

Gorby, Sara. *Unforgettable Songs of the Ghetto*. Arion 64081 (CD).

Rubin, Ruth. *Yiddish Songs of the Holocaust*. Global Village 150 (CD).

36. In Kriuvke (In the Dugout)

Standing near the old oak tree at the forest camp site,
The horses, restless, stamp the ground and they toss their manes.
We rode onward—on we rode—villages and towns flew by;
Near the quiet Don and through the Donland plains.

[See the song *Kak U Duba Starovo* /Standing by the Old Oak Tree, page 164]

For some, like the Russian partisans in the Don River region, the dark forests were a haven as well as a staging area for lightning attacks on the rear of German troops. For Jews, desperately seeking escape from the doomed ghettos, the forests to which some of them fled offered little in the way of solace. They were systematically tracked down by German soldiers and their dogs. Those who managed to elude their hunters had to face the grim realities of starvation and the freezing winters. The chances of survival under these circumstances were practically nil. Elia Magid and David Gertsman were two, who despite the odds, succeeded in eluding their pursuers and overcoming the rigors of life in a forest dugout. Both Magid and Gertsman had been soldiers in the Polish army until their capture and internment in prisoner-of-war camps. Incredibly, both managed to escape—Magid by leaping off a train heading for Maidanek, Gertsman somehow eluding his prison guards. They survived, but ironically Magid was crippled in a post-war pogrom when he was thrown from a speeding train and his legs were severed.

Words by Elia Magid and David Gertsman

Music: traditional

Ikh hob gelebt in hofnung un in strebn.
Ikh bin nokh yung—es velt zikh mir nokh lebn.
Geven zenen mir ruik in der heym;
Itst bin ikh a bandit in vald aleyn. *Tsuzung*

Mir zaynen a folk fun moykhes,
Fun tsores hobn mir shoyn nit keyn koykhes.
A yedn folk iz gut, es gist nor yidish blut—
Oy, helf undz Got in itstiker minut! *Tsuzung*

O, I have lived in hope, and ever striving.
I'm still young and I'm bent on surviving.
Once we lived quietly in our home,
Now, like a bandit in the woods I roam. *Chorus*

Our people always have shown bravery,
But we cannot long survive this slavery.
All people are the same—yet Jews they kill and maim.
O, help us, God, we ask this in Thy name! *Chorus*

37. Unter Di Khurves Fun Poyln (Under the Ruins of Poland)

December 11, 1941: Governor-General of occupied Poland, Hans Frank: *As far as the Jews are concerned, I want to tell you quite frankly that they must be done away with in one way or another. ... Gentlemen, I must ask you to rid yourself of all feeling of pity. We must annihilate the Jews.*

November 5, 1997: Bonn judge Heinz Sonnenberger (rejecting the vast majority of claims by a group of elderly women seeking payment for their work as slaves in Auschwitz): *The claims are ... not justified. ... No damage claims can be paid ... not even for slave labor.*

January 28, 1999: Chancellor Gerhardt Schröder promised prompt [*sic*] and fair compensation for people who were forced into slave labor under the Nazis.

February 10, 1999: The German Government agreed to establish a compensation fund, financed by the biggest names in German industry and banking, for victims of Nazi horrors. No company has a stronger interest in a settlement than Deutsche Bank, which provided much of the financing for the construction of Auschwitz.

December 17, 1999: *I pay tribute to all those who were subjected to slave and forced labor under German rule, and, in the name of Germany, beg forgiveness. ... Their suffering will not be forgotten.* [President Johannes Rau of Germany, announcing the establishment of a $5.1 billion dollar fund, financed equally by German industry and government to compensate the slave laborers, whose claims, among others, Judge Sonnenberg had summarily rejected two years earlier.] This agreement came almost exactly to the day, fifty-eight years after Hans Frank spoke of the annihilation of the Jews. It came at the end of the millennium and of the century that witnessed "man's inhumanity to man" at its most bestial level.

March 23, 2000: *The issue of how the money is to be shared out has been successfully settled* (Otto Lambsdorff, chief German negotiator).

Words by Itzik Manger

Music by S. Berezovsky

Iber di khurves fun poyln
Falt un falt der shney.
Der blonder kop fun mayn meydl
Tut mir mesukn vey. *Tsuzung*

Der veytik zitst baym shraybtish,
Un shraybt a langn briv.
Di trer in zayne oygn
Iz emesdik un tif. *Tsuzung*

Iber di khurves fun poyln
Flatert a foygl um.
A groyser shive-foygl,
Er tsitert mit di fligl frum. *Tsuzung*

Der groyser shive-foygl
(Mayn dershlogn gemit),
Er troygt oyf zayne fligl
Dos dozige troyer-lid. *Tsuzung*

Over the ruins of Poland
Falls and falls the snow.
The blond head of my daughter
Brings me terrible woe. *Chorus*

The pain sits at my table,
And writes an endless tale.
The tears that it is shedding.
They are profound and real. *Chorus*

Over the ruins of Poland
A fluttering bird is there.
The bird is deep in mourning,
It trembles in the air. *Chorus*

And that great bird of mourning
(O, my soul, how long!)
Upon its wings it carries
This very mourning song. *Chorus*

38. Aroys Iz In Vilne A Nayer Bafel
(In Vilna Was Issued a Brand-New Decree)

In April 1943, the Gestapo rounded up the last four thousand Jews alive in the region around Vilna, Lithuania, from the towns of Oshmene, Soler, Tal, Sventsian, Vidz, and others and brought them to the city of Vilna. From there they were supposed to be transferred to the Kovno ghetto, but this was only a pretext. The closed cattle cars in which the people were being transported went only as far as the nearby town of Ponar (Ponary, in Lithuanian), site of an infamous death camp. At that point the slaughter began, and too late did the Jews realized their deception. Desperately they threw themselves upon their German executioners, seizing anything at hand with which to defend themselves. They used fists, iron bars and clubs against machine guns and rifles. Some even sank their teeth into the throats of the guards. Several Germans were killed in the melee. About thirty Jews managed to escape.

On May 10, 1944, there was a prisoners' revolt at the camp. Once again unarmed Jews battled their tormentors. The Red Army was only weeks away, too far away to help.

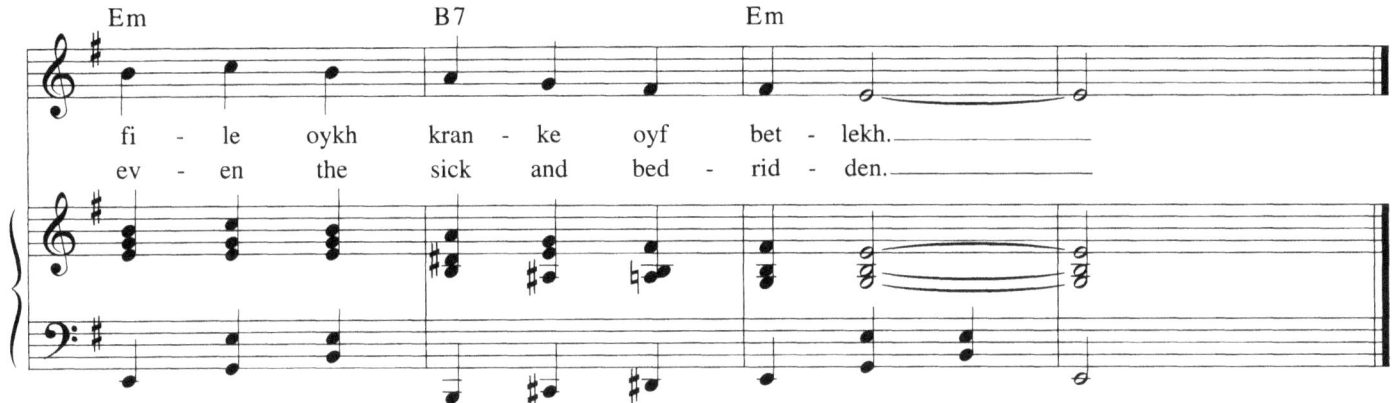

Tsunoyfgeshpart hot men dem lager,
Men hot zey genumen sortirn:
Oshmene yidn in Vilne tsu blaybn,
Un Soler in Kovne tsu firn.

Aroysgefirt hot men fun lager,
Yunge un frishe korbones.
Arayngeshpart hot men zey alemen glaykh
In di zelbe farmakhte vagones.

Der tsug is zikh langsam geforn,
Gefayft un gegebn sirenes.
Stantsie Ponar—der tsug shtelt zikh op,
Men tshepet dort op di vagones.

Zey hobn derzen az men hot zey farfirt,
Men firt tsu der shreklikhe sh'khite.
Zey hobn tsebrokhn di tir fun vagon,
Genumen aleyn makhn pletye.

Zey hobn gevorfn zikh af der geshtapo,
Un zey di kleyder tserisn.
Geblibn zaynen lign lebn di yidn,
Etlikhe daytshn tsebisn.

S'hobn di getos fun der provints,
Gegebn fir toyznt korbones.
Un opgefirt hot men di zakhn fun zey,
Tsurik in di zelbe vagones.

The camp became crowded with thousands of Jews,
And then they began the selection:
Jews from Oshmene in Vilna would stay,
Send Solers in Kovno's direction.

The first group of martyrs was led from the camp,
"More victims!" the order was worded.
Then jammed all together like animals,
They into the sealed boxcars were herded.

Then slowly the train made its way down the tracks,
The whistles and sirens were blowing.
But when it reached Ponar it came to a halt,
And then the uncoupling got going.

They realized then that they had been betrayed,
And that they would be killed at the station,
So, smashing the doors to the box cars,
They all tried escaping in great desperation.

They threw themselves bodily on the Gestapo,
Biting and clawing and crying.
And next to the bodies of Jews on the ground,
Several Germans were lying.

From ghettos of all of the province around,
Some four thousand martyrs were given.
And all their belongings were shipped back again
In the same cars in which they'd been driven.

Recommended Listening

Rubin, Ruth. *Yiddish Songs of the Holocaust.* Global Village 150 (CD)

Photographs secretly taken by Rabbi J. Cohen during the *aktion* described in the song "Aroys Iz In Vilne A Nayer Bafel," and subsequently smuggled out of Vilna.

39. Vilner Geto Lid (Song of the Vilna Ghetto)

The *Aktionen* (round-ups) and killing described in *Aroys Iz In Vilne A Nayer Bafel* continued throughout the summer of 1943. The soil of the Ponary Forest (Ponar, in Yiddish) was soaked with Jewish blood. In August Heinrich Himmler ordered the liquidation of the Vilna ghetto. Fewer than one hundred men who were deemed fit for work were shipped off to labor camps in Estonia. Some seventeen hundred young women were shipped off to the Kaiserwald Camp near Riga. The rest of the population, some five thousand, were transported to Polish extermination camps. By September 24, the Vilna Ghetto had ceased to exist.

The melody of this song is based on a Yiddish popular song, *Kupite, Koyf Bibulkes, Papirosen* (Buy, Oh, Buy Cigarette Paper, Cigarettes).

Getsoygen hot der veg zikh lang, s'iz shver geven tsu geyn,
Mir dukht az kukendik oyf unz veynen vet zikh a shteyn.
Gegangen zenen skeynim, kinder, vi tsu dem erkode rinder,
Menchens blut geflosen iz in gas. *Tsuzung*

Gevezn zenen mir tsu fil, gefaln hot der har,
Tsu bringn Yidn fun arum un shisn in Ponar.
Puste zenen gevorn shtiber, aber ful derfar di griber,
Der soyne hot dergrat zayn groysn tsil. *Tsuzung*

Itst zenen ale mir farshparte,
Farpeynigte, fun leben opgenarte.
Ver un a tate, un a mame, zelten ver er iz tsuzamen.
Der soyne hot take dergrat zayn groysn tsil. *Tsuzung*

Un oyf Ponar zet men fun di vegn,
Zakhn, hitln, durchgenetst fun regn.
Dos zenen zakhn fun carbones, fun di heylige neshomes,
Di erd hot zey af eybig tsugedekt. *Tsuzung*

It was a long, long way to go — the ghetto wasn't near;
You'd think that looking at us all, a stone would shed a tear.
Young and old, without a battle, went together, just like cattle.
People's blood was running in the street. *Chorus*

There were too many of us there, we came from near and far.
They brought the Jews from all around and shot us in Ponar.
And as our homes were emptied out, the graves were filled —
    beyond a doubt;
The enemy was getting to his goal. *Chorus*

Now we are here — together we've been herded.
We're suffering and waiting to be murdered.
Without a father or a mother, neither sister nor brother —
Indeed, the enemy has reached his goal. *Chorus*

And at Ponar there's lying in the mud now,
Rain-soaked clothing, stained with Jewish blood now.
Clothing of the martyrs killed there — holy spirits' blood was
    spilled there.
The earth has covered them eternally. *Chorus*

40. Shtil, Di Nakht (Still, the Night)

During World War I British women were urged to "keep the home fires burning 'til the boys come home." Frivolous Tin-Pan Alley songs, such as "Sister Susie's Sewing Shirts for Soldiers" and "Mother's Sitting Knitting Little Mittens for the Navy" pretty much defined women's roles as quaint auxilliaries to the epic struggle that was going on "over there." Before America entered the war in 1917, another aspect of womanhood was celebrated in "I Didn't Raise My Boy to Be a Soldier," but that pacifist cry was soon drowned out by a barrage of show-biz patriotic numbers, whose titles express the unreality of the conflict to the tunesmiths who cranked them out: "Good-bye Broadway, Hello France," "Pack Up Your Troubles in Your Old Kit Bag and Smile, Smile, Smile," and "I Don't Want to Get Well" ("I'm in love with a beautiful nurse"—yet another popular image of "femininity").

Twenty years later Dolores Ibárurri (*La Passionaria*), Spain's fiery Communist organizer, rallied Madrid's defenders with ringing oratory: "It is better to die on your feet than to live on your knees.... It is better to be the widow of a hero than the wife of a coward." But even here a woman's role was defined by her husband's heroism. During World War II Italian partisans sang *Bella ciao* (roughly translated as "So long, honey") [page 172] as once again the men march off bravely, leaving the women behind to keep those home fires burning. At the same time, however, on the Eastern front Russian women partisans were riding through field and forest on horseback or creeping on hands and knees through deep snows do do battle with the enemy, as celebrated in the song *Oi Tumany Moyi:* "There will soon be good news from the west. And along the Smolensk Road that evening they met with their most unwelcome guest." [page 166]

Vitke Kempner, celebrated in this song, was a Jewish heroine. Jewish women in pre-war Eastern Europe, by and large could not have been considered "liberated" by today's standards. Yet Vitke, and others like her, engaged in unbelievable wartime acts of heroism and self-sacrifice. It was she, in 1942, who was instrumental in the blowing up of German troop train in the Vilna sector. It was a first for the partisans and a first for Vitke, who continued carrying out numerous perilous mssions, including the incredible leading to freedom of a group of prisoners from the Kailis concentration camp near Vilna. On that occasion she was captured but managed to escape from her would-be Gestapo torturers!

The quiet beauty of this song is a fitting tribute to Vitke and her heroic Jewish sisters.

By Hirsh Glik

A moyd, a peltsl un a beret,
Un halt in hant fest a nagan.
||:A moyd mit a sametenem ponim,
Hit op dem soynes karavan.:||

Getsilt, geshosn un getrofn!
Hot ir kleyniker pistoyl.
||: An oto, a fulinkn mit vofn,
Farhaltn hot zi mit eyn koyl!:||

Fartog, fun vald aroysgekrokhn,
Mit shney girlandin oyf di hor,
||:Gemutikt fun kleyninkn nitsokhn
Far undzer nayem, frayen dor!:||

A girl in furs hides in the forest,
Holding tight a hand grenade.
||:A girl with a face as smooth as velvet,
Strikes at the German cavalcade.:||

She aims, she fires true and steady,
With her pistol smoking hot.
||:A transport, loaded down with weapons,
Has been halted with one shot.:||

At dawn she steals from out the forest;
Snowflakes garlanding her hair.
||: How proud of her one small winning battle,
Leading to freedom everywhere.:||

Recommmended Listening

Composers of the Holocaust. Leonarda LE 342 (CD)
Rubin, Ruth. *Yiddish Songs of the Holocaust.* Global Village 150 (CD).
Songs of WWII Jewish Resistance, The. Flying Fish 450 (CD)

41. Itsik Vitnberg

Itsik Vitnberg, a shoemaker from Vilna, became a leader of the United Partisan Organization. Plans to defend the ghetto were being made, when on July 15, 1943, Vitnberg was arrested by the Gestapo. Amazingly, he was rescued by his comrades, but the Nazis did not let matters rest there. An ultimatum was delivered: Give up Vitnberg or face immediate and terrible destruction of the ghetto and everyone in it. After much agonizing — and knowing full well that the Germans were not above carrying out their threat — Vitnberg bid his comrades a bitter farewell and went to his doom. It was all for naught, however. By September the Vilna ghetto was no more.

Words and Music by Shlomo Kacherginsky

Di nakht hot mit blitsn
Dos geto tserisn.
"Gefar," shrayt a moyer, a vant.
||:Khaveyrim getraye,
Fun ketn bafrayen—
Farshvunden mit dem komendant.:||

Di nakht is farfloygn,
Der toyt far di oygn,
Di geto, zi fibert in brand.
||:In umru di geto,
Es drot di geshtapo:
"Toyt—oder dem komendant!":||

Gezogt hot dan Itsik—
Un durkh vi a blits iz—
"Ikh vil nit ir zol tsulib mir.
||:Darfn dem soyne
Dos lebn opgebn . . ."
Tsum toyt geyt shtolts der komandir.:||

Der faynt vi a khaye.
Mayn mauzer er vakht in mayn hant.
||:Itst bistu mir tayer,
Zay du mayn befrayer,
Zay du itst mayn komendant!:||

The lightning flashed bright
In the ghetto that night.
"Danger," the walls seemed to chant.
||:Then our faithful brothers,
Who fight like no others,
Did free our brave commandant.:||

The night it has ended,
And death has descended.
The ghetto in fever does pant.
||:For now the Gestapo
Threatens all of the ghetto:
"Either death—or else the commandant.":||

Then Itsik spoke to us,
With words that went through us:
"To sacrifice you I just can't.
||:The cruel enemy
Will kill you for me . . ."
To death proudly went the commandant.:||

Again, off in hiding,
The enemy's biding;
My Mauser's alert in my hand.
||:Your value is greater,
Be my liberator,
For now you are my commandant.:||

Recommended Listening

Songs of WWII Jewish Resistance. Flying Fish 450 (CD).

42. Yeder Ruft Mikh Ziamele (People Call Me Ziamele)

The children in the ghetto would play and laugh, and in their games the entire tragedy was reflected. They would play at gravedigging: They would dig a pit and would put a child inside and call him Hitler . . . And they used to play funerals.

   Dr. Aaron Peretz, a survivor of the Kovno ghetto

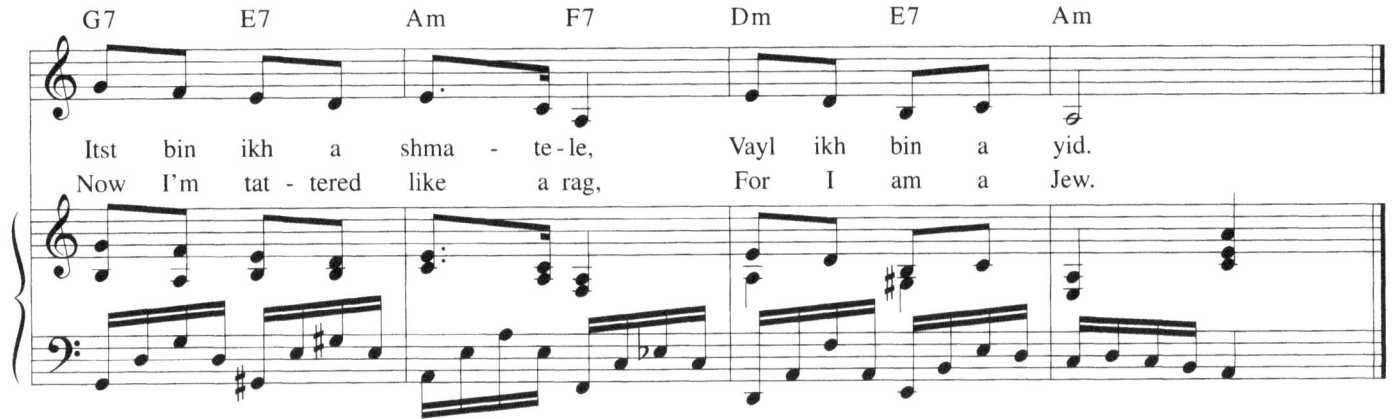

Kh'ob gehat a shvesterl,
Iz zi mer nishto.
Akh, vu biztu, Esterl,
In der shverer sho?
Ergets ba a boymele,
Ergets ba a ployt,
Ligt mayn bruder, Shloymele,
Fun a daytsh getoyt.

Kh'ob gehat a heymele,
Itster iz mir shlekht.
Ikh bin vi a beheymele,
Vos der talyen shekht.
Got, du kuk fun himele,
Af der erd arop.
Ze nor vi dayn blimele
Shaydt der talyen op.

I did have a sister, too,
Now she is no more.
Esther, what's become of you
In this awful war?
Somewhere near a little tree,
Somewhere on the ground,
Lies my brother, Shloymele—
Germans shot him down.

Once I had a little home,
Now the times are hard.
Like an animal I roam,
In the slaughter yard.
God, who looks down from the skies,
Down upon the land,
Hear the little childrens' cries—
Killed at every hand.

Recommended Listening

Rubin, Ruth. *Yiddish Songs of the Holocaust.* Global Village 150 (CD).

43. S'Dremlin Feygl (Birds Are Dozing)

In 1943, the year that Vilna ghetto poet Leah Rudnitsky was sent to her death by the Nazis, my father, Bill Silverman, wrote this poem:

He's the sweetest little fellow,
As he climbs upon my knee,
And when he says, "I love you,"
It means the world to me.

Then I think of all the children
In war-torn, bleeding lands,
Who have no one to hold them
With firm protecting hands.

Who have no one to love them,
To sing them off to sleep;
By fate ordained as victims
Of human beasts that creep.

That creep and crawl like vermin,
O'er lands so green and fair,
And like a plague of locusts,
They leave them brown and bare.

Who have no thoughts of mercy,
Whose only creed is kill;
The whole wide world they'd master,
And bend it to their will.

He's the sweetest little fellow,
As he climbs upon my knee,
But for his love to be secure,
All mankind must be free.

Words by Leah Rudnitsky

Music by Leyb Yampolsky

S'iz dayn vigl vu geshtanen,
Oysgeflokhten fun glik.
||:Un dayn mame, oy, dayn mame,
Kumt shoyn keyn-mol nit tsurik.:||
    Loo loo, loo loo loo.

Kh'hob gezen dayn taten loyfn,
Unter hogel fun shteyn.
||:Iber felder iz gefloygen
Zayn far-yosemter geveyn:||
    Loo loo, loo loo loo.

Once upon a time your cradle,
It brought joy to all.
||:But your mother, o, your mother,
She is gone beyond recall.:||
    Loo loo, loo loo loo.

I have seen your father running,
Stones falling like hail.
||:And came echoing over meadows,
His long-suffering, sad wail.:||
    Loo loo. loo loo loo.

Recommended Listening

Schlamme, Martha. *Raisins and Almonds.* Omega 6026 (CD).

44. Yugnt-Himn (Youth Hymn)

The very expression of apathy indicates submission to the enemy, which can cause our collapse morally and root out of our hearts our hatred for the invader. It can destroy within us our will to fight; it can undemine our resolution.... Our young people must walk with heads erect.

From the *Voice of Youth*, an underground publication of the Vilna ghetto

Words by Shlomo Kacherginsky

Music by Basya Rubin

Ver es voglt um oyf vegn,
Ver mit drayskayt s'shtelt zayn fus,
Brengt di yugnt zey antkegn,
Funem geto a gerus. *Tsuzung*

Mir gedenken ale sonim,
Mir gedenken ale fraynt.
Eybig veln mir dermonen,
Undzer nekhtn mitn haynt. *Tsuzung*

Kloybn mir tsunoyf di glider,
Vider shteln mir di rey.
Geyt a boyer, geyt a shmider,
Lomir ale geyn mit zey. *Tsuzung*

He who sets forth on the highway,
And with boldness strikes the blow,
Let him come and travel my way,
Greetings from us all will flow. *Chorus*

When our enemies oppress us,
We remember our friends.
Our foes cannot distress us,
For the darkest night soon ends. *Chorus*

We will gather all together,
Once again we'll form our ranks.
Workers, march through stormy weather,
You will earn eternal thanks. *Chorus*

Recommended listening

Rubin, Ruth. *Yiddish Songs of the Holocaust*. Global Village 150 (CD).

45. Neyn, Neyn, Neyn (No, No, No)

The evacuation of Jews from the town means death.... Do not go to your death of your own free will.... Defend your children.... Avenge the death of your mother.... Destroy the factories.... On leaving your home, burn it and its contents.... Do not go to Treblinka.... Jewish policemen—do not aid the hangmen.

From a leaflet distributed in the Bialystok ghetto in January 1943

46. Zog Nit Keynmol (Never Say)

If the Holocaust can be said to have an anthem, this song is it. When the April 1943 round-up of Jews began (described in the song "In Vilna Was Issued a Brand-New Decree"), the Vilna-born Hirsh Glik escaped and joined the partisans. It was also the time of the heroic uprising of the Warsaw ghetto. These stirring and tragic events inspired him to write this song, which was immediately picked up and sung by Jews—partisans and inhabitants of the ghettos alike. With the liquidation of the Vilna ghetto, Glik was captured by the Gestapo and sent to a concentration camp in Estonia. When the Red Army swept through the area the following year, he escaped from the camp, only to be killed fighting the Germans in the nearby woods. He was twenty-four.

The melody of this song was taken from a Soviet song: *To Nye Tuchi Boevyie* ("These Are Not War Clouds") by the brothers Dmitri and Daniel Pakras.

Words by Hirsh Glik

Music by Dmitri Pakras

Fun grinem palmen-land biz vaytn land fun shney,
Mir kumen on mit undzer payn, mit undzer vey.
||:Un vu gefaln s'iz a shprits fun undzer blut,
Shprotsn vet nokh undzer gvure, undzer mut.:||

Dos lid geshribn iz mit blut un nit mit blay.
S'iz nit a lidl fun a foygl oyf der fray.
||:Dos hot a folk ts'vishn falndike vent
Dos lid gezungen mit naganes in di hent!:||

From land of palm tree to the far-off land of snow,
Our people come together crushed by pain and woe.
||:But where a drop of our blood has touched the ground,
There our strength and our courage will resound.:||

This song is written down with blood and not with lead.
The birds don't sing it, for it fills the air with dread.
||:This song was sung as all around us bullets sprayed,
And walls collapsed as people hurled their hand grenades.:||

Repeat first verse

Nye skazhi chto ty idyosh' v poslyednyi put',
Khot' golubyie dni svintsom pokryla mut'—
Grianyet nash blazhennyi chas bez muk i nut,
I udarit bodryi shag nash: vsye my tut!

Iz palmovo kraia v zapoliarnyi krug
Slyshen golos nashikh volnei, nashikh muk,
Tam gdye kaplia nashei krovi udayot,
Nasha sila, nasha bodrost' zatsvetyot.

Utrom solntse vyidyot v kruge zolotom—
I vchera ischeznyet s beshennym vragom.
Yesli-zh opozdayet solntse v nyebesakh,
Grianyet nasha pesnia, kak parol' v vekakh.

Krov'iu pesnya sozdana, a nye svitsom,
To nye pesnia ptisty vol'noi v burelom.
To narod nash v rukhnuvshikh stepakh,
Etu pesniu pel s naganami v rukakh.

Russian translation by the Soviet poet Leonid Feinberg

Sage nimmermehr, du gehst den letzten Weg,
wenn vor blauen Tag ein Bleigewölk sich legt:
unsre heißersehnte Stunde sie ist nah,
unsre Tritte werden trommeln: Wir sind dah!

Vom grünen Palmenland zum weiten Land im Schnee,
so kommen wir mit unsrer Pein, mit unsrem Weh,
und wo gefallen ist ein Spritzer unsres Bluts,
dort wird sprießen unsre Stärke, unser Mut.

Einst wird Sonne sein, die unsern Tage bescheint,
und das Gestern wird verschwinden mit dem Feind.
Steigt zu spät für uns der Sonnenball—
sei dieses Lied für unsre Kinder ein Fanal.

Das Lied, geschrieben ists mit Blut und nicht mit Blei,
und kein Vogel hats gesungen, leicht und frei,
s hat ein Volk an rauchgeschwärzter Wand
das Lied gesungen mit der Waffe in der Hand

German translation by Hubert Witt

Ne dis jamais que tu prends ton dernier chemin,
Des cieux d'ardoise te cachent les beaux lendemains.
L'heure à laquelle nous rêvons arrivera,
Où notre pas martelera: nous sommes là!

Des palmeraies jusqu'aux lointains pays neigeux,
Nous arrivons le cœur souffrant et douloureux.
Où est tombé une goutte de notre sang,
Surgira notre courage jaillissant.

Soleil futur, tu embellis le jour present,
Hier est l'ombre où disparaitront nos tyrans.
Si le soleil se perd avant le jour levant,
Tel un appel d'âge en âge, soit notre chant.

Il fut écrit, ce chant, par le sang, par le feu.
Ce n'est pas le chant d'un oiseau dans le ciel bleu.
Quant tout brûlait parmi les murs qui s'écroulaient,
Fusils en mains, mon peuple a chanté ces couplets.

French translation by Charles Dobzinski

Recommended Listening

Composers of the Holocaust. Leonarda LE 342 (CD).
Gorby, Sara. *Unforgettable Songs of the Ghetto.* Arion 64081 (CD).
Robeson, Paul. *Favorite Songs.* Monitor 580/581 (CD & cassette).
Rubin, Ruth. *Yiddish Songs of the Holocaust.* Global Village 150 (CD).
Songs of WWII Jewish Resistance. Flying Fish 450 (CD).

47. Undzer Mut Vet Nit Gebrokhen (Our Courage Is Unbroken)
Le Chant De Pithiviers — The Song of Pithiviers

Excuse my audacity in writing to you, even though I am a complete stranger to you. . . . Oh, permit me to speak to you. This very Sunday morning I walked alone along the barbed wire of our camp. The sky was covered. The surrounding fields deserted . . . a humid March breeze carried the sounds of the Pithiviers church bells, and hung them on the solitude like a veil of mourning and negation. Even though a full year of internment weighed upon me with its melancholy, walling me in in my solitude, the terrible morning silence drove me to tears.

Excerpt from a letter written to an imaginary friend by Pithiviers concentration camp inmate Yossel Cukier (Tsukier).

Yoshua Cendorf (Tsendorf) fled to Danzig (Gdansk) from his native Lodz when the Germans invaded Poland. He was arrested there and transported to Pithiviers on May 5, 1941. From there, date unknown, he was transported to Auschwitz.

Pithiviers is south of Paris not far from Orléans. Jewish roots in Pithiviers date back to the twelfth century when Jews from Avignon introduced the cultivation of saffron to the region — a practice later greatly fostered by Louis XIV.

On November 16, 1941, the workers at the camp sugar factory and the camp chorus presented a program in the camp theater. The poster announcing the performance was in French and Yiddish: 1) *Le Roi Du Schnorer/Der Keynig Fun Di Shnorer* (The King of the Beggars), 2) *Menachem Mendel À Pithiviers/Menakhem Mendel In Pitivieh*, 3) *La Chorale Du Camp/Der Khor Fun Kamp*.

Yiddish Words by Yoshua-Israel Cendorf
French Translation by Henry Bulakow

Music by M. Zemelman

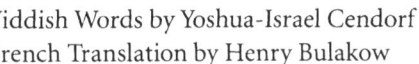

In der heym, dort vayb un kinder
Veln dokh undz vider zen.
Undzer mut vet vayzn vunder,
Un der nes vet dokh geshen. *Tsuzung*

S'iz tzu alt shoyn di geshikhte,
Funem has tzvishn krist un yid.
Shrayt dos herz es iz nit rikhtig,
I droysn s'feld far ale blit. *Tsuzung*

Hekher, hekher fun barakn
Heybn zol zikh undzer lid.
Far ale ver dos feld tseakert,
Un far ale di korn blit. *Tsuzung*

A la maison, solitaires,
Nous attendent femmes et enfants.
Loin de nous, parfois ils désespèrent,
Mais bientôt reviendra le printemps. *Refrain*

Elle est vieille cette histoire,
Qui divise Juifs et Chrétiens.
Quand viendra l'heure de la victoire,
Tous les hommes se prendront par la main. *Refrain*

Vers le ciel, nos voix altières,
Lancent très haut notre chanson.
Notre espoir va conquérir la terre,
Vois, le soleil monte à l'horizon. *Refrain*

Wives and children, they are waiting,
They will see us in our home.
Our courage celebrating,
And the miracle will come. *Chorus*

Yes, we've heard that same old song now—
Hatred 'tween Christian and Jew.
But the heart cries out: It's wrong now,
As the fields turn green anew. *Chorus*

From our barracks rising proud now,
Our singing greets the morn.
For us all the field is plowed now,
And for all men grows the corn. *Chorus*

"Le Roi de (du) Schnorer." Poster from Pithiviers camp theater.

48. Mir Lebn Ebig (We Live Forever)

This song was the finale of the revue *Moshe, Oyshalt Dos!* (Moshe, Endure It!), which was presented in 1943 in a Jewish cabaret in the Vilna ghetto. Seated in the auditorium, in addition to the Jewish spectators, were German soldiers and members of the SS. It is hard to imagine a more bizarre scene: the performers singing in Yiddish about "our enemies," and the enemies themselves listening and understanding (*Mir lebn ebig* in Yiddish translates to the practically identical *Wir leben ewig* in German). Did the performers look the SS in the eye as they sang? Did the SS enjoy the performance? Did they applaud at the end of the show? Did the Jews in the audience dare to applaud? We will never know. What we do know is that 1943 was the year of the "liquidation" of the Vilna ghetto.

Words by Leyb Rozental

49. Ani Ma-amin (I Believe)

The writings of Rabbi Moses ben Maimon (1135-1204), known as the philosopher Maimonides, and also by the acronym Rambam, exerted a tremendous influence in the thinking of both Jewish and Christian theologians in his day and beyond. He was a great exponent of reason in faith and toleration in theology. It is largely from his writings that the Church derived its medieval knowledge of the Synagogue. It was said of him: "From Moses unto Moses there arose not one like Moses." His Credo, the *Thirteen Articles of Faith*, was the inspiration for this solemn song which was sung into the very jaws of death in the concentration camps.

The Thirteen Articles of Maimonides are: 1) the existence of God, 2) His unity, 3) His incorporeality, 4) His eternalness, 5) the duty to worship only Him, 6) the fact of prophesy, 7) the superiorty of the prophecies of Moses over all those of other prophets, 8) the holiness of the Torah, 9) its immutability, 10) divine infallibility, 11) reward and punishment, 12) the coming of the Messiah, 13) the Resurrection.

Recommended Listening

Rubin, Ruth. *Yiddish Songs of the Holocaust*. Global Village 150 (CD).

50. Parpar (Butterfly)

On April 28, 1994 I received the following letter:

I am the daughter of the late composer Joseph Zvi Pinkhof. I have in my possession some sheet music written by my father during our incarceration at Bergen-Belsen, from which my sister Ada Bondi and I managed to survive. I found the sheet music somewhat by accident, in a simple envelope among my sister's possessions . . . in 1985. She doesn't remember how it got to her, and so we don't know the story behind the music. In any case, further to my investigation, I found that [the] songs were definitely composed in the camp . . . [or] possibly in a transition camp called Westerbork in Holland, or were brought by my father from home when he was taken to the camp.

. . . My late father himself taught us the . . . songs while we were in the camp; later on we taught them to others. Enclosed please find photocopies of the songs which I am certain were composed in the camp.

Leah Gola-Pinkhof, Kibbutz Saad (Israel)

Hayim Nahman Bialik (1873-1934) is the classic poet of modern Hebrew. Born in the Ukraine, he lived for a while in Germany in the 1920s before settling in Palestine in 1924. His writings paved the way for the development of Hebrew as a modern, living language.

Words by H. N. Bialik

Music by Joseph Zvi Pinkhof

51. Skharkhoret (Dizzy)

This is the second of the two songs sent to me by the daughter of the composer. The fact that her father chose these two almost playful poems of Bialik to set to music while a concentration camp prisoner underscores the essential indestructability of the human spirit — "The Undying Flame" — even under the most inhuman of conditions.

Words by H. N. Bialik

Music by Joseph Zvi Pinkhof

Hey se - khor se - khor va - sof, En la - o - lam rosh va - sof.
Hey, go 'round and 'round a - gain, In this world there is no end.

Rutz ben su - si uf ka - khez, D'e ka ne — sher tus ka nez.
Like an ar - row, run, my colt. Hawk - and ea - gle - like you bolt.

52. M'khol Masada (Oh, Masada)

During the 1920s the Hebrew poet Yitskhok Lamden wrote the dramatic poem *Masada,* which expressed the feelings brought on by the carnage of World War I from the point of view of a stateless, tormented, wandering young Jew. He saw in national emancipation the sole recourse for himself and his people. The poem describes the self-sacrifice and joy of the *khalutz*— the Jewish pioneer in Palestine. Composer and conductor Israel Fivishes was a leading figure in Jewish musical life in Poland between the wars. In 1922 he became director of the renowned Hazomir chorus in Lodz. Under his leadership it became one of the top ranked Jewish choruses in Poland, with thousands of listeners from Warsaw and the provinces attending its concerts. In 1937, his girls' Chorus won first prize in an all-Polish choral competition. Following the German occupation he moved to Warsaw, where he established a children's Chorus in the ghetto, bringing a little ray of happiness into their tortured lives. *M'khol Masada* (composed around 1935) was one of the songs performed by the children. Its recounting of Jewish resistance and sacrifice under Roman attack uncannily foretold the horrors of the Warsaw Ghetto. Fivishes himself was a member of the Ghetto Resistance Committee. With the destruction of the ghetto he was sent to the SS labor camp in Poniatowo, where he perished in November 1943. It is thanks to Israel Fivishes son, Dr. Joseph Kutrzeba (who was also a member of the Ghetto Resistance) that this song has been preserved. Joseph survived by miraculously escaping from a train bound for Treblinka. He managed to link up with a band of Soviet partisans and eventually wound up in the care of a Polish priest who supplied him with false "Catholic papers" and a Polish name, which he retained after the war.

Words by Yitskhok Lamden

Music by Israel Fajwiszys (Fivishes)

Copyright © 1993 by Joseph S. Kutrzeba. Used by permission. All rights reserved.

Eysh ragleynu avanim tatsit
Tisrefen, tisrefen.
Ba'asher sela yat hatsida
Yitakhen, yitakhen. *Pizmon*

Kof olam roshkha keyreyach
Limkholeynu hagoel.
Elohim yashir imenu,
Yisrael, Yisrael. *Pizmon*

How the fire of our feet ignites the stones—
Let them burn, let them burn.
We will trample evey stone
That tries to turn, tries to turn. *Chorus*

World on fire, head held high,
And the Redeemer dances well, dances well.
God will sing along with us.
O Israel, Israel. *Chorus*

Program in Yiddish and Polish of a concert of choral music conducted by Israel Fajwiszys (Fivishes) in Lodz, July 10, 1937.

53. Mah Ko Mashma Lon (What Is the Meaning)

What is wrong with our concentration camps? The occupation authorities have felicitated us on them. May I ask what you find wrong with them? (Dr. Limousin, Vichy official in charge of French concentration camps responding to Varian Fry of the American Emergency Relief Committee, November 1940.)

The Hebrew title of this French song is drawn from the Talmudic query: What is the meaning? The poet Avrom Reisin wrote a poem beginning with this line, which was very popular among Jews of eastern and central Europe. It was often adapted to express other states of sadness, according to circumstances. In this version it comes from the internment camp at Beaune-la-Roland, set like a canker sore on the *paysage* of the Loire River valley chateau country, not far from Orléans. The words were originally written in Yiddish by Marcel Skurnik, and the song, first sung by the Parisian artist Herman Rozenfarb, was later taken up by the inmates themselves. Incidentally, the camp at Beaune-la-Roland was not the first time that a German military presence was manifest in this region. In November 1870, during the course of the Franco-Prussian War, Beaune-la-Roland was captured by the German army.

French words by David Diamant and Annik Cherniacoski

Music adapted by Jerry Silverman

Mah ko mashma lon la marmite,
Qui donnent à nos geules semites
Rutabaga et vapeur sans fin,
Qui jamais ne calment la faim?
    Les cris stridents, le gros vacarme,
    La peur lourde, ni les alarmes,
    Les corvées, les rabiots, n'ajoutent rien
    À une ration de moins que rien.

Mah ko mashma lon les kapos?
Ils nous collent à la peau!
Ils crient, ils hurlent, ils vacarment,
Ils sont pires que les pires gendarmes.
    De jour en jour plues violents,
    Ils nous crèvent les tympans.
    Puissent-ils perdre leur boulot!
    Nous serions libres à nouveau.

Mah ko mashma lon barbelés,
Qui nous coupent de la liberté?
Servent-ils à nous faire comprendre
Que nous aussi voulons la prendre?
    Finis ces barbelés de malheur.
    Finis nos peines et nos peurs.
    Un soleil en fin devenu chaud
    Ecartera la voie des barreaux.

What's the meaning of the stew-pot?
What are we to make of all that?
Rutabaga and nothing but steam
Never will calm our hunger, it seems.
    Strident cries and noise everywhere.
    Fatigue, food scraps and despair.
    There is one thing—on that you can bet:
    There's little in the rations we get.

What's the meaning of the kapos?
Worse from day to day, goodness knows.
Screaming, cursing and raising alarms.
Soon they'll be worse than the worst gendarmes.
    There's no end to their violent shouts.
    We'll go deaf, without any doubt doubts.
    We're waiting for the end of their reign,
    For then we'll be free once again.

What's the meaning of the barbed wire,
That cut us off from all our desires?
On the outside there's liberty,
And we all have the right to be free.
    When bars and barbed wire are all away,
    Our pain will end on that day.
    The warming sun will shine down at last—
    Our nightmare will be past.

54. Le Chant des Partisans (The Song of the Partisans)

Where is the France of yesteryear?
   (Veni, Vidi, Vichy)
The France that once was loved so dear,
   (Veni, Vidi, Vichy)
Where clarioned forth the Marseillaise,
Where free men honored First of Mays;
But what is there that crawls these days?
   (Veni, Vidi, Vichy).

Where is the France of Liberty?
   (Veni, Vidi, Vichy)
Equality, Fraternity?
   (Veni, Vidi, Vichy)
Up France! Away with tear or sigh,
Now is the time to do or die.
Each freedom-loving man must cry:
   Veni, Vidi, VICI!

Bill Silverman, 1942

Montez de la mine, decendez des collines, camarades!
Sortez de la paille, les fusils, la mitraille, les grenades!
Ohé les tuers, à la balle ou au couteau, tuez vite!
Ohé saboteur, attention à ton fardeau dynamite!

      Come up from the mine, and come down from the hills, all you brave ones.
      From under the straw, take your rifles, grenades and machine guns.
      O killers, prepare all your bullets and your knives for tonight now,
      And you, saboteurs, watch with care your package of dynamite now.

C'est nous qui brisons les barreaux des prisons pour nos frères.
Las haine à nos trousses, et la faim qui nous pousse, la misère.
Il est des pays où les gens au creux des lits fond de rêves.
Ici, nous, vois-tu, nous on marche, nous l'on tue, nous l'on crève!

      It's we who are breaking the bars of our brothers in prison.
      Because of our hatred and hunger all of France is arisen.
      There are countries where people, dreaming dreams in bed are lying.
      But here, don't you see, we are marching, we are fighting and dying.

Ici chacun sait ce qu'il veut, ce qu'il fait quand il passe.
Ami, si tu tombes, un ami sort de l'ombre, prend ta place.
Demain du sang noir sèchera au grand soleil sur la route.
Sifflez, compagnons, dans la nuit la liberté nous ecoute!

      Here, each of us knows what he wants, what he does, when he passes.
      And friend, if you fall, then another will rise from the masses.
      Tomorrow, dark blood on the road, in the sun will be glistening.
      O comrades, keep whistling, for in the night Liberty's listening.

Oradour-sur-Glane, "Cité Martyre." On June 10, 1944, in repraisal for acts of sabotage and resistance, the Nazis rounded up the entire population of the town. They shot the men, herded the women and children into the church, and burned it down; then they burned down the rest of the town. The ruins have been preserved as a silent memorial to the victims of this atrocity.

55. Le Maquisard (The Resistance Fighter)

I was born French and have lived in France all my life. I feel as French as Mr. Tout-le-Monde, but I will never understand how French people could do what they did to my parents, even with the Germans breathing down their necks.

Georges Gheldman, whose parents died in Auschwitz

By Anna Marly

Personne ne m'a demandé
D'où je viens et où je vais.
Vous qui le savez,
Effacez mon passage.

J'ai changé cent fois de nom,
J'ai perdu femme et enfant.
Mais j'ai tant d'amis —
Et j'ai la France entière.

Un vieil homme dans un grenier,
Pour la nuit nous a cachés.
Les All'mandes l'ont pris.
Il est mort sans surprise.

Hier encor' nous étions trois,
Il ne reste plus que moi,
Et je tourne en ronde
Dans las prison des frontières.

Le vent passe sur les tombes,
Nous rentrerons dans les ombres,
On nous oubliera.
La Liberté reviendra!

No one asked me any questions —
Where I come from, my intentions.
You who may know it,
Just cover up my passage.

Changed my name a hundred times,
Wife and child I've left behind,
But I've many friends —
And all of France is mine now.

An old man agreed to hide us,
To his attic he did guide us,
But the Germans came.
He died without a murmur.

Yesterday we still were three,
But today there is just me,
And I'm on the run.
The frontiers are my prison.

O'er the tombs the cold wind blows,
We'll go back to the shadows,
They'll forget our names.
But Liberty will come back.

56. Das Ende (The End)

Die zur Vernichtung bestimmten Juden wurden nackt in die Gaskammer gejagt.... Die Tür wurde schnell zugeschraubt und das Gas sofort durch die Decke der Gaskammer in einem Lufstschacht bis zum Boden geworfen.
            KL Auschwitz in den Augen der SS

The Jews who have been selected for extermination were driven naked into the gas chamber... The door was quickly screwed shut and the gas was immediately thrown to the floor of the gas chamber through an air shaft in the ceiling.
            Concentration Camp Auschwitz in the eyes of the SS

Words by Wolf Hirsch

Music by Jerry Silverman

Die Sterbenden röcheln,
von Typhus durchtobt,
entsetzliches Ende,
masslos die Not.

Verloren den Willen,
den Glauben, den Mut,
es liessen Millionen
ihr jüdisches Blut.

Es geht nun zu Ende,
wir fügen uns ein,
vergebens das Flehen,
umsonst unser Schreien.

Wir haben gebetet,
gehofft und gefleht—
jetzt kommt unser Ende,
verbrannt und verweht.

The dying death rattles
From typhus proceed.
A horrible ending,
Measureless need.

We've lost our will,
Belief, courage—no more.
From millions of people
Does Jewish blood pour.

The end is approaching,
To death we're resigned.
In vain screams and pleading,
They pay us no mind.

Our prayers we have offered,
We've hoped and we've pled.
Now comes our ending—
Burnt, scattered and dead.

57. Auschwitz-Lied (Auschwitz Song)

As they marched to work each morning, the prisoners were obliged to sing to the accompaniment of the camp band. This song, marked *Autor unbekannt* (author unknown) was found without music in the files of the Paris *Memorial du Martyr Juif Inconnu*. The large manila envelope in which I carried this and other material home has printed on its exterior thirteen times in ever diminishing block letters the single word: MEMOIRE

Music by Jerry Silverman

Wo Malaria, Typhus und auch anderes ist,
Wo dir große Seelenot am Herzen frißt,
Wo so viele Tausend hier gefangen sind,
Fern von ihrer Heimat, fern von Weib und Kind.

Ausser Läuse, Flöhe plaget Fieber Dich
Viele Tausend mußten enden fürchterlich,
ja, du wirst gequälet hier bei Tag und Nacht,
und bei jedem Schritt ein Posten Dich bewacht.

Häuserreihen siehst erbaut von Häftlingshand,
bei Sturm und Regen du trägst Ziegeln, Sand.
Block um Block entstehet für viele tausend Mann,
alles ist für diese, die noch kommen dran.

Traurig siehst Kolonnen Du vorüberziehn,
Mutter, Schwester kannst Du oft dazwischensehn,
darfst sie nicht grüßen, es brachte Dir den Tod,
vergrösserst unwillkürlich dadurch ihre Not.

Traurig ziehn die Reihen nun an dir vorbei,
schallend hörst Befehle Du wie «Links, zwei, drei!»
Hier etwas zu sagen hast Du gar kein Recht,
wenn Dein Mund auch gerne um Hilfe schreien möcht!

Vater! Mutter! Ob Ihr noch zuhause seid?
Niemand weiß von unserem großen Herzeleid.
Nur träumen darfst Du noch von einem Elternhaus,
aus dem das Schicksal jagte so schnöde Dich hinaus.

Sollte ich Dich Heimat nicht mehr wiedersehen,
und wie viele durch dem Schornstein gehn.
Seid gegrüßt ihr Lieben am unbekannten Ort,
gedenket manchmal meiner, denn ich mußte fort.

Where malaria and typhus play their awful part,
And where deep depression eats away your heart,
Where so many thousand here will lose their life,
Far from their dear homeland, far from child and wife.

And the lice and fleas plague you with fever's chills.
Many thousand end up here against their wills.
Yes, you will be tortured here by day and night,
And the guards will never let you out of sight.

You see rows of houses built by prisoners' hand.
In storm and downpour you haul bricks and sand.
Block on block is built up for many thousand men,
Everything for those who will be coming in.

Mournfully you see the columns pass you by.
Mother, sister — they do often catch your eye.
Don't you dare greet them, for swift would be your fate;
It is out of your control, although your need is great.

Mournfully the rows they pass you endlessly,
And you hear the loud commands, like "One, two, three!"
Here you have no right to say a single word.
O, if you could cry for help, and know that you'd be heard!

Father! Mother! Are you still at home — who knows?
No one knows about our frightful woes.
Of you parents' house you can but dream today.
O, the cruel fate that drove you far away.

Shall I never see you, my dear home, again?
And how many rise through the chimney in flame?
Greetings, to you, loved ones, in your place unknown,
Sometimes think of me, for I must be gone.

MEMOIRE
MEMOIRE
MEMOIRE
MEMOIRE
MEMOIRE
MEMOIRE
MEMOIRE
MEMOIRE
MEMOIRE
MEMOIRE
MEMOIRE
MEMOIRE

Inscription on the stationery of the Memorial du Martyr Juif Inconnu.

58. Żywe kamienie/Die lebenden Steine (The Living Stones)

The text of this song was originally written in Polish by Włodzimierz Wnuk in 1940 in the concentration camp Mauthausen-Gusen in Upper Austria. From 1939 to 1941 he was imprisoned successively in Stutthof, Sachsenhausen, and, finally, Mauthausen-Gusen. Upon his release he went to Warsaw, where he eventually participated in the Ghetto Uprising. Mauthausen was established on Himmler's orders in 1938 in order to exploit the local granite quarry. Prisoners were brutally worked to death here. Because the men were so covered with granite dust that they resembled stones, and because on a guard's whim they could be tossed like pebbles to their death down in the abyss, they were known as the "living stones." Wnuk kept a diary in which he wrote: "The granite stones were transformed by our hands into devilishly hard, perfectly formed cobblestones. They were not only formed with the sweat that ran down on them, and not only with the blood that dripped onto them. No, we ourselves began to resemble the granite blocks. After several months of imprisonment we ourselves became stone." The words of the song drifted from camp to camp, and in 1943 Alex Kulisewiecz heard them in Sachsenhausen. Kulisewiecz spent six long years behind the barbed wire (1939–1945). He sang the songs of the camps, accompanying himself on a guitar taken from a Jewish prisoner by an SS guard. As the guard fled in the face of the advancing Allied armies, he tossed the instrument to Alex. "Hold this," he said. Alex held on to the guitar and survived. And the songs survived with him.

On May 7, 2001, in the very depths of the quarry that had witnessed such horror, the Vienna Symphony Orchestra, under the direction of Sir Simon Rattle, performed Beethoven's Ninth Symphony before a hushed audience of 11,000. Some people had criticized the very idea of holding such a concert in the place where over 100,000 prisoners were murdered. Others felt that the "Ode to Joy," with its fervent "Alle Menschen werden Brüder" (All men will become brothers) made a statement that was particularly valid precisely because of where it was being sung. After the Beethoven, Paul Chaim Eisenberg, the chief rabbi of Vienna, recited Kaddish and Samuel Barzilai, the chief cantor, sang "El Moleh Rachamim," the prayer of mourning.

Words by Włodzimierz Wnuk and Rudi Winisch

Music by Alexander Kulisewiecz

Jesteśmy jak żywe kamienie, samotne, bezdomne skały; rzeźbiły nas zimne strumienie i żarem ziejące upały.	Wir sind die lebenden Steine, Obdachlose Steine. Uns küssen keine Flüße, Uns tötet verfluchte Hitze.	We are the living stone people, Rocks bare of all shelter, Never kissed by water, And dying as we swelter.
Jesteśmy jak żywe kamienie w sercu szatańskich piramid. W swym łonie, jak żywe nasienie, pieścimy zabójczy dynamit.	Wir sind die lebenden Steine, Im Schatten der Teufelsfahne. Im Herzen die schwelende Lunte, Und täglich mehr Dynamit!	We are the living stone people, Beneath the devil's banner. Our hearts are like smoldering fuses, And each day more dynamite!
Jesteśmy jak żywe kamienie, rzucone w przepaść bezdenną, w których goreje marzenie, że stworza gore płomienną.	Wir sind die lebenden Steine, Aus der Tiefe der Hölle. Wir, Sklaven müßen doch glauben An Menschen—Menschen und Liebe.	We are the living stone people, Up from the depths of hell. We slaves, must still believe In people—people and love.

From *Concentration Camp and Ghetto Songs,* Bergen-Belsen, 1946. Artist, Yakob Nafarstek.

59. Frauenlager (Women's Camp)

The first contact with the German language that many prisoners had were the barked commands of the SS guards. It was a language of constant terror; a vocabulary of hatred and fear. Some of those words still resonate in our ears: *Lager* "the camp," *alle raus!*, "everybody out!," *Achtung!*, "attention!," *Kapo*, "Jewish 'guard'." The "sauna" (verse 1) should not be mistaken for a relaxing steam room. The term was applied sardonically to a large, ugly, concrete building which served (among other usages—disinfecting chamber, "selection" hall on days when the camp was "overpopulated") as concert hall for the prisoners' orchestra in inclement weather. The audience for these concerts was composed of SS guards and inmates. "*Blocki*" (verse 1) is the dimininutive of *blockowa*, the Polish woman in charge of a "block" (barrack) of female prisoners. Sort of a trusty, the *blocki* was herself a prisoner.

Jadwiga Leszczyńska set these terrible words to the melody of the Russian folk song *Stenka Razin* in Auschwitz-Birkenau in 1944. It is an almost surrealistic montage, chronicling the *via dolorosa* of the prisoners: arrival, daily routine, work, sickness and death.

Words by Jadwiga Leszczyńska

"Kaffee holen!" und "Aufstehen!"
"Appell, Appell!" und "Alle r-raus!"
"Und zu Fünfen!" — "Achtung!" — "Ruhe!"
"Zählappell!" — "Es stimmt genau!"

"Außenkommando ausrücken!"
Marschkolonne, Kapo, Post.
Hacke, Trage, Harke, Schaufel.
"Bemüht euch!" — "Aber los!"

Revier, Grippe und Fleckfieber,
Durchfall, Scheiße, Krätze. Laus!
"Kranke fertig!" — Leichen, Kamin,
Krematorium, Spritze, Gas! . . .

"Fetch the coffee!" and "Get up now!"
"Roll call, roll call!" — *"Alle r-raus!"*
"Lines of five!" — "Attention!" — "Quiet!"
"Counting-off!" — "Exactly right!" . . .

"Outside work squad time to turn out!"
Marching column, *kapo*, guard.
Pickaxe, basket, rake and shovel.
"Now get with it!" — "Move it now!" . . .

Sick bay, grippe and typhus fever,
Diarrhea, shit, scabies, louse!
"Sick one finished!" — corpses, chimney,
Crematorium, spraying, gas! . . .

60. Wir Singen Ein Schlager/We Zingen Een Lied (We're Singing a Song)

Robbie Gosschalk wrote this German-Dutch *Schlager* ("pop song") in Bergen-Belsen in the summer of 1944. Ina Soep Polak, who had been sent to Westerbork, the Dutch internment/transit camp in September 1943, and who then was transferred to Bergen-Belsen in May 1944 with a group of diamond workers, recalls: "We were sitting outside on a sunny summer afternoon in 1944 and Robbie came up with this song that he had composed for our amusement." There was also another bit of poetry that they would recite in unison in their barracks every night after lights out:

Liberation finally came on April 13, 1945, when U.S. troops intercepted the train that the SS had loaded with some 2,000 Hungarians, 400 Dutch, and a group of French women and children headed east.

Hoe moeilyk de dag,
Hoe zwaar ook de scheiding,
We zyn weer een dag dichter by be bevryding.

However difficult the day,
However hard the separation,
We are still one day closer to liberation.

By Robbie Gosschalk

61. Die Westerbork-Serenade (The Westerbork Serenade)

What are we to make of this 1940s pop-style ballad in the context of a Dutch internment camp? With "Strolling with my baby" along the silvery moonlit railroad tracks (*Mit einer schöne Dame*) we can almost see Fred Astaire and Ginger Rogers tap dancing over the crossties. Despite his German girl friend and the German title, it is the serenade of a Dutchman; the lyrics are almost entirely in Dutch. Then suddenly we realize that every week as many as 3,000 internees are being transported down those selfsame tracks to the camps "in the east." And then this idyllic moonlight stroll turns grotesque. The very act of kissing the girl by the barracks, so normal under other circumstances, becomes a life-affirming, almost a defiant act. Even the visit to the first-aid station, ostensibly to cure the singer's "love-sickness" can be interpreted as an attempt to get the desperately sought-after medical certificate which might delay inevitable deportation.

Max Kannenwasser and Arnold (Nol) van Wesel ("Johnny and Jones") were a popular singing duo in pre-war Holland. When they were swept into Westerbork they were assigned to the camp metal shop that stripped useful parts from wrecked airplanes, hence the reference to it in the song. At first they had difficulty getting into the cabaret troupe because they sang only in Dutch, and the official language of the camp was German. Once accepted, they became regular performers, much to the satisfaction of the Dutch inmates, who resented the total Germanization of their lives. The camp authorities thought so highly of "The Westerbork Serenade" that they sent Max and Nol on an unescorted trip from Westerbork to Amsterdam to record it in 1944. Their wives had remained as hostages in the camp, so, despite the urging of their friends, escape was out of the question for them. On the recording we hear their voices blending in close harmony accompanied by Nol's tenor guitar. By August 1944 they too had made the one-way trip down those tracks to Theresienstadt, Auschwitz, Sachsenhausen, Ohrdruf, and finally Bergen-Belsen where their voices were extinguished forever.

By "Johnny & Jones"

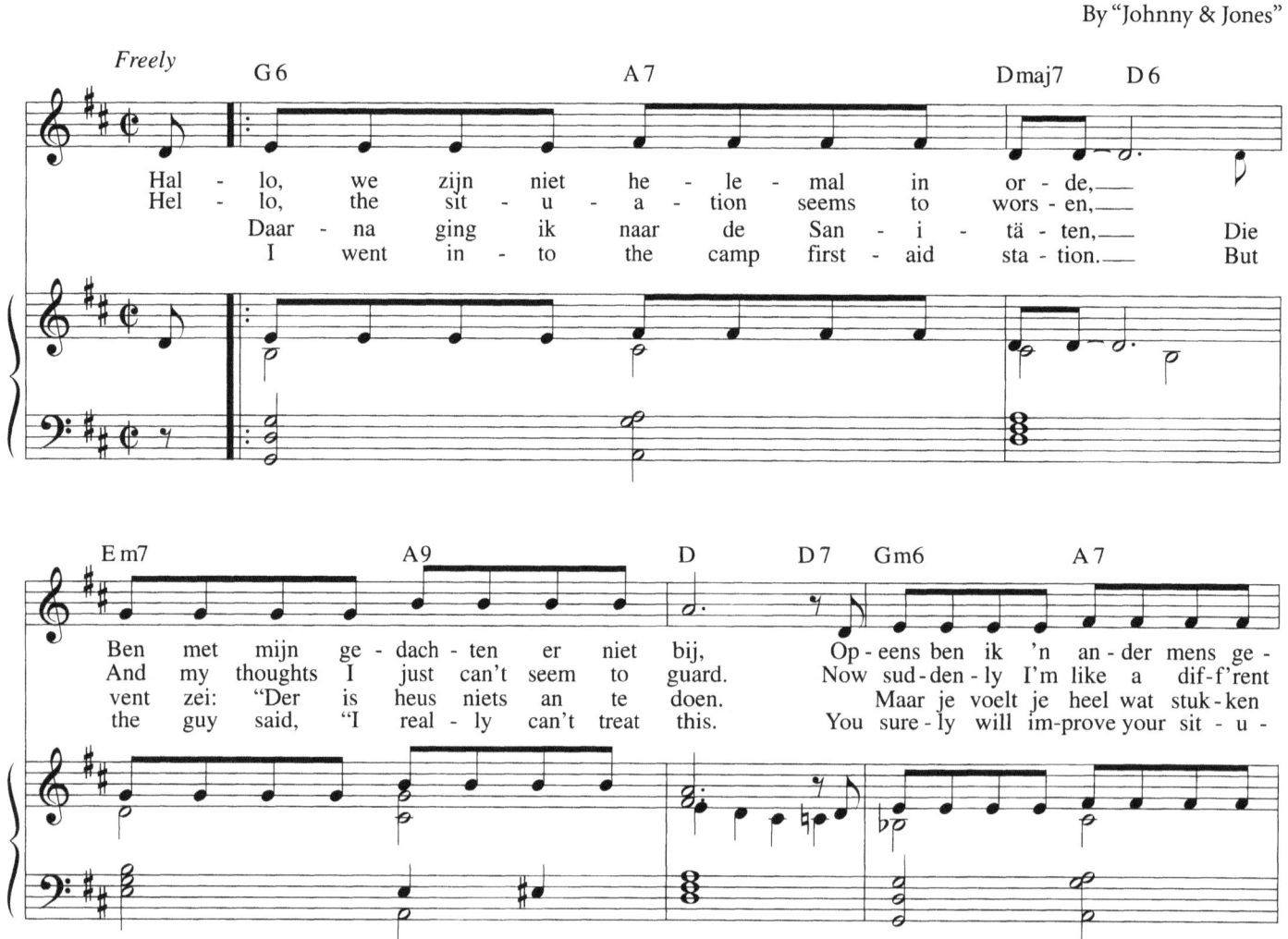

62. Wenn Ein Paketchen Kommt (When a Small Package Comes)

Westerbork Commandant Konrad Gemmeker allowed small packages of food and other necessities to be received by the prisoners from the outside, until near the end in 1944. Not, strictly speaking, a starvation diet, food in the camp was far from adequate, and these packages were looked forward to with great anticipation by the inmates. They were permitted to write their requests or thanks on small postcards that had been designated for that purpose.

By Willy Rosen

63. Det Har Vi (This Have We)

Otto Nielsen (1909–1982) was a cabaret artist and song writer who also worked for the Norwegian Broadcasting. His satirical view of life in Grini, the Norwegian concentration camp near Oslo, contrasts starkly with the experiences of Hermann Sachnowitz, a Norwegian Jew who was a trumpeter in the Auschwitz/Buna concentration camp band, 1943–1945:

Mornings we played as the work details marched out, and we did the same evenings when they all returned to the camp. We also played on other occasions, above all at executions, which took place most Sunday afternoons or evenings. Many of the condemned had tried to escape. There were many escapees, but in Buna they were almost all recaptured. I can still see them, as they dragged them through the camp, with a placard hanging in front and behind them, reading: "Hurra, hurra, ich bin wieder da!" ["Hurrah, hurrah, I'm here again"]. The poor devil had to shout these words out loudly. He had to march through the rows of thousands of prisoners while beating on a big drum. Then he was hanged, while our band played parade music. Perhaps they wanted us to drown out the last protestations and the last curses with our music. A macabre performance, ordered by the high command. And around us stood SS soldiers with loaded rifles.

Hermann Sachnowitz, *Auschwitz. Ein norwegischer Jude überlebte*

By Otto Nielsen

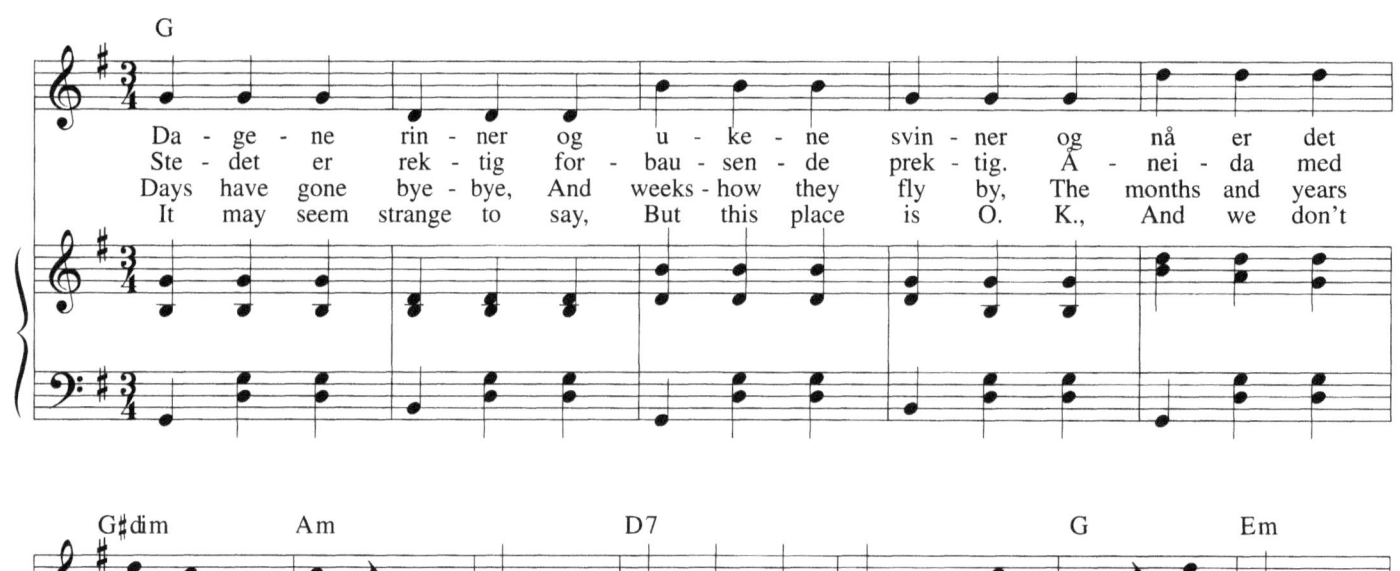

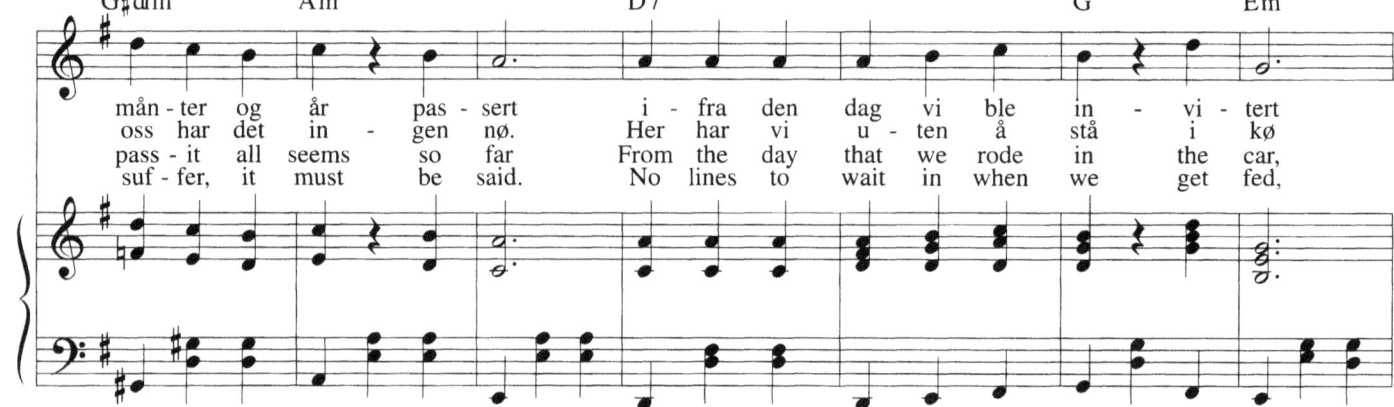

Ute i byen er middagsmenyen et spørsmål som gjør no'n og hver betenkt. Tomme er larga, og børsen sprengt, og døra til slakterbutikken stengt. Matforekomster som suppe av blomster det kjenner de ikke—å langt ifra. Peiling på midda'n den neste da' det er det jo hygg'lig å ha. *Refreng*	Out in the city The menu's a pity, And people are wondering like they're shocked. Warehouses empty—the bourse is blocked, The meatmarket's door it is all padlocked. Their food's not like ours, Their soup's made of flowers. The poor outsiders don't know a thing. Here we know what the next meal will bring, That's nice—and so we all sing: *Chorus*
Jeg tror dynamitten er blitt favoritten til folk som vil fjerne bensin og knott.* Adskillige tonn er i lufta gått, og nå arresterer de stort og smått. Det der er jo ille, nei her det stille. Her finnes det ingen slik sensasjon som bomber og sprengning og eksplosjon så trygghet for arrestasjon. *Refreng*	Dynamite sticks Are their favorite tricks For blowing up wood piles* and gas out there. Many a ton has blown in the air, Folks are arrested now everywhere. Too bad they try it, But here it is quiet. No such sensations disturb us here. Bombs and explosions do not appear, So we have nothing to fear. *Chorus*
Ute besværer de seg, mens de bærer seg for at vi har det uhyggelig, adskilt fra alt, de vet ikke de at ingen får «newsen» så fort som vi. Ingenting hender som vi ikke kjenner, forbindelsen er som seg hør og bør. Hvis en politi får et skudd og dør, har vi nyheten to dager før. *Refreng*	Folks not interned Are so very concerned. They think that conditions here are the worst. Cut off from all—they feel we're accursed, They don't know that we get news here first. We get the word here When something's occurred here, Our connection's first rate, I said. If a policeman does get shot dead, We know it two days ahead. *Chorus*
Folk tror vi gråter og sutrer og låter, kort sagt at humøret er lagt i grav. Ånei her er mye å smile av, som strekker til for vårt beskjedne krav. Ute der går de på kino, der får de tross alt lattermusklene litt på gli av Juster og Diesen og slikt, men de har ikke set Kunze på ski. *Refreng*	Folks think we're moaning, And crying and groaning, And that our humor is down and out. But there's a lot here to smile about; Of that there cannot be the slightest doubt. Out there they're going To cinemas showing. They get their laughs with the greatest ease, Juster and Diesen† are sure to please— They've not seen Kunze‡ on skis! *Chorus*

*Hardwood knots used for stoking fires in generators when gasoline supplies fell short.

†Leif Juster and Ernst Diesen, a comic duo.

‡A pointed dig at "Kunze," the sterotypically inept German skier, as seen by the Norwegians.

Jews living in Tromsö (Tromsø) were arrested, along with all other Jews living in northern Norway, on December 3, 1942, and sent on the first stage of their journey to Oslo. On February 24, 1943 they were ferried across the North Sea on the German liner Gotenland, arriving in the port of Stettin three days later. From there they were taken by train to Berlin, where they stayed in a synagogue on Levetzowstrasse for a few days. Loaded onto cattle cars, a total of 158 Norwegian Jews were transported to Auschwitz, arriving on the night of March 2–3. A monument listing the names of the seventeen residents of Tromsö who were murdered in Auschwitz on that fatal night stands on a small grassy square in that far northern town. The inscription in Hebrew reads: MAY THEIR SOULS BE BOUND IN ETERNAL LIFE. The inscription in Norwegian reads: IN MEMORY OF THE JEWS FROM TROMSÖ KILLED IN GERMAN CONCENTRATION CAMPS. ERECTED IN PROFOUND RESPECT BY THEIR COUNTRYMEN. WE MUST NEVER FORGET.

64. Przed Ostatnią Podróżą (Before the Last Journey)

A love song written in the Bialystok Ghetto in the terrible winter of 1942–43.

    Bolek Pachucki used to visit us in our Bialystok Ghetto apartment time and time again. Both of us were vociferous in our own media: I composed music to the words of various Russian and Polish poets; Bolek was a fine Polish-Jewish poet. He coaxed me to write out singable "nonsense scripts" to some of my songs, and he then wrote lovely words using these "nonsense scripts." So came into being "Before the Last Journey."... Bolek contracted hepatitis and was taken to Treblinka with his father during the final "action" in August of 1943. BOLEK PACHUCKI MADE ME BELIEVE THAT TOMORROW WILL COME. IT CAME, BUT ONLY FOR ME.   Irene Shapiro

Words by Boleslaw Pachucki
English translation by Irene Shapiro

Music by Rena Hass (Irene Shapiro)

Jak to - na - cy o - kręt przed bu - rzą, Dzi - siaj ko - ły - sze się świat. Wciąż cze - ka - my mil - cząc już os - tat - niej po - dró - ży, W ser - ca nam smu - tek się wkradł.

Bat - tered by woe, crime and great sor - row, Hu - man - kind fell to *their* blows. Qui - et - ly a - wait - ing the last jour - ney to - mor - row, Sad - ness per - vades o - ur souls.

65. Warszawo Ma (My Warsaw)

Polish was generally spoken by educated Polish Jews, and vibrant Polish-language Jewish theaters and cabarets flourished in prewar Warsaw. Even in the Warsaw ghetto this cultural life continued as long as possible. This song was sung in a 1950s Polish movie, although it may have been composed earlier. It was passed on to Irene Shapiro in New York by her sister living in Poland, who survived the war thanks to a falsely assumed Polish-Catholic birth certificate and the kindness of a righteous Gentile Polish family. The melody is borrowed from a well-known Polish-Jewish song, *Miasteczko Belz (Mayn Shtetele Belz)*.

"Shetetele" Belz is about 170 miles southeast of Warsaw on the Ukranian side of the Polish border.

English translation by Irene Shapiro

66. Pesnia Belostokskikh Partizanov (Song of the Bialystok Partisans)

On August 16, 1943, we, the United Front of the Bialystok Ghetto Underground, staged an armed uprising in the streets of the ghetto. With Molotov cocktail grenades we stood against the German tanks. ... On the Fabryczna, Zamenhof, Kupiecka, and Jurowiecka streets, there we stood and died. In February of that year, after the first "action" [round-up] that decimated the ghetto, I wrote the "Song Of The Bialystok Partisans." Shortly before the second action of the ghetto, I, along with several youths prepared to leave to join an already formed Partisan Unit hidden in the woods of the area northeast of Bialystok. But the commanding unit of the Underground "grounded" me in favor of young men who had had military training and for whom there were some Russian guns. With frozen toes I left the pre-exit bunker and returned home with a phony story of an unsuccessful "tryst." I was told to await the next partisan exit [sortie] and to write, meanwhile, a song for the fighters. So I did. The song, with Russian words, was handed over to my underground "liaison," "Berl." Berl was later accused of having betrayed the movement and of having attempted to buy his freedom by helping the Nazis locate hideout bunkers. He was eventually imprisoned in Poland and died of TB. I doubt if Berl had ever handed in my song. ... Today I sing it, both in Russian and in English—and so I pay my respects to my fallen comrades.   Irene Shapiro, January 1998

Words and Music by Rena Hass (Irene Shapiro)

Zakryty my v geto, otorvany ot mira,
I bity fashistkim knutom.
||:No esli sevodnia zhit' tiazhko i plokho.
Tak luchshevo zavtra my zhdyom.:||

V glubokom podpole zhivyom my i dyshim,
Dlia bitvy my sily kopim.
||:Za krov' beszashchitnykh, za gore i muki,
Fashistam my platu dadim.:||

Druzia partizany, podaite nam ruku,
V sovmestnoi podpol'noi bor'be.
||:Dast znak Voroshilov, ogrady razrushim,
I vyidem v shirokii, vol'nyi svet.:||

Oi, veter, ty veter, leti ty v tu storonu,
Gde solnechnyi vstayot raztsvet.
||:Nesi dorogim-to vostochnym tovarishcham,
Nash molodyozhnyi privet.:||

Cut off in the ghetto, walled in from humanity,
And beaten by brute fascist might,
||:No matter if life now is dismal and frightful,
We trust that tomorrow will be bright.:||

United and ready, we live in the underground,
We're waiting to have our day.
||:For blood of the helpless, for sorrow and torment,
We'll give to the Nazis their pay!:||

Ye partisan brothers, oh reach out your hands to us,
Unite in our underground fight.
||:And with Voroshilov* we'll smash ghetto walls down,
And proudly step into the light.:||

Oh, winds, blow ye fast, to the battlegrounds far away,
Where sunshine does blossom again,
||:And there to our brave eastern comrades advancing,
Our youthful greetings we do send.:||

*Red Army General Klementii Efremovich Voroshilov (1881–1969). Actually, Voroshilov was not involved in the fighting in this sector of the front. Irene Shapiro adds: "Historically impossible! We were simply hoping for a message that the Soviets were in the suburbs or villages nearby, so as to break out of the ghetto and also fight the surrounded Germans. Hearing the Soviet guns would have been enough!"

67. Katiusha

Written in 1938 by two Soviet Jewish composers, Mikhail Isakovsky and Matvei Blanter, *Katiusha* ("Katy") is the song of a young woman whose Red Army soldier sweetheart is off to the distant Siberian frontier to counter the ever-growing Japanese threat along the border with China and Manchuria. It became popular during the pre-war years, but with the Nazi invasion of the USSR in 1940 it took on added significance. Just as the German soldiers in World War I nicknamed their huge cannons "Big Bertha," in honor of Bertha Krupp (daughter of the arms manufacturer), Red Army troops affectionately called their devastating rockets "Katiushas."

Words by Mikhail Vasilievich Isakovskii

Music by Matvei Blanter

Vykhodila, pesniu zavodila,
Pro stepnovo sizovo orla.
||:Pro tovo, kotorova liubila,
Pro tovo, ch'i pis'ma beregla.:||

Oi ty, pesnia, pesenka devichia,
Ty leti za yasnim solntsem vsled,
||:I boitsu na dal'nem pogranich'e
Ot Katiushi peredai privet.:||

Pust' on vspomnit devushku prostuiu,
Pust' uslishit, kak ona poyot.
||:Pust' on zemliu berezhyot rodnuiu,
A liubov Katiusha sberezhyot.:||

By the river's bank she sang a love song
Of her hero in a distant land;
||:Of the one she'd dearly loved for so long,
Holding tight his letters in her hand.:||

Oh, my song, song of a maiden's true love,
To my dear one travel with the sun.
||:To the one with whom Katiusha knew love,
Bring my greetings to him one by one.:||

Let him know that I am true and faithful,
Let him hear the love song that I send.
||:Tell him as he defends our home, that grateful,
True Katiusha our love will defend.:||

Recommended Listening

Moscow Nights. Monitor 590 (CD & cassette).
Petry, Getta. *Russian Songs.* Folkways/Smithsonian FC 7743 (cassette).
Polkas for a Gloomy World. Rounder 9045 (CD & cassette).
Yulya. *Yulya Sings Russian Romantic Songs.* Monitor 597 (CD).

68. Svyashchennaya Voina (The Sacred War)

Field Headquarters, 21 November 1942

[Himmler] *told me in detail what Hitler intended to do with Russia. He would incorporate the land up to the River Ob in the Reich. The area between the River Ob and the River Lena he would hand over to be administered by the English. England would realize that this war was not being waged against her position in the world, but against the world's enemies, the Jewish Bolsheviks. The United States of America would receive the area between the River Lena, Kamschatka and the Sea of Okhotsk.*

Felix Kersten, *The Kersten Memoirs*

The war between Germany and Russia is not a war between the two states or two armies, but between two ideologies— namely, the National Socialist and the Bolshevist ideology. The Red Army must not be looked upon as a soldier in the sense of the word applying to our western opponents, but as an ideological enemy. He must be regarded as the archenemy of National Socialism, and must be treated accordingly. (General Hermann Reinecke, chief of the prisoner-of-war section of the German army.)

It was Reinecke, under direct orders from Hitler, who was responsible for the inhumane conditions suffered by Red Army prisoners of war, who died by the *millions* in Nazi camps

Words by Vasilii Ivanovich Lebedev-Kumach

Music by Alexander Vasilievich Alexandrov

Kak dva razlichnikh poliusa,
Vo vsyom vrazhdebny my:
Za svet i mir my boremsia,
Oni — za tsarstvo t'mi. *Pripev*

Dadim otpor dushiteliam
Vsekh plamennykh idei,
Nasil'nikam, grabiteliam,
Muchiteliam liudei! *Pripev*

As far apart as are the poles,
We are apart from them.
A war for light and peace, our roles;
Their aim — enslaving men. *Chorus*

We'll put to rout the murderers,
Who would destroy our dreams.
The butchers and the plunderers —
And all their evil schemes. *Chorus*

69. Kak U Duba Starovo (Standing near the Old Oak Tree)

When the Moiseyev Dance Ensemble of Moscow first visited this country as part of the cultural exchange program of the 1960s, audiences were captivated by a particularly moving number entitled "Partisans." The dancers, wearing floor-length capes, seemed literally to be riding their steeds into battle to the melody of "Standing by the Old Oak Tree." This glorification by Jewish composers and choreographers of the Don Cossacks, whose tradition of violent anti-Semitism dates back several centuries, is an interesting commentary on postwar perceptions of wartime exploits. When my Russian-born mother attended a performace of this dance she had mixed feelings about it. On the one hand she was affected by the heroics of the cossacks in the struggle against the invaders; on the other hand she could not erase from her mind the memory of the terrible historical legacy of these self-same horsemen.

Words by L. Davidovitch and Viktor Yuzefovich Dragunski

Music by Lyudmilla Alexeevna Liadova

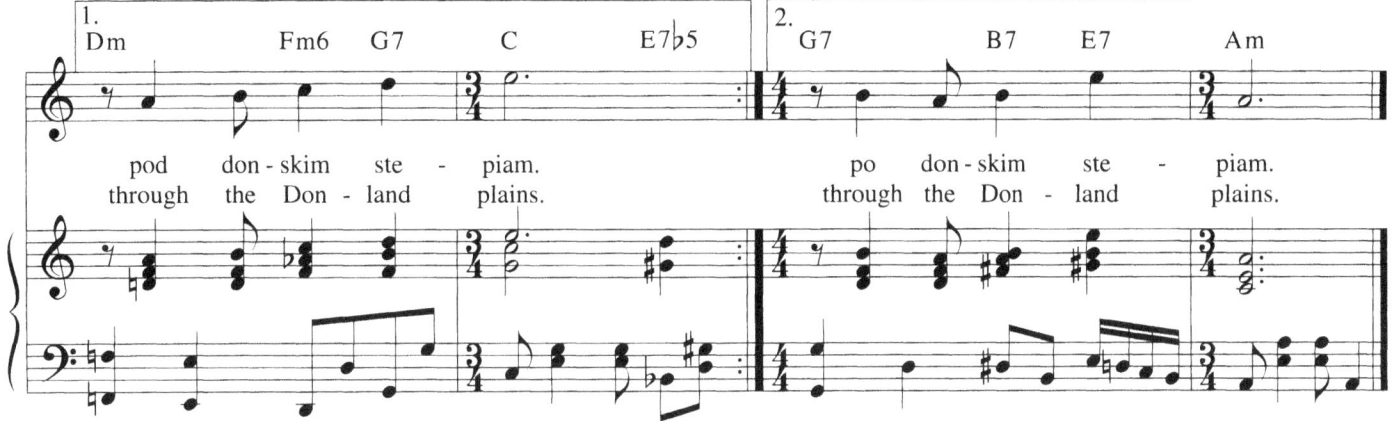

Pel v kustakh malinovykh solovei-solovushko,
Da shumeli list'iami stroiny topolia.
||:Podnimalos' solynshko—molodoye solnyshko,
Nas vstrechali devushki pesnei na poliakh.:||

Ekh ty, step' shirokaia—zhitnitsia kolkhoznaia,
Krai rodimyi, radostnyi—khorosho v nyom zhit'.
||:Edem my, kazachen'ki, edem krasnozvyozdnye,
V konnitsu Budyonnovo edem my sluzhit'.:||

Kak priedem, skazhem my boyevomu marshalu:
"My prishli, chtob Rodinu nashu zashchishchat'.
||:Ni zemli, ni travushki, ni prostora nashevo
Vsei fashistskoi svore v zhizni ne vidat'.":||

Koni b'iut kopytami nad lesnoi krinitseiu,
Posedlali konniki boyevikh konei.
||:Ekhali my, ekhali—syolami, stanitsami,
Po-nad tikhim Donom v dal' rodnykh stepei.:||

In a bush along the road, sang a wondrous nightingale,
And the poplar leaves rustled all the morning long.
||:Rising was the golden sun—rising was the young, new sun.
To the fields came young girls, greeting us with song.:||

Oh, you vast and mighty steppe—grain is growing everywhere;
Oh, my dearest Motherland—land that shall be free,
||:We are riding young cossacks, we are fearless Red horsemen;
With Budyonny* we'll serve in his cavalry.:||

And as soon as we get there, this we'll say to our marshall:
"We are here to fight for our land—to keep her free.
||:Not our land, no blade of grass, no sight of our boundless fields
Will the beastly fascists ever live to see.":||

Oh, the horses stamp the earth in the forest camping ground.
They are saddled—now the men all pull at the reins.
||:We rode onward, on we rode—villages and town flew by,
Near the quiet Don and through the Don-land plains.:||

*Red Army Marshall Semyon Mikhailovitch Budyonny (Budenny).

70. Oi, Tumany Moyi (Oh, the Fog)

The Smolensk Road (verse 2) is the main highway that leads from Brest, near the Polish border, passing through the Naliboki forest near Minsk, thence to Smolensk, and on for some 240 miles to Moscow. It was Hitler's (and Napoleon's) invasion (and retreat) route to Moscow and back. As the *Wehrmacht* swept by in 1940, thousands of Jews from Minsk joined the partisans in their camps in the wilds of the Naliboki forest. They harassed the Germans while rescuing Jews from nearby towns. I, too, drove the Smolensk Road both ways in 1959. Nearing Smolensk I saw a road sign that said "Orsha." Before the war Orsha was known for its weaving of high-quality prayer shawls (*talesim*). Orsha was also the site of the railroad station from which my mother's family left Russia on the first stage of their journey to America in 1913. They had arrived in Orsha from their neighboring home town of Dubrovno by horsecart. The feelings invoked in me by simply seeing that sign were indescribable. A generation had passed since anyone in my family had come that way. Of those who had stayed behind, there were none left. No family. *No talesim*. I asked the Soviet Intourist guide who was assigned to travel with us if a detour could be made off the highway to visit my ancestral shtetl. Came the reply: *nyet*.

Words by Mikhail Vasilievich Isakovskii

Music by Vladimir Zakharov

Na proshchan'e skazali geroi:	At the parting up spoke our heroes:
"Ozhidaite khoroshikh vestei!"	"There will soon be good news from the west."
‖: I po staroi smolenskoi doroge,	‖: And along the Smolensk Road that evening,
Povstrechali nezvanykh gostei.:‖	They met with their most unwelcome guest.:‖

Povstrechali, ognyom ugoshchali,
Navsegda ulozhili v lesu
‖: Za velikiye nashi pechali,
Za goriuchuiu nashu slezu.:‖

S toi pory da po vsei po okruge
Poteriali zlodeyi pokoi.
‖: Den' i noch' partizanskiye v'iugi
Nad razboinoi gudiat golovoi.:‖

Ne uidyot chuzhezemets nezvani,
Svoyevo ne uvidit zhilia!
‖: Oi, tumany moyi, rastumani!
Oi, rodnaia storonka moia!:‖

Yes, our guests were met with hot fire;
Our foes in the forest were slain
‖: For the sorrow, the suff'ring they brought us—
For the hot burning tears of our pain.:‖

Since that time over all of our country
The cruel murderers find no repose.
‖: Day and night our partisan whirlwinds
Roar above our foul, fascist foes.:‖

Oh, the unwelcome German will perish,
And his homeland he never will see.
‖: Oh, you blessed fog, keep us well hidden,
Till that day our dear homeland is free.:‖

"The Beast of Berlin," from *Rhymes For Our Times*, by Bill Silverman. Artist, Dr. William Avstreih.

71. Ásó Kapa Vállamon (On My Shoulder, Spade and Hoe)

Beginning in 1938, Hungarian Jewish men were pressed into service in labor batallions in the Hungarian army. The work was exhausting, dangerous, and degrading, not much different from life in the slave labor contingents of the coming concentration camps. When Hungary entered the war as an ally of Nazi Germany in 1940, these Jewsh units were sent into the Ukraine to support the regular Hungarian troops fighting the Red Army. The concept of Jews being forced to serve on the "wrong" side of the war is one of the supreme ironies of the Holocaust. Conditions on the Eastern Front were so extreme that about half of the 125,000 Jews perished. The Russian winter, disease, and starvation took their terrible toll; the brutality of their Hungarian guards also contributed to this tragedy within the larger tragedy. When the regular Hungarian army crumbled and withdrew through Poland before the advancing Red Army in 1943 (the year of the battle of Stalingrad, the turning point of the war), those Jewish "soldiers" still alive were once again forced into gruesome labor, this time burying the victims of the massacres of Polish Jews. Here again, many more died at the hands of their own guards. There was no respite for those who finally straggled back home to Hungary. In March 1944 the Germans, coming to the conclusion that Hungary could no longer be depended upon as a reliable ally, sent their troops in as occupiers. This time there was no more pretense of labor brigades. The survivers and their families were transported directly to Auschwitz.

The echoes of *Die Moorsoldaten (The Peat-Bog Soldiers)* [page 5] — marching to work with spade on shoulder, resound tragically in this song.

Zsidó szivvel dolgozunk,	With a Jewish heart we strike,
Jóban, rosszban osztozunk.	Sharing good and bad alike,
Szebb napokra készülünk,	Waiting for our better days.
A Jo-Isten van velünk, lesz velünk.	For the Good Lord is with us, always nigh,
Emelt fővel megujuló szent erővel	In God's strength we will rely with, heads held high,
Hisszük hogy felsüt a nap!	Believing the sun's rays will shine.

72. Partigiani In Montagna (Partisans in the Mountain)

Between one and three thousand Italian partisans were Jewish. While they came from a variety of backgrounds, most, like Italian Jews in general, were from the middle class. Most seem to have paid little heed to their Judaism.... A few, however ... found themselves delving deeply into this heritage that was causing so much pain. All fought in non-Jewish units, among men who had never known Jews and were quite uninterested in racial and religious issues ... all fought primarily as Italians, beside other Italians and against other Italians.

Susan Zucotti, The Italians and the Holocaust

Dove più aspra sarà la battaglia,
E a corpo a corpo verremo allemani,
||:Farem' vedere che siam partigiani,
Farem' onore al patrio valor.:||

And wherever the battle is fiercest,
Then hand to hand we'll fight the Germans.
||:They'll learn that we partisans can defeat them,
And we'll bring honor to our native land.:||

73. Bella Ciao (So Long, Dear)

The original version of *Bella Ciao* is a song about women who work in rice paddies in the Po Valley of northern Italy (as depicted in the classic post-war Italian film "Bitter Rice"). It describes the hard and demeaning life of these women, with the refrain *"bella ciao"* repeated over and over again as a sort of litany accompanying their endless labor. *Bella* means "pretty" (in this case, a pretty woman), and *ciao* (pronounced "chow") means "so long." The partisans rewrote the lyrics to describe their feelings as they went forth with premonitions of death to battle the fascists, but the refrain, *"bella ciao"* was kept.

They killed partisans, Jews and communists. Don't get excited about the Italians. The head of the SS in Trieste was Triestino. [Odilo Lotario Globocnik] This is 1 km from my father's family home. My aunt would smell the smoke.—Waldo Pagani

Much of the rice that was harvested by these women laborers was sent to the Risiera di San Sabba, the rice-cleaning and storage plant on the outskirts of Trieste. Built in 1913, the buildings of the plant were taken over by the Nazis in September 1943 to be used as a temporary prison (*Stalag* 339) for Italian soldiers captured after the Italian armistice of September 8. By the end of October the *Stalag* was transformed from a camp for prisoners of war into a *Polizeihaftlager,* a police prison camp. It now began receiving civilians who had been rounded up in Trieste, Veneto, and Slovenia for deportation to Germany and Poland. Soon thereafter it became a center for the detention and elimination of Jews, partisans, and political prisoners. In addition to the transfer of many of these prisoners to Dachau, Auschwitz, and Mauthausen, San Sabba had its own "death room" (*cella della morte*) where arrestees were murdered upon arrival. It was one of only two death camps in Italy (the other being in Gries, north of Bolzano near the Austrian border). An underground crematorium was built in the courtyard. On April 4, 1944 it was upgraded to be able to handle an ever-increasing number of bodies. Estimates by witnesses place the number of people cremated to between 3,000 and 5,000. A year later (April 29, 1945) the Nazis, fleeing before the advancing Allied troops, dynamited the structure in a vain attempt to eliminate proof of their crimes. It was not until April 1976 that the silence that had enveloped the San Sabba death camp for over thirty years was finally broken by the trial *in absentia* of the camp commandant, Joseph Oberhauser, and his superior, August Dietrich Allers, who after having organized the death camps of Treblinka, Sobibor, and Belzec, was stationed in Trieste. Allers died in 1975; Oberhauser, living in Munich at the time, escaped judgment by virtue of a nonextradition agreement signed by Germany and Italy after the war.

In April 1965, on the twentieth anniversary of the liberation of San Sabba, the site was declared a national monument by the president of Italy. It has been transformed into a museum.

Sing either "bella ciao" or "so long, dear" in the English verses.

Partigiano portami via,
O, bella ciao, bella ciao,
Bella ciao, ciao, ciao.
Partigiano portami via,
Che mi sento di morir.

E se muoio il partigiano,
O, bella ciao, bella ciao,
Bella ciao, ciao, ciao.
E se muoio il partigiano,
Tu mi devi seppellir.

Seppelire la sulla montagna,
O, bella ciao, bella ciao,
Bella ciao, ciao, ciao.
Seppelire la sulla montagna,
Sotto l'ombra di un bel fior.

E le genti che passeranno,
O, bella ciao, bella ciao
Bella ciao, ciao, ciao.
E le genti che passeranno,
Grideranno, "Che bel fior!"

Il più bel fior del partigianno,
O, bella ciao, bella ciao,
Bella ciao, ciao, ciao.
Il più bel fior del partigiano,
Morto per la libertà.

O, partisans, take me away now,
O, bella ciao, bella ciao,
Bella ciao, ciao, ciao.
O, partisans, take me away now,
For I feel I'm going to die.

And if I die a partisan,
O, bella ciao, bella ciao,
Bella ciao, ciao, ciao.
And if I die a partisan,
You will have to bury me.

So bury me up on the mountain,
O, bella ciao, bella ciao,
Bella ciao, ciao, ciao.
So bury me up on the mountain,
In the shade of a bright flower.

And all the people who will pass by me,
O, bella ciao, bella ciao,
Bella ciao, ciao, ciao.
And all the people who will pass by me,
Will cry out, "What a pretty flower!"

The brightest flower—partisans' flower,
O, bella ciao, bella ciao,
Bella ciao, ciao, ciao.
The brightest flower—partisans' flower,
He who died for liberty.

Recommended Listening

Sanacore. *All'aria.* Buda 926262 (CD).

Memorial plaques on the wall of the San Sabba Concentration Camp identifying it as a "Monumento Nazionale." Photograph: Waldo Pagani.

The inner courtyard of San Sabba, site of the underground crematorium. Photograph: Waldo Pagani.

74. Scarpe Rotte (Worn-Out Shoes)

Italian Jews fought in the resistance in a higher proportion to their national population than non-Jewish Italians. It is estimated that about 230,000 non-Jews out of a population of 45,000,000 (0.5%) took part in armed resistance, while at least 1,000 Jews out of 45,200 (about 2%) fought in the ranks of the partisans.

The tune of *Scarpe Rotte* is based on the Russian song, *Katiusha* [page 160] — with interesting melodic and harmonic variations throughout.

Ur - la il vento, fis - chia la bu - fe - ra, Scar - pe rot - te e pur bi - sogna_an - dar. A con - quis - tar la bel - la pri - ma - ve - ra, Do - ve sor - ge il sol dell' av - ve - nir. A sol dell' av - ve - nir.

Blow hard, you winds, and howl, the storm - y temp - est, Worn - out shoes, that is all we have to wear. Yet we march on to con - quer the bright spring - time. See the ris - ing bright sun of hope ap - pear. Yet sun of hope ap - pear.

Ogni contrada e' patria di ribelli,
Ogni donna lor dona un sospiro.
||:Nella notte ci guidano le stelle,
Forte il cor, il braccio nel colpir.:||

Se ci coglie la crudele morte,
Dura vendetta sarà del partigian.
||:Ormai sicuro della bella sorte
Contro il vil che tutti noi cerchiam.:||

Cessa il vento, calma la bufera,
Torna a casa il fiero partigian.
||:Sventolando l'Italia la bandiera,
Vittorioso e infin libero sarà.:||

Now every village is the land of rebels,
Every woman speeds the men along.
||:In the nighttime we have the stars to guide us.
Our hearts and our arms are strong.:||

And if cruel death should chance to overtake us,
Swift, the partisan's revenge will be.
||:We are sure that we will have good fortune
In our battle with the enemy.||

At last the winds and tempest gales are calming,
And the partisan is home again.
||:Waving high is the flag of our country,
We're victorious, and we are free men.:||

75. Domovina (Homeland)

In [April] 1941, a week after the occupation of Belgrade, the Jews were already ordered, under the threat of death, to report to German headquarters. In this situation the Communist party organized groups of youths commanded by party members. The groups met in secret, read and disseminated illegal leaflets, collected medical supplies for the partisans and saboteurs ... took part in sabotage. ... All this was done by young Jews who remained behind the front line until the mass deportations began. According to plan they were to have gradually joined the partisan ranks, but the roundups and sudden raids surprised many of them and dozens were executed. In August 1942 a first group of young Jews responded to the party appeal and went to join the partisans. Most, almost all, fell in battle all over the country. No members of their families survived. Many remain nameless heroes.

—A. Moreno, former partisan, writing in the *Yugoslav Jewish Almanac* in 1954

76. Embross, ELAS (Forward, ELAS)

ELAS is the acronym for *Ellinikos Laïkos Apeleftherotikos Stratos* — Greek People's Liberation Army.

At daylight we got our orders to move up to the front again.... We were to take over the line from Khimara to Tepeleni. [Greeks were fighting the Italian fascists in Albania.] *Night after night we trudged ahead without stopping, one behind the other, like the blind.... And the few times we'd pull up for a rest, not a word, serious and silent, we'd share our raisins one by one under the light from a bit of pine kindling.... Finally, through the darkness you'd hear a whistle signaling us to move out, and we'd push off again like pack animals to gain ground before daylight, when we'd make an open target for airplanes. Because God didn't know about targets and things, so he'd stick to this habit of making the light come up at the same time every day. That we were very near the place where you don't find weekdays or holidays, sick people or healthy people, poor or rich, we now knew. Because the roar ahead, like a storm beyond the mountains kept growing. Also because more and more we started coming across the slow procession of the wounded, heading out the other way. And when they'd hear where we were going, they'd shake their heads and start their tales of blood and terror. But we, the only thing we listened to were those other voices rising in the darkness, still scalding from the fire and brimstone of the depths. "Oi, oi, mana mou."* ["Oi, Oi, mama."] *And sometimes, less often, the sound of stifled breathing, like a snore, and those who knew said it was the rattle of death.*

From *Axion Esti* (This Is Worthy) by Greek Nobel Laureate Odysseus Elytis

Theresienstadt and the Emigrant Cabarets

77. Theresienstadt

In 1780, Emperor Joseph II of Austria (brother of Marie Antoinette) established a military garrison town and built a fortress near the confluence of the Eger and Eder rivers forty-five miles north of Prague. He named it Theresienstadt, after his late mother, Empress Maria Theresa. At that time a doctor from a prominent Jewish family named Jonas Jeitteles was practising medicine in Prague. Dr. Jeitteles came to be known as the father of the Prague Enlightenment because of his successful introduction of Edward Jenner's smallpox vaccine in that region despite intense Christian and Jewish opposition and prejudice. He inoculated his own daughter and more than 1500 persons, and the results were so dramatic, that in 1784 the emperor permitted him to treat patients "without consideration of their religion," quite a statement for the time (particularly in view of the fact that the late Empress had expelled the Jews from Prague in 1745; they were permitted to return in 1748 after international intervention on their behalf . . . and after promising to pay higher taxes). In 1816 the grandson of Dr. Jeitteles, Alois, was then a promising twenty-year-old medical student in Vienna, who moved in fashionable literary and musical circles, wrote poetry and counted Beethoven among his friends. That year he presented the composer with a cycle of poems that he had written, entitled *An die ferne Geliebte* ("To The Distant Beloved"). It was as if Alois had read Beethoven's mind. Beethoven, who was despairing of ever finding the woman of his dreams, seized upon these poems and in a short time composed the first true song cycle: a series of songs musically conceived to be sung in sequence, much as the movements of a sonata or symphony succeed one another. The Jeitteles family continued living in Prague through the years, generation after generation, producing doctors, scholars, and successful professionals. (The name Jeit[t]eles appears among the founders of the congregation *Oheb Shalom* in Newark, New Jersey, in 1848.) Berthold Jeitteles, born in 1875, continued the family tradition of scholarship. He wrote extensively on talmudic subjects, but his work was interrupted by the Nazi occupation of Prague. In 1939, one hundred and fifty-five years after the emperor who had established Theresienstadt had honored his great-great-great grandfather, Berthold was deported to Theresienstadt, where he was initially able to continue his studies. He was later transported to Auschwitz but miraculously was returned to Theresienstadt because there were "ten too many" on the transport. According to the German bureaucratic files he was considered "officially dead" and, therefore, not subject to further deportation. After the liberation in 1945 he returned to Prague, where he found all his hidden manuscripts intact. In 1948 he moved to New York and, after his death in 1958, an Institute for Publishing the Talmudic Works of Dr. Berthold Jeitteles was established in Manchester, England, but only one volume of his extensive writings was ever published.

Words by Schlesinger

Music by Jerry Silverman

Der Kaiserin gewaltge Hand
Ließ nie den Fleiß erlahmen.
Und als die Festung fertig stand,
Gab sie ihr ihnen Namen.
    Die Wälle boten Feinden Hohn,
    Die Fahne nie gestrichen,
    Uns selbst »Empereur Napoléon«
    Ist ihr stets ausgewichen.

Und jetzt—die Ironie is groß—
Es ist dahin gekommen,
Die Juden haben waffenlos
Die Festung eingenommen.
    Die starken Wälle blicken dort
    Noch dräuend gegen Norden.
    Theresienstadt, du stolzer Ort,
    Was ist aus dir geworden.

The empress's almighty hand,
The job did not distress it.
And when the fort did finished stand,
With her name she did bless it.
    The ramparts held the foe to scorn,
    The flag was never stricken.
    Napoleon himself did storm,
    And there he took a lickin'.

And now—the irony is this—
For to this place forsaken,
By Jews, completely weaponless,
The fortress it was taken.
    The mighty ramparts stony face
    The north is still defending.
    Theresienstadt, you haughty place,
    O, what has been your ending!

78. Theresienstadt, die schönste Stadt der Welt
(Theresienstadt, the Best Town in the World)

On May 29, 1942, Reinhard Heydrich, Hitler's special "Protector" of Bohemia and Moravia was mortally wounded by a bomb tossed into his open Mercedes sports car as he was driving from his country villa to Prague. When he died on June 4 the Germans began a terrible series of reprisals which touched both Czechs and Jews alike. Summary executions of innocent civilians numbered in the thousands. The little village of Lidice, not far from Prague, was obliterated by the German army, its residents either shot on the spot or transported to the concentration camp at Ravensbrück to be gassed. The Jewish inmates of Theresienstadt were not spared either: Three thousand of them were loaded on to boxcars for shipment to the extermination camps in the east.

Words by Theodore Otto Beer

Music by Jerry Silverman

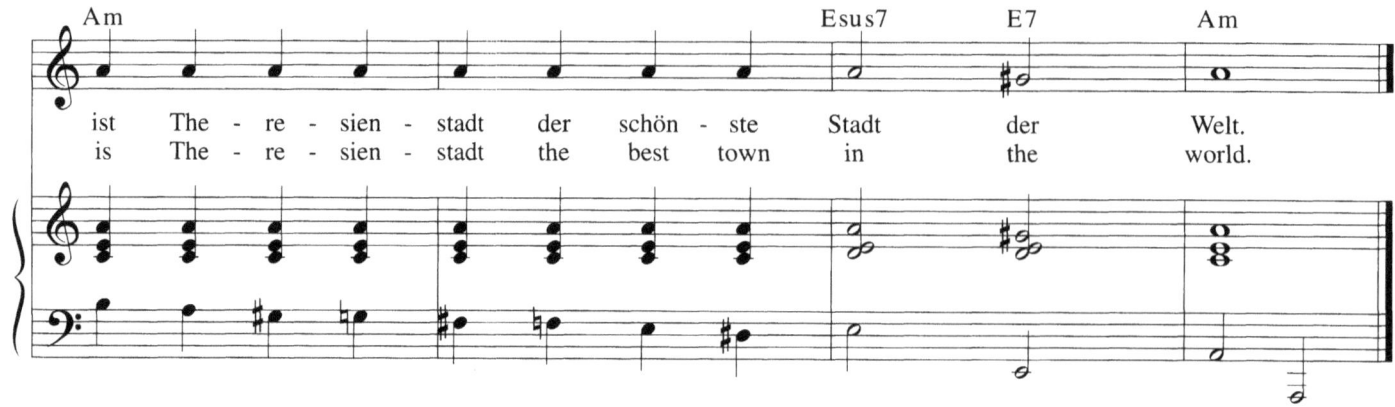

Weil Du Dich gifst, daß es kan Briefträger hier gibt,
Weil Du Dich kränkst, daß kein Salat für Dich blüht,
Weil Du nicht sprießen siehst die Blumen auf dem Feld,
Drum ist Theresienstadt uns allen so vergällt,
Drum red Dir ein, im Ghetto blühen Orchideen,
Und »prominieren« heißt, zwei Stunden Clo-Wach stehen,
Denk Dir, Du kriegst ein Wienerschnitzel, wenn Du um Menage angestellt,
Dann ist Theresienstadt die schönste Stadt der welt.

Bist Du einstens wieder mal bei Dir zu Haus,
Fährst nach Grinzing oder nach Barrandov dann hinaus.
Gehst am Abend ins Theater in die Bar,
Zu Sherry-Cobler, Gin und echtem Kaviar.
Wenn Dein Kind die kleinen Handerln um Dich legt,
Wenn Dein Familiensinn sich friedlich wieder regt,
Wenn wieder Mensch Du bist so wie es Dir gefällt,
Dann ist Theresienstadt die schönste Stadt der Welt.

Wenn die Jahre dann an Dir vorüber ziehen,
Um Dich ringsherum siehst Du neues Leben blühen,
Hast Du sicher was so sehr Dein Herz begehrt,
Und die alte, böse Welt ist ganz verkehrt.
Und eines Tages fragt Dein jüngstes Enkelein:
»Sag Opapa, war Deine Jugend wirklich fein?«
Erschütternd spricht Dein Mund, wenn die Träne Dir ins Aug' auch fällt,
Nein mein Kind — Theresienstadt war nicht die schönste Stadt der Welt.

You get upset because no mailman comes around,
And you get sick because no salad can be found,
And you don't see the flowers sprouting on the plain,
That's why Theresienstadt does cause us all such pain.
Just tell yourself that in the ghetto orchids flower.
For "promenading," you do toilet duty* for two hours.
But think, you get a wienerschnitzel when its time to eat,
That's why Theresienstadt just simply can't be beat.

When you have once again returned to your old flat,
You drive to Grinzing or Barrandov — just like that,
And in the evening in the theater and the bar
There's sherry cobblers, gin and genuine caviar.
When your child embraces you with little arms,
And when your family life regains its former charms,
When once again you feel you are the man you're worth,
Then is Theresienstadt the finest town on earth.

In the course of time, when many years have flown,
You see around you all the new lives that have grown,
Your heart's desires now have all been satisfied,
And the cruel world has changed its course — all tears have dried.
And then one day your youngest grandchild wants to know:
"Say, grandpa, tell me how your youth did really go,"
And trembling you do speak — your tears drown out all mirth:
No, my child — Theresienstadt was not the finest town on earth.

*Infectious diseases took a heavy toll of lives in Theresienstadt. Diarrhea, due to the eating of raw potato peelings and other indigestible items was a constant. *Clo-Wach* — latrine duty — trying to keep the toilets clean and functioning, was of prime importance. As a result someone was always on duty in the latrines.

79. Bad Blockhaus (Blockhouse Resort)

Born Hanus Schulhof in 1907, Hans Hofer was a performer and director in the Jewish cabaret in Prague in the 1930s. When he was deported to Theresienstadt in 1942 he founded his own cabaret ensemble, the Hofer Ensemble, that performed not only in the camp, but outside, in field hospitals, old-age homes, and even in the German army barracks in Magdeburg. After helping direct the Nazi propaganda film, *Der Führer schenkt den Juden eine Stadt* (The Führer Presents a City to the Jews) he and the actors were shipped off to Auschwitz. He was subsequently transferred to the Kaufering concentration camp, where he remained until the liberation. He then returned to Prague, and in 1960 moved to the German Democratic Republic, where he was engaged by the Rostock Volkstheater. He died in 1973.

Bad is the German word for "spa." German propaganda had convinced many Jews that they were headed for a health resort. The streets in the camp were identified by *L* (*Längs*, "Lengthwise") and *Q* (pronounced "kvé" — *Quer*, "cross"). They were all alike, and intersected each other at right angles. The barracks were numbered according to their positions either on *Längstraße* (Lengthwise Street) or *Querstraße* (Cross Street). "Brockhaus," in which the singer searched in vain for an entry on "blockhouse," is a German encyclopedia. Theresienstadt had its own autonomous post office, hence, the reference to the postmaster in verse two.

Words by Hans Hofer

Music by Jerry Silverman

Ich schrieb nach Prag ne Karte,
Daß ich auf Päckchen warte,
Denn unzureichend ist die Kost.
Und dem Herrn Postminister,
Damit dran nicht vergißt er,
Trag ich jetzt die Adresse auf die Post. *Refrain*

I wrote a card to Prague now,
I'm waiting all agog now,
For a pack of food I need the most.
And so to the postmaster,
To forestall a disaster,
I'm running with my address to the post. *Chorus*

80. Theresienstädter Fragen (Theresienstadt Questions)

Presented by the ensemble of the "Strauss Cabaret" in the Theresienstadt concentration camp between 1942 and 1944. The stage directions for this musical dialogue between two women — the first, a new arrival in the camp, and the second, a long-time inmate, specifies: *First Lady enters in a traveling outfit, with a tartan traveling rug and bird cage; Second Lady in cleaning-detail overalls, absent-mindedly sweeping the street.*

Tarnopol, (verse 2) a city and province in Poland (after the beginning of W.W. II, it was "absorbed" by the Soviet Union). The population of the city of Tarnopol was approximately half Jewish. The conversation in this verse hinges on the snobbish and superior attitude that Viennese Jews had toward their Polish brothers and sisters, even in Theresienstadt. The question of the missing belongings (verse 8) stems from the fact that the Jews were permitted to take only hand luggage with them, with the understanding that their suitcases were to be shipped later by baggage car. Naturally, the baggage cars never arrived. In the German text of verse 9, there is the Czech word *cvokárna* (pronounced "tsvokarna," derived from *cvok*, "eccentric"). In this context it means "crazy." It is "Germanized" in the subsequent duo section as *verzwockteste*, craziest.

Words by Leo Strauss

Music by Jerry Silverman

Erste Dame

Sagen Sie, wie kommt das bloß,
Gestern noch ganz sternelos,
Bin ich heute schon inmitten
Lauter polnischer Semiten?
        Theresienstadt, Theresienstadt,
        Ist das antisemitischste Ghetto, das die Welt heut hat.

Ist das Klima hier gesund?
Oder geht man hier zugrund?
Ist das Mittagessen reichlich?
Ist hier Krankheit unausweichlich?
        Theresienstadt, Theresienstadt,
        Ist das humanste Ghetto, das die Welt heut hat.

Zweite Dame

Mancher, der die Nase rümpft,
Will sich tarnen, wenn er schimpft.
Drum frag ich ganz unverholen,
Gehörn Sie zu den Tarnopolen?

Kost ist knapp für starke Esser,
Für die Kranken sorgt man besser.
Will man stets gesund hier bleiben?
Muß man dauernd krank sich schreiben?

Also nicht genug zum Essen.
Hat man uns denn ganz vergessen,
Ist das meines Lebens Schluß,
Daß ich hier verhungern muß?
   Theresienstadt, Theresienstadt,
    Ist das vornehmste Ghetto, das die Welt heut hat.

Bitte, schweigen Sie sofort!
Hunger ist ein garstig Wort.
Hier benennt man diese Chose
Vornehm Avitaminose.

Wer besorgt mir mein Logis,
Ganz bescheiden, wissen Sie.
Zimmer, Küche, Kabinett,
Aber rühig, sauber, nett?
   Theresienstadt, Theresienstadt,
    Ist das verträumteste Ghetto, das die Welt heut hat.

Mit ein wenig Phantasie,
Meine Gnädge, träumen Sie
Von Zimmer, Küche, Kabinett
Auf dem obern Cavalett.

Richtig, eh ich dran vergeß,
Wie stehts hier mit Evening-Dress?
Muß ein Mann, so möcht ich fragen,
Abends einen Frack hier tragen?
   Theresienstadt, Theresienstadt,
    Ist das mondänste Ghetto, das die Welt heut hat.

Meistens geht man hier salopp,
Und nur manche tun als ob.
Schmücken sich je nach Geschmack,
Mein Mann geht hier nur als Wrack.

Ich bin zwar recht abgespannt
Von der Reise in dies Land,
Dennoch möcht ich mich bequemen,
Heute noch ein Bad zu nehmen.
   Theresienstadt, Theresienstadt,
    Ist das hygienschste Ghetto, das die Welt heut hat.

Gehn Sie nur direkt nach Haus,
Schlafen Sie sich richtig aus.
Denn die ersten Badekarten
Können Sie im Mai erwarten.

Ach, noch etwas, mein Gepäck
Ist zum größten Teile weg.
Sagen Sie mir bitte an,
Wie ichs holen lassen kann.
   Theresienstadt, Theresienstadt,
    Ist das kulanteste Ghetto, das die Welt heut hat.

Lassen Sie das Zeug nicht holen,
Denken Sie sich, Gott befohlen,
Jeder Schritt ist für die Katz,
Und Sie haben doch eh kein Platz.

Apropos, ich möchte morgen
Vogelfutter hier besorgen.
Ach, mein Vogel braucht Diät,
Frißt nur prima Qualität.
   Theresienstadt, Theresienstadt,
    Ist das verzwockteste Ghetto, das die Welt heut hat.

Dafür gibts hier kein Import,
Gebens rasch den Vogel fort.
Wer hier einen Vogel hat,
Ist Cvokárna-Kandidat.

Sagen Sie mir noch zum Schluß,
Was ich dringend wissen muß,
Denn ich will nach Hause schreiben,
Wie lang werden wir hier bleiben?
   Theresienstadt, Theresienstadt,
    Ist das informierteste Ghetto, das die Welt heut hat.

Ja, da kann man sich nur richten
Nach denn neuesten Berichten.
Heute hört ich beispielweise ...
Musik übertönt ihre Worte.

First Lady

Tell me, please, how can it be?
Yesterday I was quite free.
Now today I cannot choose,
Here with noisy Polish Jews.
   Theresienstadt, Theresienstadt,
    Is the most antisemitic ghetto that the world has got.

Second Lady

Many who turn up their nose,
Try to fool us—so it goes.
No offense, upon my soul,
Do you come from Tarnopol?

Is the climate healthy here?
Or do people "disappear"?
Is the midday meal enjoyable?
And is sickness unavoidable?

Food is tight for heavy eaters,
Sick folks here are treated better.
To stay healthy, learn the trick here.
You must sign up to be sick here.

    Theresienstadt, Theresienstadt,
        Is the most humane ghetto that the world has got.

So, the eating here is rotten.
Is it that we've been forgotten?
Will I draw here my last breath,
As I slowly starve to death?

Quiet! Please don't be absurd.
Hunger is a dirty word.
Here we call it—don't you see?
Vitamin deficiency.

    Theresienstadt, Theresienstadt,
        Is the most distinguished ghetto that the world has got.

Who takes care of housing me?
Something simple—don't you see?
Bedroom, kitchen, cabinet.
Quiet, cozy, pretty yet.

With a little fantasy,
Just keep dreaming, dear lady,
Of those rooms and all that junk,
Atop your double-decker bunk.

    Theresienstadt, Theresienstadt,
        Is the daydreamingest ghetto that the world has got.

Ah, there's one thing more, I guess,
What gives here with evening dress?
Must a man, I'd like to know,
Evenings, wear a tuxedo?

Worn-out clothes are what we wear,
Most of us don't even care.
Wear what you like—what the heck.
My man looks just like a wreck.

    Theresienstadt, Theresienstadt,
        Is the most stylish ghetto that the world has got.

I am really all tired out
From this traveling about.
So, I'd like to have the pleasure
Of a hot bath at my leisure.

Just go to your house directly,
Go to bed and sleep correctly.
And your first bath-card, I say,
You'll expect some time in May.

    Theresienstadt, Theresienstadt,
        Is the most hygienic ghetto that the world has got.

My belongings, by the way,
For the most part, gone astray.
Won't you tell me, if you can,
How I can fetch them again?

Leave your things, don't even bother.
It's the will of God the Father.
Every step here's a disgrace,
And you hardly have a place.

    Theresienstadt, Theresienstadt,
        Is the most obliging ghetto that the world has got.

Apropos, tomorrow morning,
I'll need bird food—that's a warning.
On a diet's my birdie;
Eats just first-class quality.

This is getting quite absurd,
Quickly get rid of that bird.
Anyone here with a pet
Is a nuthouse candidate.

    Thersienstadt, Theresienstadt,
        Is the craziest ghetto that the world has got.

Tell me this, before I go,
What I really want to know,
So that I can write home today,
How long will we have to stay?

Yes, I've gotten confirmation
From the latest information.
Today I heard—just for example . . .
Music drowns out her words.

    Theresienstadt, Theresienstadt,
        Is the best informed ghetto that the world has got.

81. Als Ob (As If)

Leo Strauss (1897–1944), son of Viennese operetta composer Oscar Strauss (*The Chocolate Soldier*), was a cabaretist and author. He arrived in Theresienstadt in 1942, where he became active in camp-cabaret (*Lager-Kabarett*) musical productions, both as librettist and performer. In January 1943, a coffee-house was opened in Theresienstadt as part of an effort to give the camp a "friendlier" aspect. It was in this cafe that a group of inmates, calling themselves (in English) the "Ghetto-Swingers" [!], performed the latest camp songs (*Lager-Lieder*). According to survivors, *Als Ob* was the most popular of these songs. In October 1944, Strauss and his wife Myra were deported to Auschwitz where they were murdered shortly after their arrival.

Since Strauss used the English expression "tip top" (*tipp-topp*) as a rhyme for *als ob*, I have left that combination intact in the English lyrics as well. (*Ob* is pronounced "op.")

Words by Leo Strauss
Music by Jerry Silverman

Die leben dort ihr Leben,	There you can live your life out,
Als ob ein Leben wär,	As if it were a life;
Und freun sich mit Gerüchten,	Also rejoice in rumors,
Als ob die Wärheit wär.	As if the truth were rife.
Die Menschen auf den Straßen,	The people in the streets here,
Die laufen im Galopp—	Do run at a *Galopp*.
Wenn man auch nichts zu tun hat,	When one has nothing to do,
Tut man doch so als ob.	Then one just does *als ob*.
Es gibt auch ein Kaffeehaus,	There is a coffee-house here,
Gleich dem Café de l'Europe,	Like the Café de l'Europe;
Und bei Musikbegleitung,	And with the background music,
Fühlt man sich dort als ob.	You feel you're there *als ob*.
Und mancher ist mit manchem,	And this one toward that one,
Auch manchmal ziemlich grob—	At times acts like a slob.
Daheim war er kein Großer,	At home he was no big shot,
Hier macht er so als ob.	Here he behaves *als ob*.
Des Morgens und des Abends	At morning and at evening,
Trinkt man Als-ob-Kaffee.	*Als ob* coffee's a treat.
Am Samstag, ja am Samstag,	On Saturday, yes, Saturday,
Da gibts Als-ob-Haché.	There is *als ob* chopped meat.
Man stellt sich an um Suppe,	One sits down to eat supper,
Als ob da etwas drin,	As if we could dig in,
Und man genießt die Dorsche,	And we enjoy dry stalks here,
Als Als-ob-Vitamin.	Like *als ob* vitamin.
Man legt sich auf den Boden,	One lies down on the hard floor,
Als ob das wär ein Bett,	As if 'twere bed or cot,
Und denkt an seine Lieben,	And thinks about his loved ones,
Als ob man Nachricht hätt.	As if some news he's got.
Man trägt das schwere Schicksal,	One is weighed down by fate here,
Als ob es nicht so schwer,	As if one weren't so numb,
Und spricht von schönrer Zukunft,	And speaks of a brighter future,
Als obs schon morgen wär.	As if the dawn had come.

82. Der Reisepaß Erzählt (The Passport Relates)

Jewish exile political cabarets came into being in cities all over the world, as writers and musicians sought refuge from the Holocaust. One such establishment in New York, called The Ark, was the setting in 1943 for a production entitled *Reisende der Weltgeschichte* (Traveler Through World History). Viennese refugee Oskar Teller, one of the founders of The Ark, sang this song from that show there to an understanding and appreciative audience.

The "affadavit" mentioned in the last verse was the certificate of guarantee of support that a refugee needed to obtain from a citizen of the country in which he was seeking asylum.

Words by Hugo F. Königsgarten

Music by Jerry Silverman

Das Leben führte mich durch viele Hände,
Nicht alle schmutzig, doch nicht alle rein.
Man prüfte mich von Anfang bis zu Ende,
Und jede drückte mir'n Stempel rein.
So wurden meine ehmals weißen Blätter
Beschrieben und bestempelt Jahr um Jahr,
Bis von der einstgen reineren Unschuldsfarbe,
Nicht mehr ein einziges Fleckschen übrig war.
Fast wundert's mich, daß ich noch immer führ
Die Nummer Kf Strich 3 6 0 4.

Ich wanderte durch mancher Herren Länder,
Freiwillig manchmal, aber manchmal nicht.
An jeder Grenze ward ich neu bestempelt,
Nicht immer mit dem freundlichsten Gesicht.
Und eines Tages hab ich mich vermählet
Mit Kf Strich 3 6 0 4 b,
Und eh ich richtig noch bis drei gezählet,
Gab's auch 3 6 0 4 Strich c und d.
So lebten traulich im Vereine wir,
Die Nummer Kf Strich 3 6 0 4.

Dann ward ein Affadavit mir verliehen—
Das war mein schönster Lebensaugenblick!
Doch später habe ich dann eingesehen,
Auch das allein bedeutet nicht das Glück!
Und jetzt, da meine Blätter lose werden,
Mein Rücken nicht mehr ganz zusammenhält,
Nun stempeln mich »ungültig« die Behörden,
Und ich geh ein in eine bessere Welt.
Ich bitte: Schreibet auf den Grabstein mir:
»Hier ruht in Gott Kf 3 6 0 4«.

Well, life conducted me through many strange hands,
Not all of them were dirty, not all clean.
I was examined from the start to finish,
And each one added his stamp to the scene.
And so, my pages that had all been so white,
Were written on and stamped year after year,
Until from all that innocent blank paper,
The smallest little space did not appear.
It struck me very strange that I still bore
The number Kf dash 3 6 0 4.

Through many foreign lands I then was tramping,
Sometimes by choice, sometimes the other way.
At every border I received re-stamping,
Rarely by friendly faces, I must say.
And one fine day I happily did marry—
With Kf dash 3 6 0 4 dash b.
And one-two-three, we didn't stop to tarry,
Soon came 3 6 0 4 dash c and d.
And so we lived in comfortable rapport—
The number Kf dash 3 6 0 4.

Then one day I received an affadavit—
It was the sweetest moment of my life.
But later on I realized, though I crave it,
That by itself it does not end one's strife.
And now, when all my pages dangle loosely,
My spine does not support me any more,
Authorities now stamp me as "invalid,"
And to a better world I pass the door.
Please write this on my tombstone—nothing more:
"Here lies in God Kf 3 6 0 4."

Theresienstadt-Gelt (Theresienstadt Money). Scrip issued for the prisoners' use in Theresienstadt. Printed in German with denominations in fictitious Czech kronen and signed, to preserve the illusion of "authenticity," by Jakob Edelstein, *der Älteste der Juden* (the "Elder" of the Jews).

83. Die Novaks aus Prag (The Novaks from Prague)

The 1938 Nazi *Anschluss* in Austria effectively spelled the doom of the Viennese cabaret scene. Among the performers caught up in the terror was the well-known singer Hermann Leopoldi, who was arrested and sent to Buchenwald. Miraculously, in 1939 he was freed from that concentration camp and subsequently emigrated to New York. He performed this song in the New York emigrant-cabaret, Kadeko with humor and *tristesse*. Kurt Robitschek's German lyrics are full of delicious rhymes, not the least of which pairs *Señoras* with *Zoras* (verse 2), which is the German spelling of that most Yiddish of words: *tsores,* "troubles."

The Sunday roast goose at the Novaks was part of a national tradition which "placed great emphasis on pleasures of the table. Robust, with sophisticated overtones, it was well known for its soups; its roast birds and smoked meats; its savory sausages and wild mushrooms . . . its goulash and wiener schnitzel; its large variety of dumplings . . . its cheeses . . . yeasted pastries . . . sweet crepelike pancakes; and, of course, beer." (Clara De Silva, *In Memory's Kitchen*)

Words by Kurt Robitschek

Music by Jerry Silverman

Der Fußtritt der Zeit	The footstep of time
Hat die Novaks geknickt.	Struck the Novaks a blow.
Sie wurden aus Träumen geweckt.	They were wakened out of their dreams.
Den böhmischen Löwen, den hat man verkauft,	The Bohemian lions were treacherously sold,
Die Gänseln, die hab'n sich versteckt.	The geese were all hidden, it seems.
Marschierende Schritte: »Ein Führer, ein Volk ... «	Then came marching footsteps: "One Führer, one folk!"*
Da hat man in Schnellzug gesehn:	And in the express train were seen
Die Wrbas, die Krejcis, die Bilys, die Krcs.	The Wrbas, the Kejcis, the Bilys, Krcs.
Doch was ist mit Novaks geschehn?	The Novaks, where could they have been?
Es sitzt jetzt der Leo	Now sitting is Leo
In Montevideo.	In Montevideo.
Er denkt nicht mehr an die Señoras,	He thinks no more of the *señoras*,
Er hat jetzt ganz andere Zoras.	For he now has quite different *tsores*.
Die Tante, die Anna,	And dear Aunty Anna,
Die sitzt in Havanna	She sits in Havana
Und wartet auf Arthur, den Jüngsten,	And waits there for Arthur, the young son,
Denn der Dampfer aus Lisbon kommt Pfingsten.	On the steamship from Lisbon on Whitsun.
Die Köchin Marianka	The cook, Marianka
Sitzt in Casablanca.	Sits in Casablanca.
Die Tochter, die Mali,	Their daughter, named Molly
Hat kein Visum von Bali	Has no visa from Bali
Nach Schanghai und Bombay.	For Shanghai and Bombay.
Und lang wird der Tag!	And as in a fog,
Die Novaks, die träumen	The Novaks are dreaming,
In gemieteten Räumen	In strange places scheming,
Von einem Ort nur.	Of only one place.
Sie träumen von Prag.	They're dreaming of Prague.

Another look at the ramifications of the worldwide scattering of emigrés was offered in the poem *Greenhorn Denkt Nach (Greenhorn Reflects)* by Carl Farkas in 1940. Farkas was an actor and director in Viennese cabarets who managed to escape to Paris in 1938 before the trap was sprung. From Paris he made his way to New York, where he lived until his return to Vienna in 1946. Only a few verses of his long poem are given here.

Nun hab' ich meine Frau in Frankreich,	In France my wife's now living,
Un meine Schwester noch in Wien.	And my sister's still in Vienna.
Es sitzt mein Sohn, der Börseaner	You'll find my son, the stockbroker,
In Zürich als Costaricaner	A Costa Rican Züricher
Aus Krotoschin ...	From Krotoczyn ... [a city in Poland]
Mein Schwiegervater lebt in China,	My father-in-law lives in China,
Im gelben Himmelreich der Mings;	In the yellow heavenly empire of the Ming.
Assimiliert sich in die Tiefe,	He's assimilated better,
Und schriebt mir vertikale Briefe,	And writes me vertical letters,
Anstatt wie einst von rechts nach links ...	For right to left's no more his thing ... [Yiddish, that is.]
Mein Töchterl ward durch Heirat Griechin—	My little daughter is a Greek by marriage—
(Bevor der Krieg so weit gedieh'n.)	(Before the war she became one.)
Ihr Paß ist leider aus Wolhynien,	Her passport, though, is from Volhynia,
Sonst wär' sie längst in Argentinien	Although she lived long in Argentinia
Als Ungarin ...	As a Hungarian ...
Was für Geschlechter einst entstehen	What kind of offsprings will come forth
Aus dieser polyglotten Sauce?	From such a polyglottal sauce?
Hindo-Slovaken, Nil-Hussiten,	Hindo-Slovaks, Nilo-Hussites,
Vermischt mit Fidschi-Israeliten,	Mixed with Fiji-Israelites,
Und strammen Czecho-Eskimos?	And also Czecho-Eskimos?

*One of Hitler's favorite expressions.

84. Die Kosmopolitin (The Cosmopolitain)

Egon Larsen, born Egon Lehrburger, was a cabaret author and journalist. Before 1933 he was on the staff of the *Berliner Tageblatt*. When the Nazis came to power, like so many others, he was forbidden to exercise his profession in Germany. He fled to Prague and was engaged by the *New York Times* as a correspondent. In 1938 he emigrated to London where he worked for the German Service of the BBC. Because of his lingusitic proficiency he also began broadcasting over the military network "Calais" to France in 1944. He wrote lyrics for the London emigrant-cabaret, Four-and-Twenty Black Sheep and for the cabaret (*die Kleinkunstbühne*) of the Free German Cultural Alliance.

It was at the cabaret that Agnes Bernelle first performed this song in a revue in 1940, entitled "What's in the Newspaper?" As a true "cosmopolitain," Larsen injected lines in French and English into the song. I have retained the French in the body of the song to give the flavor of the original.

Words by Egon Larsen

Music by Jerry Silverman

Shanghai was raided by the Japs.
I saw our boarding house collapse.
In Hollywood, without a cent,
I couldn't even pay the rent.
In Rio ein Mann wollt mich haben—
Ich glaub, als seine Frau sogar.
Ich dachte an Hans nur in Deutschland,
Und ob er auch draußen schon war?
    Ich kenn die Welt,
    Sie läßt mich kalt.
    Ich bin schon ganze zwanzig Jahre alt.

Vom Reisen träumt' ich als Kind
Von Abenteuern, Seefahrt und Wind.
Jetzt ist's ein Haus, vom dem ich träum',
Und eine Stadt, die heißt Daheim.
Ich möcht sie einmal wiedersehn,
Und hörn, wie man deutsch spricht zuhaus.
Ich könnt' dort die Menschen verstehen,
Ist alles dies erst einmal aus,
    Ich kenn die Welt,
    Sie ist so kalt.
    Ich bin erst ganze zwanzig Jahre alt.

Shanghai was raided by the Japs.
I saw our boarding house collapse.
In Hollywood, without a cent,
I couldn't even pay the rent.
In Rio, there a man did want me—
Believed he wanted me as wife.
I only thought of Hans in Germany,
And did he get out with his life?
    I know the world.
    It leaves me cold.
    I am already twenty long years old.

When I was young I dreamt of trips,
Adventures, ocean winds, and ships.
But now I dream, where'er I roam,
Of house and town—that is, of home
For I must see them all once more,
And hear them speak German again.
I'll understand them as before,
When all of this comes to an end.
    I know the world.
    It is so cold.
    I am already twenty long years old.

Translation of the French lyrics:

I know the whole neighborhood,
And in Montmartre the cabarets.
Life is good when one is rich,
But like [since I am] a refugee—I don't give a damn!

85. Transport

Author Manfred Greiffenhagen (1896–1945) was arrested and sent to Theresienstadt in January 1944. He played an active role in the presentation of outstanding cabaret productions there in association with Leo Strauss. His texts were bitterly ironic in their tone, describing the precarious situation in which the prisoners all found themselves. In early October 1944 he was deported to Auschwitz. He survived that death camp, only to perish in Dachau in January 1945.

Words by Manfred Greiffenhagen
Music by Jerry Silverman

Es brennt die Welt, es lodern die Flammen,
Darin die Erde schaurig sich erhellt,
Und krachend stürtzt in Rauch und Glut zusammen,
Was sich der Mensch erbaut als seine Welt.
Was segensreich dem Frieden konnte dienen,
Gibt seine Kraft nun der Zerstörung her,
In Tempokampf der Menschen und Maschinen
Erzeugt der Krieg gesteigerten Verkehr.
    Transport, Transport
    In einem fort
    Rollen die Wagen, donnern und tragen
    Millionenheere von Meer zu Meere,
    Leistungsrekord!
    Transport.

Wie häufig führte man das Wort im Munde,
Wie ahnungslos sprach man es vor sich hin,
Bis für uns alle kam die schwere Stunde,
Da wir erfaßten seinen wahren Sinn.
Man rollt die Decken, ein paar Abschiedsküsse,
Ein rascher Händedruck, ein letzte Blick,
Es dampft ein Zug hinaus in Ungewisse,
Und leere Schienen bleiben uns zurück.
    Transport, Transport,
    Kennst du das Wort,
    Kennst du die Wagen, hörst du die Klagen?
    Eh du begriffen, ist abgepfiffen,
    Und sie sind fort—
    Transport.

Doch eines bleibt, es bleibt uns bis zum Tode,
Das ist der Glaube, ihm gehört der Sieg.
Einmal wird alles für uns Episode,
Und einmal, einmal endet auch der Krieg.
Wir fragen nicht nach Sieg und Niederlage,
Wir fragen nur, wann kommt ihr uns zurück?
Wir Juden wolln den Frieden unsrer Tage,
Und irgendwo ein ganz bescheidenes Glück.
    Transport, Transport
    Tönt's dann sofort!
    Wir sehen uns wieder, Schwestern und Brüder,
    Lachend und weinend, sich wieder vereinend
    Am Schlußakkord—
    Transport!

The world's on fire, the flames are blazing,
The earth is lit up by their gruesome light,
And crackling, all in smoke and fire is razing
This world that man has built for his delight.
What blessedly can serve the cause of world peace,
Devotes its power only to destroy.
In battle-speed with men and with machinery,
The war reverses all we did enjoy.
    Transport, transport,
    As one, go forth.
    Wagons are rolling, thundering and hauling,
    Millions in motion from ocean to ocean,
    Performance record!
    Transport.

How often does that word exert its power,
How unsuspectingly we say it here,
Until for us arrives that fatal hour,
And then its awful meaning becomes clear.
Roll up the covers, and some farewell kisses,
And then a quick handshake and a last glance.
The train bound for the unknown steams and hisses,
Behind us, empty tracks—we have no chance.
    Transport, transport,
    You know that word?
    Cars full of moaning, crying and groaning.
    Ready or not now, you're on the spot now,
    And you go forth—
    Transport.

Yet there is one thing that cannot be shaken,
We believe firmly in our victory.
One day this, too, shall pass—we shall awaken,
The war will then be a faint memory.
We do not ask who will win and who will lose,
We ask but one thing: When will you return?
Living in peace remains the goal of all Jews,
And happiness for all—for that we yearn.
    Transport, transport,
    Sound the report!
    We'll see one another—sister and brother,
    Laughing and crying as one—no denying,
    At the final accord.
    Transport!

86. Diese Emigranten! (These Emigrants!)

This satirical text of unknown authorship circulated in exile-cabarets in Holland in 1934. Its barbs were directed at a number of well-known Nazi figures. Hjalmar Horace Greeley [sic] Schacht, financial wizard was, at the time of the composition of this song, president of the *Reichsbank* and minister in Hitler's cabinet. Nazi army chaplain Ludwig Müller was appointed "Reich Bishop" and was charged by Hitler to bring the more than forty million Protestants "into line" (he committed suicide in 1945). Ernest Röhm, leader of the S. A. (*Sturmabteilung*—Storm Troopers or Brownshirts) and Edmund Heines, convicted murderer and head of the Munich S. A. Both were known for their homosexual quarrels and jealousies (while persecuting and imprisoning homosexuals). On Hitler's orders they were both murdered on June 30, 1934, along with a number of other early Hitler supporters, in the blood purge known as the "Night of the Long Knives."

Music by Jerry Silverman

An jedem Übel, wie bekannt, Trägt Schuld allein der Emigrant.
For ev-'ry e-vil it is known, The em-i-grant's at fault a-lone.

In Deutschland droht ein harter Winter—
Da steckt ein Emigrant dahinter!
    Verloren ist die Arbeitsschlacht,
    Ein Emigrant hat das gemacht!
        Dem Schacht entgleiten die Devisen—
        Die Emigranten ziehn an diesen!

Kein Leder, keine Woll im Land—
Ha—wiederum der Emigrant!
    Reischsbischof Müller steckt in Nöten—
    O, diese Emigrantenkröten!
        Wie Röhm mit Heines hat verkehrt,
        Hat sie ein Emigrant gelehrt!

Das Braune Reich voll Defraudanten?
Die Treue floh—zu Emigranten!
    Die haben, eh sie abkosackt,
    Flugs allen Vorrat eingepackt.
        Der nun bei Emigranten steckt—
        Daher in Deutschland der Defekt!

Das braune Lumpenpack in Massen,
Schmarotzt in Ämtern, in den Kassen.
    Sie werden fett, die Kassen leer,
    Die Erlichkeit, die gibt's nicht mehr.
        Die ist abhanden ganz gekommen,
        Da sie ins Ausland mitgenommen.

Nimmt nun das Laster überhand,
Wer ist dran Schuld?—Der Emigrant!

The winter's hard in Germany—
Just blame the Emigrant, you see!
    You've lost your job, your daily bread—
    Just blame the emigrant instead!
        To Schacht our money slips away—
        The emigrant has a field day!

There's neither wool nor leather here—
The emigrant again, I fear!
    Reischsbishop Müller, that good German—
    Bankrupted by emigrant vermin!
        Consider Röhm and Heines now,
        An emigrant did teach them how!

The brown-shirt Reich is rife with fraud?
It is the emigrant abroad!
    They filled their sacks year after year,
    And took all our goods from here.
        So, that's the problem, don't you see—
        The emigrant from Germany.

The brown-shirt riff-raff—it's not funny,
Sponge wherever there is money.
    They grow fat as the banks grow thin,
    Honor just never enters in.
        All our wealth, it's simply lost now,
        Gone abroad, at what a cost now!

Then seize the wicked by the pants—
For who's to blame?—The emigrants!

87. Und die Musik spielt dazu (And the Music Just Plays On)

Just about everybody in Theresienstadt would have been familiar with Fredy Raymond's light-hearted operetta, *Salzburger Nockerln* (a favorite Austrian pastry). They would also have heard the recording made by Rosita Serrano of *Und die Musik spielt dazu*, one of the hit tunes from the show. Walter Lindenbaum's parody, with its implied suggestion that beneath the façade of normalcy in Theresienstadt, other terrible events were taking place while the music was playing, found its mark all too well.

Words by Walter Lindenbaum

Music by Fredy Raymond, 1900–1954

Ob Meyerbeer, ob Mozart,
Bei uns klingt alles so zart,
Denn das Forte ist im diesem Orte
Streng verpönt, streng verpönt.
Obwohl Musik hier chronisch,
Leben viele disharmonisch,
Sie haben ans Zsammenspieln
Sich leider nicht gewönt.
Denn alle wolln hier zeigen,
Sie spielen die ersten Geigen.
Ein jeder ist hier Dirigent,
Zumindest Prominent. *Refrain*

And Meyerbeer and Mozart,
We do consider so smart.
But to play it loud before this crowd,
Is not allowed — just not allowed.
Though music here is chronic,
Many lives are disharmonic.
They're not used to playing in ensemble,
They're too proud — they're just too proud.
Here everyone is saying,
First fiddle they are playing,
For here each one conducts the band,
They'd have you understand. *Chorus*

88. Doch auch für uns kommt mal die Zeit
(Yet Soon for Us Will Come the Time)

Otto Halle (1903–1987) was a political prisoner almost uninterruptedly from 1933 until 1945. While in Buchenwald he took part in various cultural presentations and cabaret productions. He wrote theatrical sketches with provocative titles like *Bomber über Buchenwald* ("Bomber over Buchenwald") and "Yet Soon for Us Will Come the Time" which was produced in 1944. That same year he took part in a performance of Shakespeare's "As You Like It" (*Was Ihr wollt*) — in German in the camp's canteen. After the liberation he lived in the German Democratic Republic, where he wrote a novel based on his experiences (*Hart auf Hart*—"Hard Times").

"Yet Soon for Us Will Come the Time" was staged with chorus, orchestra, scenery and props. Halle's stage directions are given here along with the song, which begins as might a Schubert *Lied*, but soon turns into a nightmare.

Words by Otto Halle

Music by Jerry Silverman

The orchestra softly accompanies the singing to underscore the continuing play. In the left foreground are four prisoners, busy with laying stones. One of them kneels and lays the stone while the others stand in readiness with the pile driver. They are not working but are looking at their tools and are listening to the singing backstage. The stream of stone haulers flows over the stage in such a manner that the prisoners enter on one side and disappear on the other— but always reappearing, so that the impression is given that hundreds are busily engaged. The scene must continually flow by. An old prisoners steps out of the ranks and looks back at the model of the crematorium. He repeats this in his next appearance, so that the impression must be made that the old prisoner is occupied in thought only by his own death. The stone layers begin their work. After several hammer blows the kneeling workers let their hammers sink down. The others stop, during which time the first ones sing a verse, to which the hammerers beat out the rhythm.

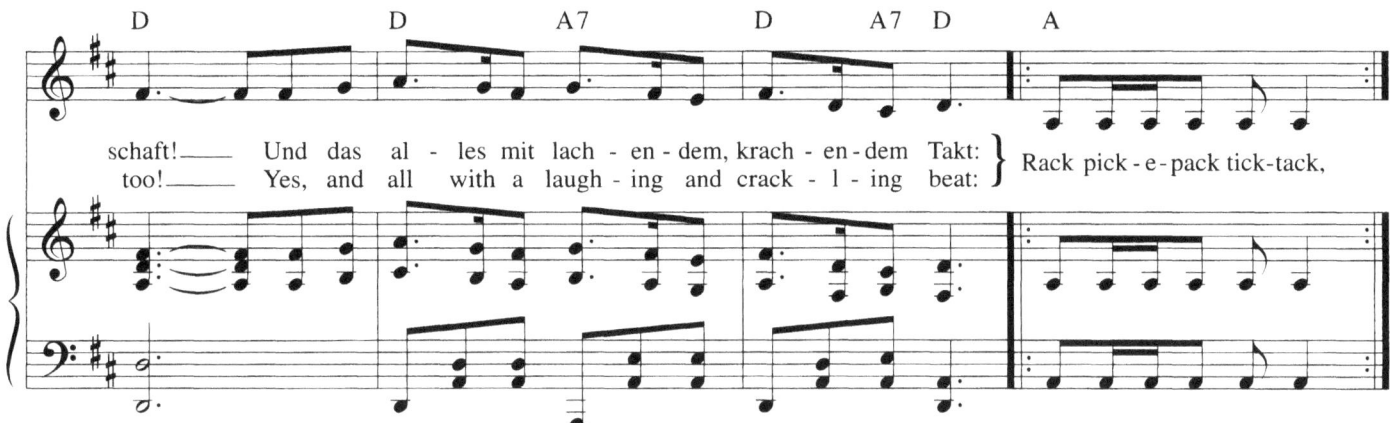

The stone-haulers have resumed working, but towards the end of the song they have slowed down. They eat furtively, sitting down individually. The scene is one of weariness and fatigue . . . The old man totters out of his row and collapses. Several workers silently help him. The others just stare emptily and remain indifferent. Suddenly a clap of thunder. The light goes out for a moment, and when it comes on again a supernaturally large kapo is seen. Gesture of power. Another clap of thunder. The kapo has disappeared. The prisoners sit frozen in terror. The old man straightens himself up, clutches his stone to his breast and is himself dragged away. The stage empties. Even the stone layers have disappeared. The chimney of the crematorium begins to smoke heavily. A large red question mark rises up from stage left, remains standing for a moment and then sinks slowly down to the right. While the question mark is standing erect, there appears in white, shining script — cut-out letters:

SEIN ODER NICHTSEIN, DAS IST HIER DIE FRAGE!

TO BE OR NOT TO BE, THAT IS THE QUESTION HERE!

The music rises and breaks off with a loud drum beat. Then it begins again. The column of stone haulers appears again, carrying effortlessly and confidently and singing.

89. Dopis (The Letter)

Jiří Stein:
Born in Prague, August 8, 1923.
Transported to Theresienstadt, December 12, 1941.
Transported to Auschwitz, April 29, 1944 . . .

Words by Jiří Stein

Music by Jerry Silverman

2. Není tu chléb a děti chtějí jíst,
   a mrtví ktěří prchli ze hřebitova,
   po ztichlých koutech umírají znova,
   v pohaslých očích strach a nenávist.

4. Dnes chtěl jsem víno — pelyněk me spil,
   dnes horký plamen šlehl černou nocí,
   dnes místo loutny nůž jsem uchopil.

2. The children are crying for bread,
   Even the dead from the graveyard are flying,
   And once again in dark corners are dying,
   With lifeless eyes, hatred and dread.

4. Now wormwood replaces the sweet wine of life.
   A glowing flame stings me and burns in the dark of night.
   Instead of the lute I picked up the jagged knife.

90. Motýl (Butterfly)

Pavel Friedmann's composed his vision of a "ghettoized" butterfly in Theresienstadt on June 4, 1942. He had been transported there from Prague on April 26. On September 26, 1944, he was transported to Auschwitz.

It is interesting to compare Friedmann's tragic butterfly with Bialik's playful butterfly in the song *Parpar,* [page 118], which was written years before the Holocaust, but which composer Joseph Zvi Pinkhof set to music during his incarceration while either in Westerbork or Bergen-Belsen.

Words by Pavel Friedmann

Music by Jerry Silverman

91. Máj 1945 (May 1945)

In 1840, Robert Schumann composed a song cycle, setting Heinrich Heine's poems *Dichterliebe* (A Poet's Love) to music. The first song in that cycle, *Im wunderschönen Monat mai* (In the Wondrously Beautiful Month of May) is an achingly beautiful ode to love and longing. Dagmar Hilarová was transported to Theresienstadt from her native Prague on transport CV-190 on June 3, 1943. Two years later she was able to witness the wondrously beautiful month of May 1945; the end of the war and her liberation from the camp.

I have set her words to an adaptation of Schumann's inspired melody.

Words by Dagmar Hilarová

Music adapted by Jerry Silverman

Byl máj
Haluze rozvěsily
praporky svych kvetu
opilé včely hledaly svůj úl.
Ta hořká léta přešla.
Jarní vítr
poslední bolest
z hrudi vyvanul.

Coda:
Byl máj
a všechno kvetlo do svobody.

'Twas May
And twigs their flags did hoist up,
While drunken bees were busy
Searching for their hive.
The bitter years have passed by;
Springtime wind
The last sharp pain
Has swept away.

Coda:
'Twas May
And all the blossoms bloomed in freedom.

Kaddish: A Post-War Retrospective

92. A Mol Iz Geven A Mayse (I'll Tell to You All a Story)

Hartzvalde, 14th March, 1945
I went with Himmler today into the question of releasing Jews in the Bergen-Belsen camp. They are all to receive South American passports and permission to enter Sweden.... [15th March] Himmler told me ... that he would go fully into the question of releasing definite categories of Jewish prisoners to Sweden and Switzerland. ... He also promised to discuss it with Count Bernadotte. (Dr. Felix Kersten, Heinrich Himmler's Finnish personal physician and practitioner of Chinese "manual therapy." His ability to alleviate the intense stomach pains of the head of the SS afforded him the opportunity to exercise a certain "humanitarian" influence upon this monster of the Third Reich.)

Swedish iron ore had been a vital component of the Nazi war machine. Tens of millions of tons were transported over the Baltic Sea and by rail across occupied Norway to the port of Narvik, thence down the Norwegian coast to Germany. But as the tide of the war turned, the attitude of neutral Sweden began swinging toward the winning side. Himmler (literally prodded by Kersten's manual therapy) entered into covert negotiations with Swedish Count Folke Bernadotte over the fate of the Jews still remaining alive in German concentration camps. As a result of these negotiations a convoy of one hundred buses (known as "the white buses") of the Swedish Red Cross "secretly" entered Germany and Denmark to convey some of the remnants of European Jewry to freedom. Among the last to be liberated before the final conflagration were the Danish Jews from Theresienstadt.

Salomon Schulman's mother was a passenger on one of the "white buses." He wrote the bitterly ironic words to this song in 1995 as "some kind of hymn to the survivors from that terrible war who landed in Sweden."

Words by Salomon Schulman

Music: traditional

Ikh bin gekumen do aher fun Poyln,	I've come to this land from Poland,
Tsu veys ikh bloyz fun ergetsvu...	I barely remember from where...
Kemat farbrent bin ikh gevorn fun koyln,	I was almost burned just like coal, and
Got-tsu-danken geratevet di letste shu.	Thanks to God that my life was spared.
Di vayse busn fun Folke Bernadotte,	The white buses of Folke Bernadotte,
Un a sheyne khevre mit blonde hor,	And a pretty comrade with blonde hair,
Iz gekumen tsu undz fun a vayter shtot,	From a far-off city came to this spot,
Un hot undz gegebn nadoves, dos iz vor.	And gave us alms from over there.
Mir hobn gezen in zeyre oygn,	In their eyes we saw it clear,
Az der emes iz nisht azoy sheyn.	And the truth was very plain.
Vos ken dos efsher toygn,	What does it matter to us here,
Ven fun undz iz geblibn bloyz beyn?	When from us just bones remain?
Di shvedlekh hobn gut fardint—	The "little Swedes" made out quite well—
Derloybt di daytshn transitirn zeyer ban.	The German trains passed through their land.
Ven mir hobn gehorevet erger vi hint,	While worse than dogs we slaved in hell,
Hobn zey bagrist dem natsi-karavan.	They welcomed the Nazi caravan.
Vos veys ikh tsi di busn zenen geven vays,	What do I know if the buses were white,
Oder Bernadotte hot zikh oyfgefirt vi a meylekh.	Or if Bernadotte did prove so brave.
Ikh veys bloys az di krematorien zenen geven heys,	I only know the crematoriums burned bright,
Un az shvedish ayzn hot undz gelegt in keyver.	And that Swedish iron laid us in the grave.
Kent ir kumen mit ayre vayse busn,	You can come now with your white buses,
Getribn mit kerosin on humanitet,	Driven with gasoline—not humanity,
Azoy-tsi-azoy vil ikh aykh nisht kushn—	In any case, you'll not get my kisses—
Ir hot geholfn a velt fun brutalitet.	You helped a world of brutality.
Di mayse iz gornisht freylekh,	The story is far from cheering,
Un iz nisht geven a mol.	And never has been, you see.
Mir shrayen nokh in undzer keyver,	In our graves we still are screaming,
Un ir hot geholfn hitleristn on a tsol.	And you helped the Hitlerites willingly.

The reference to a *yiddishn melekh,* "a Jewish king," in the first verse stems from the original folk song upon which this song is based. The original, a lullaby, with the same title as this one, does "begin with a Jewish king" and moves on through interlinked verses to a queen, her vinyard, a tree in the vinyard, a branch on the tree, a nest on the branch, a bird in the nest, the death of the king, the ruination of the queen, the breaking of the branch, the disappearing of the bird, finally ending with the plaintive:

Vu nemt men aza khokhem,	Where can one find such a wise man,
Er zol kenen di shtern tseylen?	Who can count the stars?
Vu nemt men aza doktor,	Where can one find such a doctor,
Er zol kenen mayn harts heyln?	Who can heal my heart?

93. Én Még Most Kicsi Vagyok (I Am Still a Little Child)

I remember standing onstage with a group of little children in 1945–46, at age eight singing it at a Jewish children's home located on Domonkos Street in Budapest, Hungary. The teacher's or houseparent's name, Rózsi Steiner. When the orphanage closed some years later, she dedicated her life to raise four to five girls whose family did not return. She is living in Vienna since 1956. (Greta Fischman Elbogen's family fled Vienna for Budapest in 1939 when she was one-and-a-half years old. She, her mother, sister and two brothers survived the war in hiding. Her father perished in Dachau.)

en - ged még lát - nom E drá - ga or - cák - at
see their dear fac - es, Their fac - es once more now.

Greta Elbogen (center) with her mother behind her and her three siblings and aunt in Budapest, 1944.

94. Waterlooplein (Waterloo Square)

Waterloo Square, the site of a flea market in Amsterdam, was once the center of the so-called Jewish quarter of the city (Amsterdam never had a ghetto). The "Dockworker" mentioned in the song is in reality a statue which stands in front of the Portuguese Synagogue in Waterloo Square. It was erected after the war in commemoration of a general strike called by the dockworkers on February 25, 1941, to protest the Nazis' first deportation of Jews from the Netherlands to the Buchenwald and Mauthausen concentration camps. The round-up of the Jews took place near Waterloo Square. The song (in Dutch, with an occasional Yiddish word thrown in, and one verse in Yiddish) is an affectionate and nostalgic look at "the old neighborhood," which has changed so much over the years. The reference to *"Rembrandt van Jansen"* is a sly wink at the false "Rembrants" for sale at the flea market (Jansen is a common Dutch name). The ecumenically named Moses and Aaron Church also looks down upon the square.

The song was written around 1960, and was often sung by Jossy Halland, accompanied at the piano by her composer-husband Jacques.

By Jacques Halland

Dos harts blaybt mir shteyn
Vi ikh hob derzeyn,
Mayn altishker Yidengas fun Amsterdam iz nisht mer do.
Vu ist gebliben mayn shtib,
Vus iz mir geveyn azoy lib.
Khaloymes fun yoren tsurik a sakh gliklikhe sho.
Oys hoys fun Rembrandt dortn dartselt mir di mayses,
Der dokker vos shteyt oyf dem platz bay der shul, er vays es.
Mayn harts blaybt mir shteyn,
Vi ikh hob derzeyn,
Di altishker Yidengas fun Amsterdam iz nisht mer do.

How my heart does pound,
When I look around.
The old Jewish Street of Amsterdam's no longer here.
My home I don't see,
That was so dear to me.
And memories of happy times gone by won't disappear.
And Rembrandt's house over there tells of past glories.
The Docker who stands in the square by the shul knows the stories.
How my heart does pound,
When I look around.
The old Jewish Street of Amsterdam's no longer there.

Composer's Dutch Translation from the Yiddish

Mijn hart bleef stilstaan,
Toen ik zag,
Dat mijn oude Jodenbreestraat niet meer bestond.
Waar is mijn kamer,
Waar ik zo van hield,
Herinneeringen van vervlogen jaren, van gelukkige uren.
Het huis van Rembrandt vertelt mij al die verhalen,
En de Dokwerker, die bij de synagoge staat, kent ze allemaal.
Mijn hart blijft stil staan,
Als ik zie,
Dat de ouderwetse Jodenbreestraat van Amsterdam niet meer bestaat.

COMITÉ INTERNATIONAL DE LA CROIX-ROUGE

GENÈVE (Suisse)

Service Hollandais
RHOC/C IV
FD/ls

DEMANDEUR — ANFRAGESTELLER — ENQUIRER

Nom - Name: JEWISH AGENCY

Prénom - Vorname - Christian name:

Rue - Strasse - Street:

Localité - Ortschaft - Locality: JERUSALEM

Département - Provinz - County:

Pays - Land - Country: Palestine

Message à transmettre — Mitteilung — Message
(25 mots au maximum, nouvelles de caractère strictement personnel et familial) — (nicht über 25 Worte, nur persönliche Familiennachrichten) - (not over 25 words, family news of strictly personal character).

Message of 3.11.43 : Family Jacob POLAK, Croix-Rouge Néerlandaise Amsterdam. You have been registered on exchange list for immigration in Palestine. Your number is : EL/43/2364

Date - Datum: 10.11.43.

DESTINATAIRE — EMPFÄNGER — ADDRESSEE

Nom - Name: JOODSCHE RAAD

Prénom - Vorname - Christian name:

Rue - Strasse - Street: Jan van Eyckstr. 15

Localité - Ortschaft - Locality: AMSTERDAM

Province - Provinz - County:

Pays - Land - Country: Hollande

RÉPONSE AU VERSO — ANTWORT UMSEITIG — REPLY OVERLEAF
Prière d'écrire très lisiblement — Bitte sehr deutlich schreiben — Please write very clearly

A precious document, but one which unfortunately did not always guarantee safety. Jacob Polak was sent, not to Palestine, but to Westerbork and Bergen-Belsen. Fortunately, he survived both camps and arrived with his family in the U. S. after the war.

95. O Mis Hermanos (O My Brothers)

It was at her brother Albert's home near Seattle, Washington, that I met Jennie Adatto Tarabulus, a writer living in Jerusalem. Her husband David had, as a child, moved with his family from Turkey to Xanthi in Greece. While he was temporarily at work in Baghdad, most of his family was taken by the Nazis. His letters to Greece in search of them were returned, marked, "Moved to Cracow. Address unknown." When Jennie went to visit her husband's city, she found that more than 60,000 Greek Jews lost in the Holocaust had been all but forgotten. "I wanted to memorialize their existence," she said.

She returned to Jerusalem and wrote this poem as part of her documentary "The Greek Jews In The Holocaust," which aired on Kol Israel Radio. (Judy Frankel)

The lingua franca of the Sephardic Jews of the Mediterranean Basin is Ladino (*Judeo-Español*). Pronunciation and spelling are not consistent among Ladino speakers. In an attempt to make the song universally accessible the composer has opted for Spanish orthography, with a couple of minor exceptions.

Words by Jennie Adatto Tarabulus

Music by Judy Frankel

Used by permission of Judy Frankel.

Recommended Listening

Frankel, Judy. *Sephardic Songs of Love and Hope.* JFR Records (CD), P.O.B. 470515, San Francisco, Calif. 94147-0515.

96. Asma Asmaton (Song of Songs)

On the face of it, the Greek Jews whom we met in the concentration camp [Maidanek] seemed to have little in common with their brethren from Poland, Hungary, Czechoslovakia or France. Their hair, eyebrows, and eyelashes were black, and their skin was the color of light chocolate. They were tough and stubborn, and they talked very fast. They spoke to each other in Greek, and sometimes also in French, Spanish, Italian, or even Hebrew, but they knew neither Yiddish nor German. As a result, Jewish inmates who wanted to talk to them had to do it through a Jewish fellow prisoner who happened to speak both Hebrew and Yiddish. . . . That first night, two voices out of the darkness began to sing; they were two men from the Greek contingent. It was the first time we had ever heard such a strangely intimate style of singing; it went straight to our hearts like the words of a mother, a sister or a sweetheart. . . . When the song ended, everyone heaved a great sigh. Although we could not understand the words, the melody had stirred us to inmost depths of our hearts.   Paul Trepman, *Among Men and Beasts*

Although written some twenty years after those two unknown Greek Jews so moved their fellow prisoners by their singing, we can be similarly enthralled by the passionate lyrics and haunting melody of *Asma Asmaton*. Poet and playwright Iakovos Kambanellis was himself imprisoned in the Mauthausen concentration camp from the summer of 1943 until the arrival of the American army on May 5, 1945. He had been active in the Greek Resistance, and after liberation he was elected as representative of the Greek delegation, staying behind in the camp with the Greek Jews who were too ill to leave. In 1965 he published his book *Mauthausen*, a novel based on his terrible experiences in that slave labor camp. He also wrote a cycle of four poems based on episodes in the book, which were lovingly set to music by Mikis Theodorakis. Asma Asmaton is one of those poems. Theodorakis had also fought in the Resistance and had been arrested, tortured, and interned on several occasions. In 1947, during the Greek Civil War, he was imprisoned for protesting against the right-wing monarchy, and spent five years behind bars. In 1967, with the military coup in Greece, he was again imprisoned and his music (including the score for the film *Zorba the Greek*) was banned in Greece. Now his music has gained worldwide recognition as expressive of Greek history and traditions.

Words by Iakovos Kambanellis   Music by Mikis Theodorakis

Copyright © 2000 by Mikis Theodorakis, Romanos Productions Ltd. All rights reserved for the world. Printed in Greece by Romanos Productions Ltd.

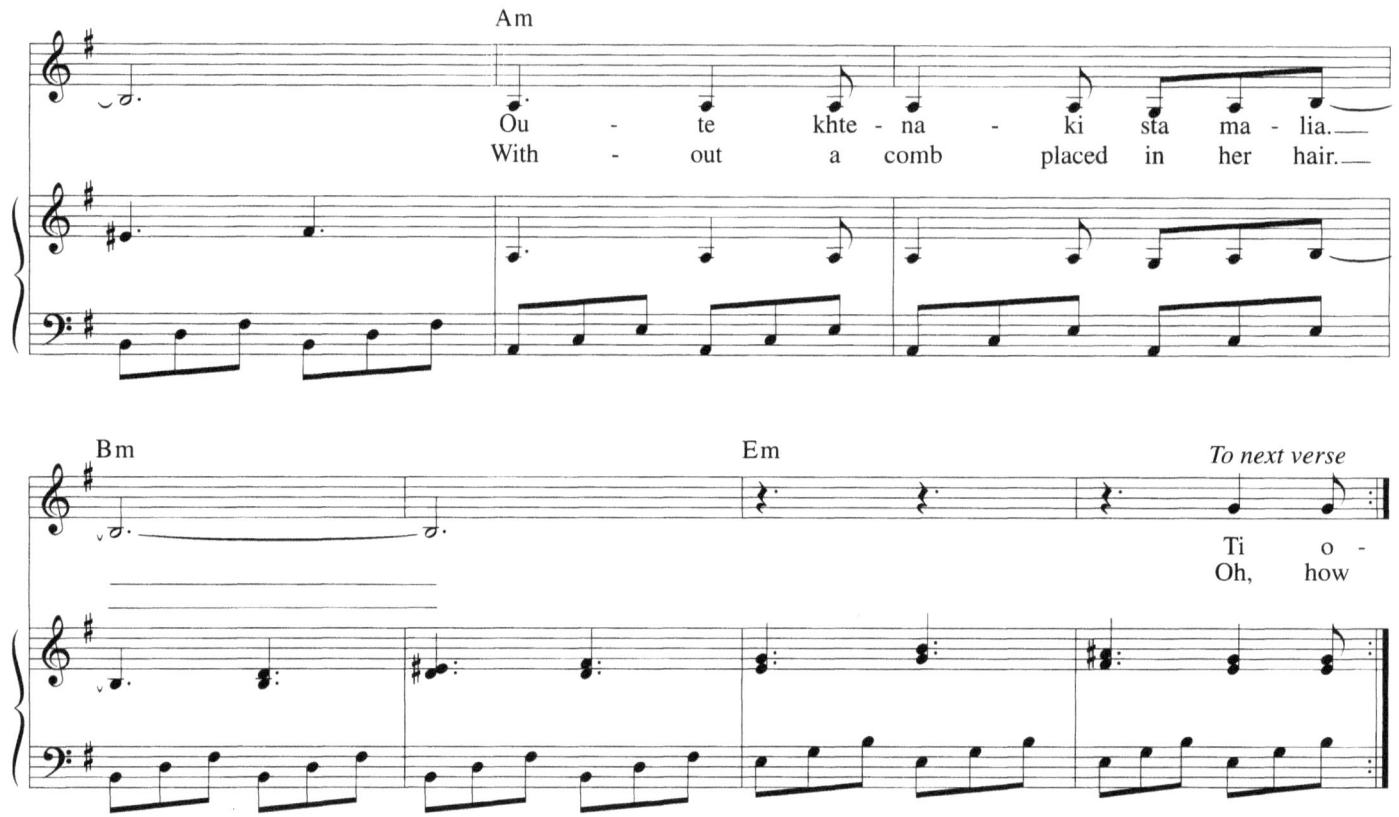

Ti orea pou ine agapi mou!
I khaithemeni apoti mematis,
Ke tou adelfou tis ta filia.
‖:Kanis then ixere pos ine toso orea.:‖ (3)
    Kopeles tou Mauthauzen,
    Kopeles tou Belsen,
    ‖:Min itathe tin agapi mou?:‖ (3)
Tin ithame stin payeri platia,
Me ena arithmo sto aspro sto heri,
Me kitrino astro stin karthia.

Oh, how beautiful is my beloved one!
She was caressed by her loving mother dear,
And by her brother she was kissed.
‖:No one could ever know how beautiful she used to be:‖ (3)
    You maidens of Mauthausen,
    You maidens of Belsen,
    ‖:Oh, have you seen the one I love?:‖ (3)
We saw her standing in the frozen courtyard,
Upon her white arm was a number,
A yellow star over her heart.

Repeat from beginning to "Final Ending"

Ti orea pou ine agapi mou!
I kaithemiapo ti mana tis,
Ke tou adelfou tis ta filia.
‖:Kanis then ixere pos ine toso orea.:‖ (3)

Oh, how beautiful is my beloved one!
She was caressed by her loving mother dear,
And by her brother she was kissed.
‖:No one could ever know how beautiful she used to be.:‖ (3)

Recommended Listening

Farandouri, Maria. *Ballads of Mauthausen.* EMI 7020-42.

97. Bukhenval'dskii Nabat (Buchenwald Alarm)

Keep Faith ...
(1914–1918)

Hear that ghostly rhythmic beat,
The tramp of a million marching feet.
Left, Right. Hep, Hep.
How they keep that ghostly step.
Marching along in grim array,
From midnight dark till break of day,
While all about a rumble swells
Into a million bursting hells,
But no man falls, they show no fear,
For they are the men of yesteryear.
Left, Right. Hep. Hep.
How they keep that ghostly step.

In Flanders Field, where poppies grow,
They fell that man should onward go
In peace.
At Vimy Ridge and Armentières,
Vale of a million women's tears,
They fell that strife
Should cease.

Hear that ghostly, muffled drum,
Still they come, still they come.
Rising from eternal beds,
Marching firm with measured treads.
Left, right. Hep, Hep.
How they keep that ghostly step.

They fought and died, were crucified,
To keep this world from pain;
A ghostly murmur sweeps the ranks—
"Keep faith or we'll have died in vain."

Bill Silverman, 1940

The Russian author of the lyrics of this song was himself a prisoner in Buchenwald.

Words by A. Sobolev   Music by Vaino Muradeli

Sotni tysiach zazhivo sozhzhyonykh,	Countless hundred thousands were cremated.
Stroiatsta, stroiatsia v sherengi k riadu riad.	Now they form, now they form in ranks row after row.
Internatsional'nye kolonny	Men from many lands—how long they've waited.
S nami govoriat, s nami govoriat.	Hear their voices grow, hear their voices grow.
Slyshite gromovye raskaty?	Can't you hear that terrible commotion?
Eto ne groza, ne uragan.	Neither thunderstorm nor hurricane—
Eto vikhrem atomnym ob″iatyi	An atomic whirlwind o'er the ocean,
Stonet okean, tikhii okean.	Like a cry of pain, like a cry of pain.
Eto stonet, eto stonet tikhii okean.	O'er the ocean, o'er the ocean, like a cry of pain.

Last verse begins with first 4 lines of verse one.

. . . Zvon plyvyot, plyvyot nad vsei zemloiu,	. . . Spreading o'er the earth we hear the pealing.
I gudit vzvolnovanno efir:	In the air its volume does increase.
Liudi mira, bud'te zorche vtroe,	People of the world all know the feeling:
Beregite mir, beregite mir!	Stand on guard for peace, stand on guard for peace!
Beregite, beregite, beregite mir.	Let us stand guard, let us stand guard, stand on guard for peace.

Drawn in Buchenwald. "Hear their voices grow, hear their voices grow . . ."

98. Lady of the Harbor

In America's a golden portal,
Opened by a lady who's immortal.
   Open was the gate I saw before me,
   She herself did open it wide for me.
     She gazed down on me and then demanded:
     Where are you bound, dear soul, now you've landed?

                            Ukranian immigrant song, © 1900

On May 13, 1939, 930 Jewish refugees boarded the German luxury liner *St. Louis* bound for Cuba from the port of Hamburg. They all held precious Cuban landing certificates, but on arrival they were not allowed to disembark. After intense but fruitless financial dickering between the Cuban government and the Jewish Joint Distribution Committee in New York, the ship set sail for Miami (a number of the passengers held U.S. immigration quota numbers). The U.S. State Department refused permission for the ship to land. President Roosevelt did not intercede. One by one, the governments of Colombia, Chile, Paraguay, and Argentina closed their doors. Finally, there was no choice for Captain Schroeder but to return to Hamburg with his cargo of distraught passengers. He was sympathetic to their plight and had secretly considered beaching the *St. Louis* on the coast of England if no port were found. However, en route, they were informed on July 13 that France, Holland, Belgium, and England would accept a total of 906 of the refugees. The two dozen unfortunate souls who were not granted refuge were swallowed up by the Nazi monster.

By Si Kahn

Copyright © 1986 Joe Hill Music (administered by Copyright Management International). All Rights Reserved. International Copyright Secured. Used by Permission.

Imagine then how beautiful that torchlight must have seemed
To a frightened Jewish immigrant caught up in freedom's dream.
But the land had room for many, and he studied while he worked,
By the lamplight of the Lady of the Harbor. *Chorus*

In nineteen thirty-seven* with war on every hand,
A band of Jewish refugees sought shelter in this land.
With the Nazis close behind them they sailed their leaky boat†
Towards the safety of the Lady of the Harbor.
> But every door was closed to them, no port would take
> them in,
> 'Til sick at heart they sailed back home to Gemany again,
> Where their dreams were turned to ashes and their bodies
> turned to smoke,
> That drifted past the Lady of the Harbor. *Chorus*

So, if these silent lips could speak, what reasons would they say,
Why some are sheltered freely, but others turned away.
Now as the terror rises a fleeing world awaits
An answer from the Lady of the Harbor.
> For all along the borders the nightmare comes again,
> As homeless, stateless refugees seek shelter in this land.
> Will the lamp be raised to welcome them, or turn them
> back once more?
> Only silence from the Lady of the Harbor. *Chorus*

Recommended Listening

Kahn, Si. *In My Heart.* Philo 1169 (CD).

*The date, of course, should be 1939.
†Poetic licence has transformed the luxury liner *St. Louis* into a "leaky boat."

THE NEW COLOSSUS

NOT LIKE THE BRAZEN GIANT OF GREEK FAME,
WITH CONQUERING LIMBS ASTRIDE FROM LAND TO LAND;
HERE AT OUR SEA-WASHED, SUNSET GATES SHALL STAND
A MIGHTY WOMAN WITH A TORCH, WHOSE FLAME
IS THE IMPRISONED LIGHTNING, AND HER NAME
MOTHER OF EXILES. FROM HER BEACON-HAND
GLOWS WORLD-WIDE WELCOME; HER MILD EYES COMMAND
THE AIR-BRIDGED HARBOR THAT TWIN CITIES FRAME.
"KEEP ANCIENT LANDS, YOUR STORIED POMP!"
    CRIES SHE
WITH SILENT LIPS. "GIVE ME YOUR TIRED, YOUR
    POOR,
YOUR HUDDLED MASSES YEARNING TO BREATHE FREE,
THE WRETCHED REFUSE OF YOUR TEEMING SHORE.
SEND THESE, THE HOMELESS, TEMPEST-TOST TO ME,
I LIFT MY LAMP BESIDE THE GOLDEN DOOR!"

THIS TABLET, WITH HER SONNET TO THE BARTHOLDI STATUE
OF LIBERTY ENGRAVED UPON IT, IS PLACED UPON THESE WALLS
IN LOVING MEMORY OF
EMMA LAZARUS
BORN IN NEW YORK CITY, JULY 22, 1849
DIED NOVEMBER 19, 1887.

Inscription on the base of the Statue of Liberty.

99. Children of Poland

In the May 5th, 1938, issue of *Ken* magazine, Ernest Hemingway wrote: *There are two pictures . . . with this article. Take the picture of the children first. In the bombing of Barcelona on Saint Patrick's Day there were 118 children killed along with 245 women and 512 men. That makes a total of 875 dead . . . remember that the picture shows only a few of the 118 children that the fascists' planes killed. We won't have any picture of the men and women. Perhaps it is all right to kill men and women and maybe their politics were wrong too. The prosecution for murder, if there was any prosecution for this kind of murder, and there is not, rests on the case of the 118 dead children. Take as good a look at them as you can stand. . . . Maybe there isn't any moral to these pictures. But the children of Barcelona are dead as you can see from the picture, and millions of other people will die long before it is their time to die because of the policy that might makes right that that strange outstretched arm salute stands for.*

The distance between Barcelona and Warsaw is about 1300 miles . . . as the *Luftwaffe* flies.

By Si Kahn

In the city of Warsaw, such a long time ago.
Two hundred children stand lined row on row; With their freshly washed faces and freshly washed clothes, The children of Poland who never grow old.

Copyright © 1981 Joe Hill Music (administered by Copyright Management International). All Rights Reserved. International Copyright Secured. Used by Permission.

In the orphanage yard not a child remains.
The soldiers have herded them down to the trains,
Carrying small flasks of water and bags of dry bread,
To march in the ranks of the unquiet dead.

With their small Jewish faces and pale haunted eyes,
They march hand in hand down the street—no one cries.
No one laughs, no one looks, no one turns, no one talks,
As they walk down the streets where my grandparents walked.

Had my grandparents stayed in that dark bloody land,
My own children, too, would have marched hand in hand
To the beat of the soldiers—the jackbooted stamp
That would measure their lives 'til they died in those camps.

The cries of the children at night take me back
To those pale hollow faces in stark white and black.
Only the blood of the children remains;
It runs in the streets—and it runs in our veins.

At about the same time as Ernest Hemingway's article appeared, "children of Poland," never imagining that death would soon be raining down upon them, were singing to the tune of a Red Army song:

Madrid iz oysgeflakert.	*Madrid in flames is blazing,*
Un shikt di beste zin.	*Her bravest sons march in.*
Nor bombes shikt Italye	*But Italy sends bombs down,*
Un pulver shikt Berlin.	*Gunpowder sends Berlin.*

Recommended Listening

Kahn, Si. *In My Heart.* Philo 1169 (CD).

100. Unter Der Gelber Late: A Vig-Lid (Under the Yellow Patch: A Lullaby)

Poet Leivick Halpern (1886–1962), writing under the pen-name H. Leivick, was born in Igumen, Belarus. He spent the war years in the U.S., but his wartime and post-war poems reflect a deep, personal understanding of the horrors that had befallen the Jews in the concentration camps. After the liberation he visited Dachau. This song (composer unknown) is the result of that pilgrimage.

Just as the Jews were forced to wear yellow patches, non-Jewish Polish prisoners wore red ones (verse 3).

Words by H. Leivick

Tsum knut, tsum shlos in grate,
A kop in blut falt tsu.
O neyn—s'iz nit dayn tate,
Nit fiber, kind, lyu-lyu.
    Kh'vel mer dikh nit dershrokn
    Mit blut, mit vey un vund.
    A mol iz di late mit ekn,
    A mol iz di late rund.

A mol iz royt di late,
Un a mol iz di late gel.
A kholem, kind, dayn tate
Bavayst zikh oyf undzer shvel.
    Er git di tir an efn,
    Er kumt in shtub arayn,
    Dayn hengbetl tsu trefn,
    Far vos zol shver im zayn?

Er nemt dikh vign, vign,
Un vigt zikh ayn aleyn.
Der tate ligt, blaybt lign,
Darf mer shoyn in Dakhau nit geyn.
    An eybiker—dayn tate,
    Azoy vi di eybike ru,
    Azoy vi di gele late—
    Shlof, mayn kind, lyu-lyu.

Behind bars, whipped and martyred,
A bloody head's in view.
O no—it's not your father,
Don't worry child, lyu-lyu.
    I'll frighten you no more now,
    With blood, wounds, pain profound.
    Sometimes the patch has corners,
    Sometimes the patch is round.

Some people wear a red one,
Others a yellow patch.
In dreams, my child, your father
Will open our door latch.
    He opens up the door then,
    He comes in once again.
    To see you in your cradle.
    Why should he be in pain?

He starts to rock and rock you.
He rocks himself as well.
Your father lies forever,
No more in Dachau's hell.
    Your father is eternal,
    His suffering is through,
    Like the yellow patch infernal—
    Sleep, my child, lyu-lyu.

101. Denmark 1943

Adolf Hitler sent birthday greetings to King Christian X of Denmark on the occasion of the king's seventy-fifth birthday in November 1942. He expressed his wish that some day the two "'Aryan" nations would be united. "What a wonderful idea," Christian replied in a telegram, "but frankly, I'm too old to rule Germany." *Der Führer* was not amused.

The Germans had invaded neutral Denmark on April 9, 1940, in preparation for an eventual assault on Norway. Their ultimate goal was the establishment of a nautical line of defense against the British navy. Denmark was to be considered a "protectorate" of Germany and, by and large, Danes (including Danish Jews) were pretty much left alone. During the first few years of the occupation this uneasy relationship continued, a tacit *modus vivendi* of "cooperation" between all parties ensured relative normalcy in the daily affairs of the country and its people. The Jewish congregation, aware of the thin ice it was treading, followed a "lie-low" policy in order not to provoke the Germans—not that the Nazis would have needed much in the way of "provocation" to institute repressive measures against the Jews, in light of their unprovoked atrocities in Eastern Europe which were taking place during this period.

But by April 1942 the first stirrings of a Danish resistance movement, with coordinated activities between *Frit Danmark* (Free Denmark) in London and brave local patriots in Denmark, began to make themselves felt. Then came the so-called November Telegram Crisis precipitated by the remarkable exchange between Hitler and the king. The German minister in Copenhagen was recalled; the Danish minister in Berlin was undiplomatically handed his passport. A governmental crisis ensued in Denmark, with parliamentary elections called for March 1943. Although the German "protectors" presence was keenly felt during the election campaign, the result was a resounding defeat for Danish Nazism.

During the summer and fall of 1943, acts of sabotage increased dramatically despite admonitions from the king and the prime minister. In August violent riots exploded across the country. Italy had capitulated to the Allies, and the sense that the tide of the war was turning emboldened the underground forces. On August 29 the German army assumed full control and martial law was declared. The king was imprisoned in his castle, parliament was dissolved, ships of the Danish navy were scuttled to prevent them from falling into German hands, and the Germans now turned their attention toward the Jews.

The Chief Rabbi of Denmark, Max Friediger, was arrested in September and sent to Horesod, a detention center and transit point to the concentration camps of the east. From there he was transported to Theresienstadt. The stage was being set for the next act. It was the eve of *Rosh Hashanah* and there were terrible rumors in the air. A German shipping agent, Georg Duckwitz, overheard the SS plans for an *Aktion*—a roundup—and alerted some Danish friends. What better time for such a sweep than when Jews would be gathered together to celebrate the new year!

Acting Rabbi Marcus Melchior had warned his people to stay indoors during the holiday. But things had already progressed beyond the point where merely staying home would have done any good. The *Aktion* was imminent. They would have to escape now!

The Danish underground had been alerted and an evacuation plan was put into operation. Leaving their *Rosh Hashanah* tables set for the new year's feast, 5,800 Danish Jews quietly slipped away into the night for the perilous ocean crossing to Sweden. In the days between *Rosh Hashanah* and *Yom Kippur* they gathered in small groups in seaside homes awaiting their turns to be ferried across the Øresund, the strait dividing the North Sea from the Baltic, for the six-hour voyage to safety.

Due to their ever-increasing military difficulties, the German naval presence in these waters had been reduced. Nevertheless, there were a number of enemy gunboats patrolling along the coast. These craft had to be avoided at all cost, and the skillful Danish sailors managed to do just that. Miraculously, they all got through. Some boats arrived in Sweden on Yom Kippur eve.

Of Denmark's almost 6,300 Jews, about 470 were captured and transported to Theresienstadt. They were confined in more "comfortable" surroundings than prisoners from other countries. None was sent to Auschwitz. More than 400 survived, including Rabbi Friediger who was among those who returned to Denmark after the war.

The day that the German army marched into Copenhagen, a performance of *Porgy and Bess* had been scheduled at the Royal Opera House. The opera was given that evening, but a repeat performance of this work, by a Jewish-American composer on a "Negro" subject, was immediately banned. The SS threatened to blow up the opera house if the order were ignored. The Danes complied, but from then on every time one of Hitler's speeches was broadcast they jammed it with a recording of *It Ain't Necessarily So*.

Victor Borge (born Borge Rosenbaum) fled Denmark shortly after the German occupation. "They were Nazis and I was Jewish," he recalled in an interview with the *New York Times* (January 21, 1999). It was impossible for him to continue his career as an entertainer in Denmark, especially after jokes like: "What is the difference between a Nazi and a dog? A Nazi lifts his arm."

Sompolinski the tailor on the eve of Rosh Hashanah,
Gathers his family near.
"The Lord is my light and salvation.
Whom on this earth shall I fear?"
When a young Danish gentile steps into the glow
Of the candle, with tears flowing down.
"Good neighbors, flee — I pray you, believe me."
And as quickly, the young man is gone.

Christian policemen, shopkeepers, and teachers,
Tell their friends in the quickening storm,
While students on bicycles race through the streets,
Searching for Jews to be warned.
And Katlev the forman blurts out to the trainman,
"My family has no place to hide."
"Well, bring 'em to my house," the stranger replies,
"And we'll spit in the damn Nazis' eyes." *Chorus*

Rabbi Melchior hires a young trawlerman
To ferry his family across.
After twelve hours afloat in a scurfy old boat,
Morning light shows the same Danish coast.
Says the skipper, "I'm afraid of the German blockade,
So we've motored in circles around."
The rabbi gives a shout — with one blow knocks him out,
And steers a straight line 'cross the sound. *To Bridge*

Seven thousands of Jews smuggled over to Sweden,
By fisherman, nurses, and priests.
Hitler sends Eichmann to hunt them down,
But his quarry have vanished like mist.
When the war's over the Jews return;
Cheers and flowers adorn their way home.
"We're not heroes or martyrs," so say the Danes.
"We were just looking after our own." *Chorus*

Fred Small adds: *After writing this song, I learned from Rabbi Melchior's son that the story of his father slugging the skipper, which I had read in historical accounts, is an exaggeration. His father, he said, would never have struck anyone in anger, but he could knock you down with his words. So I like to think the song is still metaphorically true.*

Recommended Listening

Small, Fred. *I Will Stand Fast.* Flying Fish 70491 (CD)

102. Tattoo

We could see the tall smokestacks from some distance away before we actually came to the entrance of the camp. When we entered everybody suddenly became very quiet. We were in a terrible and yet somehow sacred place. . . . What we saw in the museum itself is indelibly stamped on my mind: Mountains of eyeglasses, human hair, dentures, artificial limbs, crutches, shoes, and other personal belongings taken away from the hundreds of thousands of people before they were led to the "showers" or before they were cremated. . . . You couldn't stand it there too long; it was just too horrible to contemplate, and I soon made my way into the sunlight once more. . . . Of course, we have all heard of Auschwitz. It is a name to everybody. But after actually being here myself and seeing these unspeakable things, it will no longer be just a name to me. (From a letter from my friend, Russian musicologist Alexander Medvedev in 1966. He has written the libretto to an opera [music by Moshe Weinberg] entitled Passazhirka [The Passenger], based on the experiences of an inmate of Auschwitz.)

With their shaven heads, shrunken faces, emaciated bodies, and tattered uniforms, it was often difficult for the sex of the prisoners to be distinguished by the guards. To overcome this "problem," the number tattooed on the arms of female prisoners was often followed by a triangle.

Words and Music by Janis Ian

Copyright © 1992 Rude Girl Publishing (BMI). Administered by Bug Music. All Rights Reserved. Used by permission.

She steps out of the line to the left,
And her father to the right.
One side's a cold clean death,
The other is an endless night.
Gold from a grandmother's tooth,
Mountains of jewelry and toys
Piled in the corners,
Mailed across the borders—
Presents for the girls and boys,
Presents for the girls and boys.
Tattoo. *To Bridge*

Soldiers on the other side
Liberated them at dawn.

Gave her water, gave her life;
She still had all her clothes on.
She lived until she died,
Empty as the autumn leaves that fly.
Surgeons took the mark,
But they could not take it far.
It was written on her heart—
Written on her empty heart:
Tattooed.

Recommended Listening

Ian, Janis. *Breaking the Silence.* Morgan Creek 20023 (CD & cassette) www.janisian.com

103. Last Train to Nuremberg

[*New York Times* reporter] *Seymour Hersh broke the story on the My Lai massacre. Later there was a trial and the two officers most immediately responsible got light sentences. I sang the song during the 70s. The American media ignored it, but the song got on Swedish TV. Nuremberg refers to the 1947 [1945–46, JS] war-crimes trials of some of Hitler's accomplices.* (Hersh won the Pulitzer Prize in 1970 for his reporting on My Lai.)

Pete Seeger, *Where Have All the Flowers Gone*

On March 16, 1968 in the little Vietnamese hamlet of My Lai in Quang Ngai Province, a platoon of American soldiers under the command of Lieutenant William L. Calley rounded up about 150 old men, women, children, and babies, herded them into a ditch and gunned them down. Captain Ernest L. Medina, Calley's superior officer, did not report this gross violation of standing orders, military law, and human decency. The Division Commander, Major General Samuel H. Koster, likewise took no action to investigate conflicting statements in the battle reports submitted by the unit. When this "incident" was brought to light a year later (March 29, 1969), an investigation was launched by the Army. In the subsequent court martial Major General Koster was reduced in rank to Brigadier General, and Captain Medina and other officers and enlisted men were found not guilty. Lieutenant Calley was found guilty of war crimes (the first time that term had ever been applied to the conduct of an American soldier) and sentenced to life imprisonment. The Secretary of the Army eventually reduced the sentence to ten years. On March 19, 1974, Lieutenant Calley was paroled.

On March 6, 1998, two American soldiers who risked their own lives by interposing themselves between their fellow soldiers and fleeing Vietnamese civilians in My Lai, and aiming their weapons at the rampaging GIs in order to stop the massacre, received the Soldier's Medal, the highest award for bravery not involving conflict with an enemy. At the awards ceremony by the granite walls of the Vietnam Veterans Memorial in Washington, the following words were spoken: "Remembering a dark point in time, we are now a richer nation as their personal heroic service is woven into the fabric of our history." The key word is *remembering*.

Words and Music By Pete Seeger

Copyright © 1970 (renewed) by SANGA MUSIC INC. All Rights reserved. Used By Permission.

Who held the rifle? Who gave the orders?
Who planned the campaign to lay waste the land?
Who manufactured the bullet? Who paid the taxes?
Tell me, is that blood upon my hands. *Chorus*

Go tell all the young people, tell all the little children,
Don't, don't you get aboard this train!
See where it's coming from, see where it's going.
Don't, don't you ride it ever again. *Chorus*

If five hundred thousand mothers went to Washington,
And said, "Bring all of our sons home without delay!"
Would the man they came to see say he was too *bizzee*?
Would he say he had to watch a football game? *Chorus*

Recommended Listening

Seeger, Pete. *A Link in the Chain.* Legacy 64772 (CD).
———. *The World of Pete Seeger.* Columbia 31949 (CD).

104. My Name Is Lisa Kalvelage

This story was in a [May 1966] newspaper clipping sent me from San Jose, California. Lisa Kalvelage and two other women, dressed in their Sunday best, stopped a shipment of napalm [bound for Vietnam] by standing on a loading platform and refusing to budge. Arrested— and in court she told this story to a newspaper reporter.
—Pete Seeger, *Where Have All the Flowers Gone*

Words and Music By Pete Seeger

Copyright © 1966 (renewed) by SANGA MUSIC INC. All Rights reserved. Used By Permission.

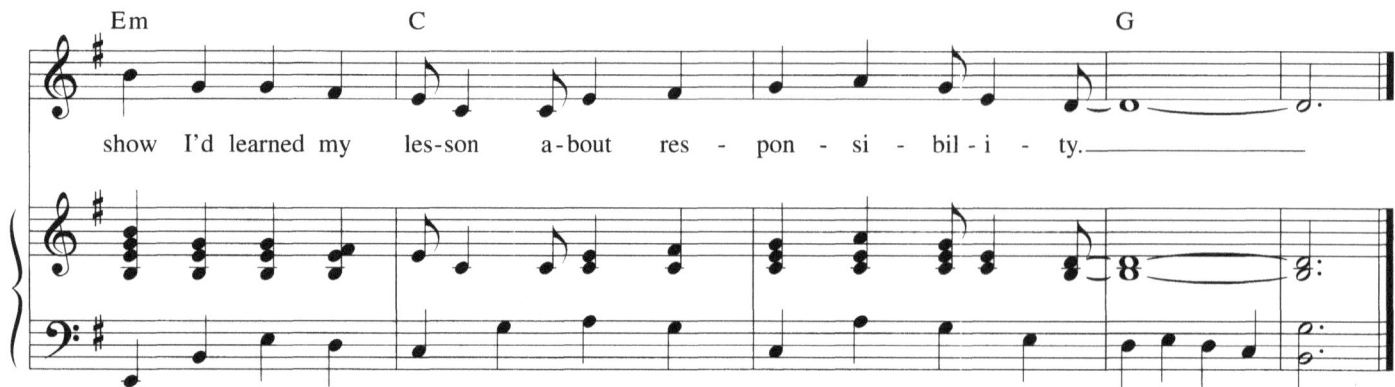

Thus suddenly I was forced to start thinking on this theme,
And when later I was permitted to emigrate,
I must have been asked a hundred times where I was and what I did
In those years when Hitler ruled our state.
I said I was a teen-ager,
But that only extended the questioning.
They'd ask, where were my parents — my father, my mother,
And to this I could answer not a thing.

The seed planted there in Nuremberg in nineteen forty-seven*
Started to sprout and to grow.
Gradually I understood what that verdict meant to me,
When there are crimes that I can see and I can know.
And now I also know what it is to be charged with mass guilt;
Once in a lifetime is enough for me.
No, I could not take it for a second time,
And that is why I am here today.

The events of May twenty-fifth, the day of our protest,
Put a small balance weight on the other side.
Hopefully, some day my contribution to peace
Will help just a bit to turn the tide.
And, perhaps, I can tell my children six,
And later on their own children,
That, at least, in the future they need not be silent
When they are asked, "Where was your mother, *when?*"

Recommended Listening

King, Charlie. *Food Phone Gas Lodging.* Flying Fish 70536 (CD & cassette).
Seeger, Pete. *Waist Deep in the Big Muddy.* Columbia 9505 (LP).

*The composer is referring to the Nuremberg War Crimes Trials, which took place from 1945 to 1946.

105. Anton Schmidt

Anton Schmidt was a sergeant in the German army stationed in Vilna. Shocked by what he saw in the death camp in nearby Ponary, he made the incredible decision in late 1941 to do whatever he could do to help the Jews survive. His activities included securing the release of Jewish prisoners from the notorious Lakishki jail, supplying food to other Jews inside the ghetto, and even transporting some Jews in his truck to Warsaw and Bialystok in order that they might bring word of the mass killings at Ponary. His clandestine operations soon were uncovered and he was arrested in January 1942, sentenced to death by a military tribunal, and executed the following April 13. In 1964, Schmidt was posthumously recognized by Yad Vashem as a "Righteous among the Nations."

Words by Norman Chansky

Music by Pete Seeger

Copyright © 2000 by Sanga Music, Inc. All rights reserved. Used by Permission.

106. We Didn't Know

I have this good friend who was a flight cadet in the Air Force a few years ago. During the course of his training he was called before a board of examining officers and asked whether or not he would obey an order by a superior officer to drop a nuclear bomb on an American city. The mere fact that questions like this are being asked of elite military personnel points up graphically, I think, how far into limbo the Cold War and the arms race have carried us. The fact that the big brass in the Pentagon are approaching such questions scares hell out of me, because you can bet your last dollar that they can find the people who could be persuaded that their duty lay in doing just that unspeakable thing. The world is full of zealots and most of them are content to hold their beliefs and attempt to persuade others. But when those zealots get their hot little hands on a nuclear arsenal, I think it's time to get worried. The Nuremberg War Crimes trials examined only German atrocities. The standard cop-out was either "Orders are orders" or "We had no idea that such things were going on." There will be no war crimes trials, apparently, in Mississippi, Alabama, or in Viet Nam. Political considerations must, of course, come first.

Tom Paxton, *Sing Out!*. Vol. 16, No. 2, April–May 1966

Einstein says he's scared . . . and when Einstein's scared . . . I'm scared. Vern Partlow, "Talking Atomic Blues."

Copyright © 1965 (renewed 1993) United Artists Co., Inc. Rights assigned to EMI Catalogue Partnership. All rights controlled and administered by EMI Catalog Inc. (Publishing) and Warner Bros. Publications U.S. Inc. (Print). All rights reserved. Used by permission.

"We didn't know," said the congregation,
Singing a hymn in their church of white.
"The press was full of lies about us;
Preacher told us we were right.
The outside agitators came,
They burned some churches and put the blame
On decent southern people's names,
To set our colored people aflame.
     (*Sung to music of measures 9–16*)
And maybe some of our boys got hot,
And a couple of niggers and reds got shot.
They should have stayed where they belong,
And preacher would've told us if we'd done wrong." *Chorus*

"We didn't know," said the puzzled voter,
Watching the president on tv.
"I guess we've got to drop those bombs
If we're gonna keep South Asia free.
The president's such a peaceful man,
I guess he's got some kind of plan.
They say we're torturing prisoners of war,
But I don't believe that stuff no more.
Torturing prisoners is a communist game,
And you can bet they're doing the same.
I wish this war was over and through,
But what do you expect me to do? *Chorus*

107. Auschwitz

The train is a familiar image in American folk music. While revolutionizing transportation "from sea to shining sea," it also came to symbolize both parting and return, love and loss, reliability and danger. It was used as a metaphor, for "going to Heaven" (*Gospel Train*), "freedom" (*The Midnight Special*), and "workers' rights" (*Union Train*). Some of our most memorable heroes made their mark "a-workin' on the railroad" one way or another: John Henry, Jesse James, Casey Jones, to name but three. *The Wabash Cannonball* meant "speed"; Jay Gould (*Jay Gould's Daughter*) equaled "greed." Abraham Lincoln's funeral train took on mythic dimensions, "crying Freedom," in the cantata by Millard Lampell and Earl Robinson, *The Lonesome Train*. But all these images pale before Tom Paxton's "long train coming across the Polish plain." Written in the vernacular and musical lingo of the American narrative ballad, the terrible story is retold in a straightforward manner that only serves to accentuate the underlying unfolding horror.

Words and Music By Tom Paxton

Copyright © 1961; renewed 1989 Cherry Lane Music Publishing Company, Inc. (ASCAP) and DreamWorks Songs (ASCAP). Worldwide Rights for DreamWorks Songs Administered by Cherry Lane Music Publishing Company, Inc. International Copyright Secured. All Rights Reserved.

This train is bound for Auschwitz,
Like many another one.
The passengers condemned to die,
But no crime have they done.

They are packed into boxcars,
So tight against the wall,
And in those cars the dead men stand,
There is no room to fall.

The reason they are dying,
I will explain to you:
Adolph Hitler has decided
To exterminate the Jews.

He ships them off to Auschwitz,
The train unloads them there,
And standing by the railroad track,
They take their last breath of fresh air.

The SS troopers herd them
Right down a well-worn path,
Into a hall where they are told
They are to take a bath.

When they're undressed they're led inside
A giant shower room.
The door is sealed behind them;
It also seals their doom.

Into the room there drops a bomb
Of Nazi poison gas,
And not one soul is left alive
When fifteen minutes pass.

Now those who did those awful crimes,
They wish they'd murdered more.
The only thing they're sorry for,
Is that they lost the war.

And hundreds of these murderers
Still walk the earth today,
Just hoping for a chance to kill
The ones that got away.

108. Rain Falls Down in Amsterdam

While living in Europe in the early nineties, I began to notice the rise of nationalism and increase of right wing skinhead violence after the Berlin wall fell. Stories appeared with increasing frequency of violence against immigrants, brutal cops, immigrant house burnings, murders, Jewish graveyard desecrations, unbelievable stuff. . . . The activity was in America, too; homegrown militias, Oklahoma bombing, a black man being dragged to death behind a truck by white men in Texas, the teenagers in Littleton, Colorado [On April 20, 1999, two students at Columbine High School shot and killed 12 fellow students and one teacher before shooting themselves] . . . all displaced orphans of the Klan and under the spell of the Nazi and fundamentalist church propaganda. . . . I've come to realize that the old maxim is true: those who don't learn from their history are doomed to repeat it. While the war in Bosnia was cooking to a holocaust boil, I realized that Europe was doing nothing about it. Strange, since they had that war and ethnic cleansing right in their backyards not fifty years ago.

Eric Andersen. *Sing Out,* Fall 1999, vol. 44, no. 1

Words and Music by Eric Anderson

The rain falls down in Amsterdam, The streets are wet and black. Midnight's like November, By the glow of a cigarette. The girls on hash in station square Looking stupid from the drugs.

Copyright © 1998 Wind and Sand Music

Fire-bomb those houses,
Burn those refugees.
Be the crowd and do your work,
Applauding silently.
Round up all the gypsies,
Go send them on the trains.
Can't you smell the smoke now,
Drifting through the rain?
Jews, better draw your curtains,
You better lock your doors up tight.
They're snarling up in Rostock,
In the beer hall-belly nights.
The Fourth Reich's coming, baby,
They're writing out the page.
In Rome, Berlin, and Stockholm
The beast has left the cage. *Chorus*

Those canals and cozy houses,
Those reflections in the lights;
You can almost feel it moving—
The monster in the night.
It's looking with its yellow eyes,
It's out to settle scores.
In the dim medieval distance,
Feel it breathing down your pores.
In Salt Lake and in Rio
The beast can smell the flames.
It's faxing hate out in Marseilles,
Typing out your name.
You can hear the windows shatter
As the time is drawing near.
Kristallnacht is back in town.
Welcome back to the house of mirrors. *Bridge*

Now, I have been here thinking
How lucky I have been.
I never touched barb-wire,
Never saw the monkey grin.
No rifle ever smashed my face,
No bare electric shock.
But I'll confess up all I know
Who I am and who I'm not.
To see retired killers is
To see the lion yawn.
The skinheads do their dirty work
For the cloak and dagger pawns.
The dark eyes will be waiting there
When the borders will be crossed.
So keep your filthy swastikas,
And shove your iron cross. *Chorus*
Coda

Recommended Listening

Anderson, Eric. *Memory of the Future.* Appleseed Records 1028.

109. We Are Here

Rosalie Gerut is the daughter of survivors from Lodz, Poland, and Vilna, Lithuania. Her parents lived through the Lodz ghetto, Auschwitz and Dachau. From early childhood Rosalie's parents spoke to her about their terrible experiences in the Shoah. This view of life's dark side has inspired her to transform pain into creativity, rage into acts of social justice, and fear into compassion and love. One of the avenues through which she works is the organization One By One, created by Jews and Christians whose lives have been deeply affected by the Holocaust: "We are the children of survivors of Nazi atrocities who grew up in the shadow of our parents' suffering and trauma.... We are also the descendants of the Third Reich whose parents or grandparents were perpetrators or bystanders in one of the most evil chapters of human history.... Together we seek to bear witness to the reality of the Holocaust, to speak out against denial and revisionist history and to work for social justice wherever it is needed."

By Rosalie Gerut

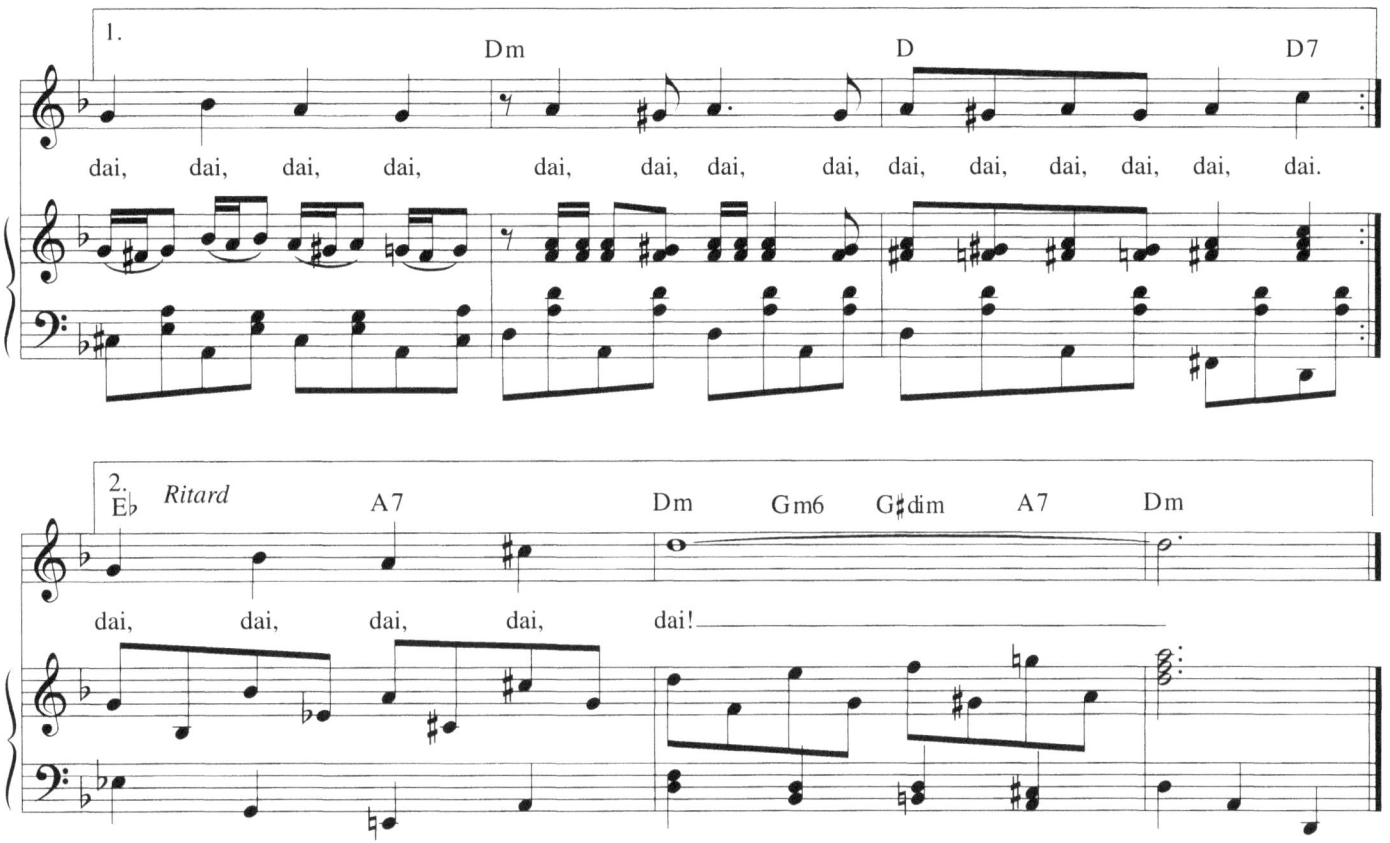

Recommended Listening

Gerut, Rosalie. *We Are Here.* Blue Hill Recordings BHR 101 (CD).

110. Kaddish

Words by Z. Segalovitch
Music by Ben Yomen

In Memoriam — Warsaw Ghetto

Shed no tears for the ones who fell,
Away with thoughts of grief;
Shed no tears for those valiant ones,
Brave beyond belief.

Sing loud hosannas to the skies,
Chant praises far and wide —
With heads unbowed they faced the foe,
And fiercely burned their pride.

Though fascist monsters hemmed them in,
No quarter there was sought;
Their Maccabeean strength prevailed —
Unto the death they fought.

All hallowed is the ground wherein
Eternally they sleep;
And hallowed, too, their memory
Which we must ever keep.

Shed no tears for those valiant ones,
Brave beyond belief;
Sing loud hosannas to the skies
Of triumph — not of grief.

      Bill Silverman, 1945

Notes

1. When Israel was in Egypt land,
   Let my people go,
   Oppressed so hard they could not stand,
   Let my people go.
   Go down, Moses, 'way down in Egypt land.
   Tell old pharaoh to let my people go.
   Let My People Go, Negro Spiritual

2. Oh, the praties [potatoes] they grow small over here, over here,
   Oh, the praties they grow small over here.
   Oh, the praties they grow small,
   And we dig them in the fall,
   And we eat them skin and all, over here, over here . . .
   The Famine Song (The Praties), c. 1848

3. *The Kishinev Pogrom* (1903):

   Dem ershten tog peysakh
   Hobn yidelekh gants freylakh farbrakht
   Un dem letsten tog khoge,
   Hot men Keshenev khorev gemakht.

   Keshenev arumgeringelt,
   Azoy vi a bonder di fas.
   Tates un mames un kinder
   Zaynen gefaln in gas.

   O, du got in himl
   Kuk shoyn arop tsu undz,
   Batracht nor dem rash mit dem tuml,
   Vi di goyim zenen zikh noykem in undz.

   It was on Passover's first day,
   That the Jewish people gathered in their joy.
   And the last day of Easter,
   It was Kishenev that was destroyed.

   Kishenev was surrounded,
   As a hoop holds a barrel's staves.
   Fathers and mothers and children
   Right on the street found their graves.

   O, you God in heaven,
   Gaze downward if you choose,
   And look at the scene of destruction,
   What the *goyim* are doing to Jews.

   Forty-nine Jews were murdered and some five hundred injured. Jewish homes and property were destroyed. The pogrom was instigated by the age-old anti-Semitic legend, reborn every Passover/Easter, about the alleged Jewish need for the blood of a Christian child for the preparation of Passover matzohs.

4. Actually the name and concept of the concentration camp were first devised by the British under Kitchener in 1900 during the Boer War, when the women and children of the Boer commandos were interned behind barbed wire under extremely harsh conditions. However, it remained for the Nazis to refine and perfect this system.

5. One of their most famous songs, *Das Einheitsfrontlied* ("The United Front Song") appears in this collection in the original German as well as in English, Spanish, French, and Russian translations. A Yiddish variant will also be found under the title *Tsu Eyns, Tsvey, Dray!* ("So, One, Two, Three!"). Both men eventually emigrated to the U.S., where they spent the war years. They both got caught up in the postwar anti-Communist witch hunts and were both subpoenaed by Congressional "un-American activities" committees. Their welcome to this country at an end (despite worldwide protests by Thomas Mann, Einstein, Picasso, Matisse, Jean Cocteau, Aaron Copland, and others), they opted for "voluntary deportation" and returned to (East) Germany in 1948.

6. One of the "four insurgent generals" referred to in the song *Los Cuatro Generales,* (see p. 41).

7. Speaking at the dedication of a memorial to the Veterans of the Abraham Lincoln Brigade (VALB) in Madison, Wis., Oct. 31, 1999. *The Volunteer* (Journal of the VALB), vol. 21, no. 4, Fall 1999.

8. "They Shall Not Pass!,"—the rallying cry of the Republican defenders of Madrid. It was subsequently adopted as a universal appeal to anti-fascist resistance.

9. *Tiempo de Historia,* Madrid, Sept. 1975.

10. "Jews in the International Brigades," *Jewish Currents,* Feb. 1979.

11. Organized in 1916, primarily to educate Jewish youth for kibbutz life in *Eretz Israel,* its members were notably active in resistance to Nazi occupation in eastern Europe. Mordecai Anielowicz, the commander of the Warsaw Ghetto revolt, was a member of Hashomer Hatzair, as were resistance fighers in other Polish ghettos.

12. On July 15, 1918, the Germans made their last major attack of WWI, crossing the Marne River near Reims. The fighting continued until August 2. Allied casualties were about 112,000; German 168,000. Canadian songwriter Lieut. Ingraham (Gitz) Rice, a member of the Canadian Expeditionary Force in France, incorporating several other battles into the lyrics, wrote *We Stopped Them at the Marne,* which a scant nineteen years later, with a few changes, could almost have been sung in Spain:

    We stopped them at the Marne,
    We beat them on the Aisne,
    We gave them hell at Neuve Chappelle,
    And here we are, yes, here we are again.
    The French stopped them at Verdun,
    And you can't forget Ypres.
    Now America's here to help us,
    So, it's to hell with Germany.

13. Ernest Hemingway described Wolff as: "Tall as Lincoln, and as brave and as good a soldier as any that commanded battalions at Gettysburg."

14. *The Volunteer* (Journal of the VALB), vol. 21, no. 4, Fall 1999. op. cit.

15. Two weeks earlier, on Oct. 16, the first French monument was unveiled in Champigny, near Paris, "*En hommage aux 9000 Voluntaires antifascistes Français partis de 1936 à 1939 en Espagne combattre pour la République et la Démocratie contre le coup d'état du Général* FRANCO" ("In homage to the 9000 French antifascist volunteers who went to Spain from 1936 to 1939 to fight for the Republic and Democracy against the *coup d'état* of General FRANCO.")

16. In Barcelona, on Mar. 3, 1990, a monument was dedicated on Mont Juich (Jewish Mountain) in homage to the "Jewish heroes who fell among the 7,000 Jewish volunteers from all the countries, fighting for liberty in Spain." It was inscribed in the Catalan language of that region of Spain: *Homenatge als herois jueus—Caiguts entre 7000 voluntaris jueus de tots els països—Combatants de la libertat a Espanya—1936-1939.*

17. In 1940, Keynote Records issued an album entitled "Six Songs for Democracy," in German and Spanish, recorded in part during a *Luftwaffe* airraid in Barcelona in 1938, by Ernst Busch and a chorus made up of members of the XI International Brigade. In 1961, Folkways Records ("Songs of the Spanish Civil War," vol. 1, FH 5436) reissued that historic album, with additional songs performed by Pete Seeger, Tom Glazer, Baldwin Hawes, and Bess Hawes. The following year "Songs of

the Spanish Civil War," vol. 2, (FH 5437) was released. It was produced by the Veterans of the Abraham Lincoln Brigade in conjunction with Folkways. Performers included Ernst Busch, Woody Guthrie, Bart van der Schelling (a Dutch veteran of the war), and the "Exiles' Chorus." These albums have been reissued by Smithsonian/Folkways. Incidentally, Folkways Records was founded by Moses (Moe) Asch, son of the Yiddish author Sholem Asch.

18. Composer W. C. Handy, "The Father of the Blues," participated in a project to raise money for an ambulance to be shipped to Spain. Inscribed in bold letters on its side was the message: " From the Negro People of America to the People of Republican Spain."

19. German anti-fascist song writer, singer, and actor; fled Germany in 1933; lived in exile in a number European countries before moving to Moscow in 1936; traveled to Spain in 1937 where he performed in besieged Madrid, in the trenches of the Ebro and in military hospitals in Barcelona and Benicasim.

20. German Communist leader. See the song *Die Thälmann-Kolonne,* page 30.

21. See the song *Hans Beimler,* page 26.

22. A union leader decapitated by axe in Hamburg, November 4, 1936.

23. Cited in album notes to the above-mentioned "Songs of the Spanish Civil War," vol. 2., and used by permission of the Veterans of the Abraham Lincoln Brigade, which supplied much of the material for the production of the album. Journalist and author Egon Erwin Kisch (1885-1948) was active in pre-war Czech-Jewish literary circles. He led an adventurous life as a prolific leftist writer and activist. In 1913 he joined the staff of the *Berliner Tageblatt;* in 1918 he led the Communist "Red Guard" in Vienna (which earned him three months imprisonment and expulsion from Austria); in Berlin once again, arrested after the Reichstag fire (1933) and deported to Czechoslovakia; choosing exile in Australia in 1934, he was refused admission as an "undesirable alien," whereupon he leaped from the ship into Perth harbor; sentenced to six months imprisonment and deportation; fought in the Spanish Republican Army (1937-1938); passed through Paris before emigrating to New York (1939); settled in Mexico; returned to Prague (1946), where he became the honorary president of the Prague Jewish community.

24. French poet Louis Aragon, on hearing of the establishing of the camp in the spring of 1939 wrote: "Gurs, une drôle de syllable. Comme un sanglot qui ne sort pas de la gorge" ("Gurs, a strange syllable. Like a sob that does not escape the throat."). Eberhard Schmitt, a veteran of the Thaelmann Battalion imprisoned in Gurs, inscribed his song *Wir Hinterm Draht* ("We Behind Barbed Wire") in the camp book, *Lagerstimme* ("Camp Voice"):

Gray are the barracks, gray the enclosures,
Fourfold surround us the wire barbs.
Gray are the days here, gray are the fences,
All day and night we're confronted by guards.

25. Some prisoners wound up in a camp in Djelfa, Algeria. Polish citizens from the just recently Soviet-occupied part of Poland (as a result of the 1939 Soviet-German Non-Aggression Pact, the so-called Molotov-Ribbentrop Pact which divided Poland between Germany and the USSR) were allowed to opt for deportation to the Soviet Union.

26. Article 19 of the June 1940 armistice between France and Germany stipulated in part: "The French government is obliged to surrender upon demand all Germans named by the German Government in France." By this was meant, political refugees — Jews and non-Jews alike — who had fled to France to escape the rising terror in the "Greater Reich" (Germany, Austria, Czechoslovakia, and part of Poland). This rather imprecise category was gradually expanded to include anybody that the Nazis wanted to detain. In this regard the Vichy government proved itself all too willing to cooperate, handing 74,721 Jews over to the Germans between 1941 and 1944. Most perished in the extermination camps.

27. HICEM was organized in Paris in 1939 to deal with the problem of refugees. Its name is an acronym derived from the names of three other agencies, whose efforts were now combined: HIAS (Hebrew Immigrant Aid Society), ICA (Jewish Colonization Association, founded by Baron Maurice de Hirsch in 1891), and Emig-direkt (set up in Berlin in 1921). On November 24, 1999, some sixty years after the founding of HICEM, an Israeli officer, perhaps a descendant of refugees, on duty with troops in Nazareth separating Muslims from Christians, who were protesting the building of a mosque at the foot of the Basilica of the Annunciation, was quoted in the *New York Times:* "We are in the middle, because we are not Muslims and we are not Christians. . . . The Muslims are a lot stronger than the Christians, a lot more deadly. Without the protection of the Jews, I don't think there would be any Christians left here." *O tempora. o mores.*

28. In his memoir, *Et la mer n'est pas remplie* (And the Sea Is Not Filled Up) (Paris: *Éditions du Seuil,* 1996, published in New York in 1999 by Knopf) Elie Wiesel touches on the very subject of "the undying flame:" "Après la libération . . . Il leur fallait bien recommencer à vivre, à fonder des foyers, à bâtir sur des ruines; réapprendre à rire, à chanter. . . . Encore dans les camps pour Personnes Déplacées, ils avaient célébré fiançailles et mariages, ouvert des écoles et des centres culturels dans des baraques." ("After the liberation . . . They indeed had to begin to live again, to establish families, to build upon the ruins; to learn once more to laugh, to sing. . . . While still in the Displaced Persons camps, they celebrated engagements and marriages, opened schools and cultural centers in the barracks.")

29. Despite the façade of "normalcy" for the benefit of the Red Cross inspectors, the ultimate fate of the inmates was always intended to be Auschwitz. The total number of arrivals in the camp from 1941 to 1945 was about 150,000 Jews. The average population was about 30,000. At the moment of liberation there were 17,521 survivors.

30. In 1845, the Bohemian-Jewish poet Moritz Hartmann wrote this prophetic verse in his *Böhmische Elegien* (*Bohemian Elegies*):

Ein slavisches Jerusalem,
Das bist Du, wie Dein Kind Dich nennet,
O Prag! das Dich von ehedem
Und das in Deinem Gram Dich kennet.

A Slavic Jerusalem,
You are, just as your child does call you,
O Prague! that from time immemorial
Knows you in your sorrow.

31. In a 1931 interview with the New York Yiddish-language newspaper *Der Tog* (The Day), Albert Einstein was quoted as saying, "The Yiddish folk songs, why they are the most heartfelt I have heard anywhere. They are the truest expression of the soul of a people." When the reporter asked him if he knew any, Einstein replied, "Yes — very many (*suddenly starting to sing a Yiddish folk song, but stopping short*). If I only had my violin with me, I could have played it," The song he was attempting to sing was *Oyfn Pripetchik* (At the Hearth).

32. In 1888, fifty years before Goebbels' diatribe, Dr. Moritz Gruenwald, the Chief Rabbi of Bulgaria had published a volume entitled *Über den jüdisch-deutschen Jargon vulgo Kauderwälsch genannt* (On the Jewish-German Jargon Vulgarly Called a Mishmash Language), which contains this remarkably farsighted passage directed at the German-language snobs of his day: "Gently, Herr von X, Frau von Y, or perhaps Mademoiselle von Z. This very miserable, detestable, and heaven knows how else dubbed language [Yiddish] is entitled to its existence, is perhaps more entitled to live than *your* German language, which is so interlarded and distorted with so many French and other foreign words that, happily, you yourself don't understand."

In an interview with a British journalist, published on July 30, 1933, in the *Sunday Referee,* Goebbels had no compunction about expressing his innermost thoughts: "Death to the Jews! has been our war cry for fourteen years." (That is, since the end of WWI.) Now with Goebbels in charge, an irrational fear of so-called foreign influences upon all aspects of German life (including the language itself: the Greek-rooted word *Telefon,* for example, was translated to its German equivalent,

Fernsprecher; (Rabbi Gruenwald would have smiled at that one) had by October 12, 1935, caused German radio to ban the playing of "Nigger jazz" (the English adjective is theirs). Ten so-called "Swing Boys" from Hamburg were interned in the euphemistically named Moringen "youth protective-custody camp" (*Jugendschutzlager*) near Göttingen for the duration of the war, for the "crime" of listening to "enemy radio broadcasts" (jazz on the BBC) and trading swing music records. Evenings in their barracks, when the SS guards had gone off duty, they passed their time singing softly under their blankets (shades of summer camp and boarding school!) such "subversive" songs as "Sweet Sue," "Jeepers Creepers," "Some of These Days" and "Flat-Foot Floogie." When they were sent to work in a dangerous munitions factory they found the opportunity (once again, when the SS were absent) to sing and play "drums" on empty munitions boxes *"wie die Mills Brothers."* Paradoxically, jazz bands and orchestras were formed in some other concentration camps. Guitarist Coco Schumann, of the Theresienstadt "Ghetto Swingers," [!] who survived a 1944 deportation from that camp to Auschwitz, felt that music had saved his life: He was compelled to play while other prisoners were sent to the gas chambers.

33. Goebbels may have had something like the following in mind: Hitler comes into a Vienna coffee-house where a Jew is reading the newspapers that are placed at the disposal of the customers. The Jew studiously reads all the papers but does not put them back on the rack. After a while, Hitler comes to his table and politely asks: "Please, is the *Wiener Journal* free?" Relishing the moment, the Jew replies, "Not for you, Herr Hitler, not for you!"

And did you hear the one about the "ideal Nazi"? In 1935 the following picture of the "ideal Nazi" was formulated by Viennese cabarettist Oskar Teller: Blond as Hitler, slim as Göring, handsome as Goebbels and named at least Rosenberg. (Alfred Rosenberg, despite his "Jewish-sounding" name, was the "intellectual leader" of the Nazi party. He was executed in Nuremberg for war crimes on October 16, 1946.)

Even during the desperate year of 1942, Jewish humor made it possible to imagine Churchill consulting a wonder-working rabbi on the question of how to defeat Germany: "There are two possibilities," says the rabbi, "the natural and the supernatural. The natural way would be for God to send down upon Germany a million angels with flaming swords. The supernatural would be the debarcation of a million British soldiers."

Perhaps the most "amusing" story of all is this charming description of his pal Adolf by automobile manufacturer Ferdinand Porsche (whose fortune was founded on the Hitler-inspired "people's car," the Volkswagen): "Simpatico, if you knew him personally."

34. "The Ark" was located in a Jewish community center at 270 West 89th Street. That neighborhood, in the Upper West Side of Manhattan was heavily populated by German-speaking Jewish refugees. The building now houses a Hebrew school.

Writing in the New York German-language newspaper *Aufbau* (April 30, 1943), exiled Viennese actress Ellen Schwanneke headlined her article with the defiant: *"Nein, Herr Goebbels! Ich spiele lieber in der Arche'"* ("No, Herr Goebbels! I'd rather play in 'The Ark'"). "I had really—thank God—by now almost forgotten that I (as the barbarians put it) am an 'Aryan.' I work a lot in the American radio, I feel at home here, and it doesn't occur to anyone to ask about race and religion.— Again: thank God! However, there is always somebody . . . About two weeks ago two men came to me, who once again posed the 'race question.' I was terribly surprised. My visitors smiled understandingly and said: 'It doesn't make any difference to us. Would you like, in spite of that, to perform with us? The two men were Erich Juhn and Oskar Teller of the Jewish-political cabaret 'The Ark,' and the role that they proposed was the young Jacob in Richard Beer-Hoffman's masterful 'Jacob's Dream.' I was enchanted . . . But somewhere I thought: Would the 'Ark's' public think of me as an interloper in this Old Testament role? But my visitors smilingly calmed me down: 'We Jews are very tolerant. And besides,' they continued earnestly, 'in the difficult times of persecution you were so well known to us for your bravery that we are convinced that our public will embrace you with open hearts.' I was assured—and thus it came about that I joined 'The Ark.' This small group of talented and dedicated actors, who earn their daily bread in mundane callings and in the evenings tirelessly try—and in a few short months have presented the evidence that in New York a German-language cabaret has the right to exist. And why? Because it has political convictions, spirit, wit and class! [*Niveau*]."

35. The original *Kadeko* (*Kabarett der Komiker*—Cabaret of the Comics) was founded in Berlin in 1924 by Kurt Robitschek and Paul Morgan. Robitschek's attempts to recreate *Kadeko* in New York in 1941 were ultimately unsuccessful.

36. The first exile cabaret in Holland. It opened in Amsterdam in 1933.

37. Some lyricists borrowed familiar tunes for their barbs, a sure-fire method to get people to sing their parodies. A song that every German knew (indeed, it was also sung by the British army, known in France and even sung in the Soviet Union) was the sentimental ballad, *Lili Marleen* (made famous all over the world by Marlene Dietrich). In the original version Lili waits patiently for her soldier lover underneath the streetlight by the barracks gate. In the underground version which circulated in Germany during the war she waits on line at "Meier's" butcher shop hoping to buy some meat: *"Ob er noch Knochen hat"* ("But he has only bones"), or, better still:

Unter der Laterne vor der Reichskanzlei,
Hängen alle Bonzen, der Führer hängt dabei.
Und alle Leute bleiben stehn,
Sie wollen ihren Führer sehn
Wie einst Lili Marleen,
Wie einst Lili Marleen.

Underneath the streetlight by the Reichschancellery,
The bigshots are all hanging, the Führer hangs nearby.
And all the people just remain,
To see their Führer once again,
Just like Lili Marlene,
Just like Lili Marlene.

Another song known to every German schoolchild is Heinrich Heine's 1823 poem "Die Lorelei," set to music in 1838 by Friedrich Silcher, which in exiled Viennese cabaret composer Jimmy Berg's 1943 take-off, performed at The Ark in New York, goes in part:

Ich weiß nicht, was soll es bedeuten,
Daß ich so unruhig bin,
Das sind wohl die neudeutschen Zeiten,
Die lasten auf Magen und Sinn . . .
Da hab ich auf einmal ein Brüllen gehört:
Hepp Hepp und den Juden der Tod!
Das hat mich erheblich beim Singen gestört,
Bis man es mir gänzlich verbot!
Lore Lore Lore Lorelei,
Kein Wunder, daß du so vergrämt bist,
Weil dein Papa Heine verfemt ist,
Heil, deutsche Treu!

I do not know what it may mean now,
That all these troubles I find.
It could well be the new German times now,
That weigh on my stomach and mind . . .
Then suddenly I heard a loud roaring:
Hep, Hep, and now death to the Jews!
That considerably disturbed my singing,
Till they then forbade me my muse.
Lore Lore Lore Lorelei,
No wonder you've troubles at hand now,
For your Papa Heine is banned now,
Hail, German fidelity!

The expression "Hep, Hep" (sometimes spelled *Hepp, Hepp* in German) refers to the anti-Semitic German "Hep! Hep!" movement which dates from 1819. It took as its rallying cry, "Hep! Hep! Hep! Death and destruction to all the Jews," (*Den Juden der Tod und die Vernichtung*). It is noteworthy because it was the *first* major organized movement in Germany which specifically singled out Jews as "the enemy." It had been preceded by the abrogation of Jewish rights in 1813, with its attendant violence and pogroms. Further exacerbation of the situation grew out of the Congress of Vienna (1814–15), which in attempting to sort out post-Napoleonic Europe, failed to take positive action regarding the civil status of Jews.

The origin of the slogan itself is unclear. One theory has it that the cry "hep" is derived from goatherds' calls employed in driving their animals, with the obvious intent of ridiculing Jews' beards by comparing them to "goatees." Another possibility suggests an abbreviation of the word *Hebräer* (Hebrew person) or "heb,"—in which the letter *b* is pronounced more like a *p*. The most intriguing explanation is that it is a crusaders' Latin rallying cry, derived from the initials of *Hierosolyma est perdita* (Jerusalem is lost), to which the Jews supposedly riposted with *Jep! Jep!*, signifying *Jesus est perditus*.

38. From the introduction to the memoir, *Steal a Pencil for Me: Love Letters Written by Jaap Polak and Ina Soep in the Concentration Camps Westerbork and Bergen-Belsen, 1943-1945* (Scarsdale, N.Y.: Lion Books, 2000). They were married on January 29, 1946, in Amsterdam.

39. *Conférenciers* Josef Baar, Franz Engel; comedians Hermann Feiner; actresses Chaja Goldstein, Camilla Spira; dancer, Otto Aurich; musician Erich Ziegler; actor Kurt Gerron, among others. All had sought refuge in Holland.

40. The Nazi law of August 26, 1938, compelled every Jewish man to adopt the name "Israel" and every Jewish woman, "Sara."

41. Rudolf Nelson's son, Herbert, was also a cabaret composer and performer. He arrived in Holland in 1939 and soon became active in the Amsterdam exile-cabaret scene. In the summer of 1943 he and some of his fellow performers organized a clandestine cabaret that put on Sunday afternoon performances in his own apartment! They were taking a terrible chance of discovery (incredibly the Germans never caught on), but they nevertheless felt compelled to carry on the tradition of political satire which their audience (by discreet invitation only) so appreciated. Often American popular songs served as vehicles for their up-to-the minute barbs. Rommel's retreating Afrika Corps was serenaded with "Give Me Five Minutes More, Only Five Minutes More." As the Allies slowly closed in, they had Hitler singing Cole Porter's "Don't Fence Me In" (popularized by Bing Crosby's 1944 hit recording). One scene ended with a rendition of "Happy Days Are Here Again."

42. Sometimes spelled "Gemmecker." He was sentenced to ten years imprisonment by a Dutch court after the war.

43. It wasn't for lack of trying that nobody was fooled. The German press often outdid itself in trying to portray the "humanitarian" aspect of the *Wehrmacht*'s activities: "They tell us from Amsterdam that Dutch citizens manifest an intense animosity toward the Jews. The Jews have turned to the German *Wehrmacht* for protection. In spite of their eternal hostility, the *Wehrmacht* has taken the Jews under its protection and, by their own demand, have transferred them to Germany, where they will be employed according to their capacities. In order to express their appreciation for this generosity, the Jews have placed their furniture and apartments at the disposition of suffering Germans, victims of British bombardment." (*Hamburger Fremdenblatt*, July 24, 1942.)

44. Some inmates lived in private bungalows.

45. "Too bad," or "what a pity," in Yiddish in the original.

46. The repairman.

47. In Dutch in the original.

48. In Dutch in the original.

49. *Erste Hilfe bei Unfällen*—"First aid for accidents," that is, the First-Aid Station.

50. "Troubles," in Yiddish in the original.

51. Mara Rosen was also a member of the cabaret troupe.

52. *Fliegende Kolonne* (Flying Column), a detachment of mostly young men who assisted with the luggage when a train arrived or departed.

53. *Verwaltung*—Administration

54. An ironical Westerbork prisoners' code word for *Israelitische Presse-Agentur*, Jewish Press Agency, which, of course, did not exist in the camp but was the "source" of the rumors that fed the inmates' hopes and fears. Other "press agencies" circulated fantastic "bulletins" as well. In the Warsaw Ghetto, historian Emmanuel Ringelblum kept a diary which survived the destruction of the ghetto. In his entry for May 8, 1942, Ringelbaum noted: "What is in these communiqués? First, Smolensk was captured by a debarquement of 60,000 soldiers, who joined up with the Red Army. The same communiqué also captured Kharkov. It landed an army in Murmansk brought in by 160 ships, none of which was sunk. If that weren't enough, Mussolini was assassinated and there was a revolution in Italy. Finally, there was an ultimatum by Roosevelt addressed to the German people, expiring May 15."

55. Johnny and Jones were deported to Bergen-Belsen, where they perished in April 1945.

56. The Allied invasion of Normandy.

57. In Norman Corwin's 1945 CBS radio drama "On A Note Of Triumph," celebrating the end of the war in Europe, this song is sung variously in Serbian (*Obil osimo okolo nokolo Hitlerovog groba, okolo nokolo*), Danish (*Og saa vi rundt om Hitler's grav, Hitler's grav, Hitler's grav*) and Greek (*Gyro sto mnima too Hitler gyro gyro pername*).

58. Trepman's *nom de camp* was Pawel Kolodziejczyk. He was the editor of *Unzer Shtimme* ("Our Voice"), a Yiddish newsletter which was the first periodical to be published in Germany after the war. Later, he edited the *Vokhenblatt* ("Weekly Journal"). Both these publications were put out by the previously mentioned Central Jewish Committee in Bergen-Belsen.

59. On March 5, 1998, the *New York Times* reported: "Ex-Nazi Is Seized; Accused of Gunning Down 500 at Maidanek." The article went on to say that one Alfons Goetzfried, a member of the Gestapo, who had been captured by Soviet forces in 1945, sentenced to thirteen years in a labor camp, freed in 1958, and after living in Kazakhstan until his return to Germany in 1991, was arrested in Stuttgart, "accused of a catalogue of murders, including his killing of 500 camp prisoners, mostly Jews, during a systematic massacre gruesomely code-named 'Operation Harvest Festival' *[Unternehmung Erntfest]* . . . during a two-day period in November 1943."

60. The power of music was likewise felt by French poet Louis Aragon, who, inspired by a Catalonian patriotic song which was taken up by the Spanish loyalist fighters, wrote:

Je me souviens d'un air qu'on ne pouvait pas entendre
Sans que le cœur battit et le sang fût en feu,
Sans que le feu reprit comme un cœur sous la cendre
Et l'on savait enfin pourquoi le ciel est bleu.

I recall an air which I could not hear
Without my heart pounding and my blood on fire,
Without the fire rekindling like a heart beneath the ashes,
And finally knowing why the sky is blue.

61. Julius Freund, *O Buchenwald!* Klagenfurt, 1945.

Bibliography

Corwin, Norman. *On a Note of Triumph.* New York: Simon & Schuster, 1945.

De Silva, Clara, ed. *In Memory's Kitchen: A Legacy from the Women of Terezín.* Northvale, N.J.: Jason Aronson, 1996.

Feder, Zami, ed. *Katset Un Geto Lider* (Concentration Camp and Ghetto Songs) Bergen-Belsen, Germany: Central Jewish Committee in Bergen-Belsen, 1946.

Fry, Varian. *Surrender on Demand.* Boulder, Colo.: Johnson Books, 1997.

Gilbert, Martin. *The Atlas of Jewish History.* New York: William Morrow, 1992.

Kalisch, Shoshanna, with Barbara Meister. *Yes, We Sang: Songs of the Ghettos and Concentration Camps.* New York: Harper and Row, 1985.

Katz, William Loren, and Marc Crawford. *The Lincoln Brigade.* New York: Atheneum, 1989.

Kersten, Felix. *The Kersten Memoirs.* London: Hutchinson, 1956.

Klarsfeld, Serge, *French Children of the Holocaust.* New York: New York Univ. Press, 1966.

Kühn, Volker, ed. *Kabarett unterm Hakenkreuz* (Cabaret under the Swastika). Weinheim, Germany: Quadriga, 1989.

Lipshitz, Reuben. *Tsu Zingen Un Zogn (To Sing and to Say).* Munich, Germany: Privately Published, 1949.

Migdal, Ulrike. *Und die Muzik Spielt Dazu: Chansons und Satiren aus dem KZ Theresienstadt* (The Music Plays Along: Songs and Satires From The Theresienstadt Concentration Camp). Munich, Germany: Serie Piper, 1986.

Mlotek, Eleanor, and Malke Gottlieb. *We Are Here: Songs of the Holocaust.* New York: Educational Department of the Workman's Circle, 1983.

Morse, Arthur D. *While Six Million Died.* New York: Random House, 1967.

Musik in Konzentrationslagern (Music in Concentration Camps). Freiburg im Breisgau, Germany: Projektgruppe, 1991.

Partlow, Vern. "Talking Atomic Blues." *People's Song Bulletin* 1, no. 12 (Jan. 1947).

Polak, Jaap, and Ina Soep. *Steal a Pencil for Me.* Scarsdale, N.Y.: Lion Books, 2000.

Reik, Theodore. *Jewish Wit.* New York: Gamut Press, 1962.

Sachnowitz, Hermann. *Auschwitz. Ein norwegischer Jude uberlebte.* Frankfurt-am-Main, 1981.

Shirer, William L. *The Rise and Fall of the Third Reich.* New York: Simon & Schuster, 1959.

Silverman, Bill. *Rhymes for Our Times.* Bronx, New York: International Workers Order, 1946.

Silverman, Jerry. *Songs of the Jewish People.* Pacific, Mo.: Mel Bay, 1997.

Szpilman, Wladyslaw, *The Pianist.* New York: Picador, 1999.

Taylor, Telford. *The Anatomy of the Nuremberg Trials.* New York: Knopf, 1992.

Teller, Oskar. *David's Witz-Schleuder: Jüdisches-Politisches Cabaret: 50 Jahre Kleinkunstbuhnen in Wien, Berlin, London, New York, Warschau, Tel Aviv.* (David's Wit-Slingshot: Jewish Political Cabaret: 50 Years of Cabaret in Vienna, Berlin, London, New York, Warsaw, Tel Aviv). Darmstadt, Germany: Verlag Darmstadter Blatter, 1982.

Trepman, Paul. *Among Men and Beasts.* Cranbury, N.J.: A. S. Barnes, 1978.

Yahil, Leni. *The Holocaust.* New York: Oxford Univ. Press, 1990.

Zucotti, Susan. *The Italians and the Holocaust.* New York: Basic Books, 1987.

Index of Song Titles

English titles are in roman type; all other languages are in italic.

Als Ob, 194
A Mol Iz Geven A Mayse, 228
And Must It Be This Way?, 59
And the Music Just Plays On, 212
Ani Ma-amin, 116
Anton Schmidt, 275
Aroys Iz In Vilne A Nayer Bafel, 90
As If, 194
Asma Asmaton, 245
Áso Kapa Vállamon, 168
Auschwitz, 280
Auschwitz-Lied, 133
Auschwitz Song, 133

Bad Blockaus, 187
Ballade von der Judenhure Marie Sanders, 23
Ballad of the Jews'-Whore Marie Sanders, 23
Before the Last Journey, 152
Bella Ciao, 172
Birds Are Dozing, 102
Bless the Child That Cries to Thee, 48
Blockhouse Resort, 187
Buchenwald Alarm, 249
Buchenwald-Lied, 15
Buchenwald Song, 15
Bukhenval'dskii Nabat, 249
Butterfly (*Motýl*), 222
Butterfly (*Parpar*), 118

Children of Poland, 256
Cosmopolitain, The, 204

Dachau Lied (a), 18
Dachau-Lied (b), 21
Dachau Song (a), 18
Dachau Song (b), 21
Das Einheitsfrontlied, 6
Das Ende, 132
Das jüdische Kind, 11
Denmark 1943, 260
Der Hof-Zinger Fun Varshaver Geto, 74
Der Reisepaß Erzählt, 196
Det Har Vi, 148
Die Kosmopolitin, 204
Die Lebende Steine, 136
Die Moorsoldaten, 3
Die Novaks aus Prag, 200
Diese Emigranten!, 210
Die Thälmann-Kolonne, 30
Die Westerbork-Serenade, 142
Dizzy, 120
Doch auch für uns kommt mal die Zeit, 216
Domovina, 178
Dopis, 220

Embross, ELAS, 179

Én Még Most Kicsi Vagyok, 230
End, The, 132

Far Vos Iz Der Himl?, 68
Forward, ELAS, 179
Four Insurgent Generals, The, 41
Frauenlager, 139
Freedom. See Thaelmann Column, The, 30
Freiheit. See Die Thälmann-Kolonne, 30

Gehat Hot Ikh A Heym, 44
Gib A Brokhe Tsu Dayn Kind, 48
Gypsy Song, 65

Hans Beimler, 26
Homeland, 178

I Am Still a Little Child, 230
I Believe, 116
Ich hab' kein Heimatland, 13
If You Want to Write to Me, 36
I Have No Native Land, 13
I'll Tell To You All a Story, 228
In Kriuvke, 86
In Memoriam—Warsaw Ghetto (poem), 293
In the Dugout, 86
In Vilna Was Issued a Brand-New Decree, 90
Itsik Vitnberg, 98

Jarama Valley, 32
Jewish Child, The, 11
Join in the Struggle, 39

Kaddish, 292
Kak U Duba Starovo, 164
Katiusha, 160

Lady of the Harbor, 252
Last Train to Nuremberg, 270
Le Chant de Pithiviers, 111
Le Chant des Partisans, 128
Le Maquisard, 131
Letter, The, 220
Lid Fun Bug, 52
Lied der Internationalen Brigaden, 28
Living Stones, The, 136
Long Live the Fifteenth Brigade, 34
Los cuatro Generales, 41

Mah Ko Mashma Lon?, 125
Máj 1945, 224
Makh Tsu Di Eygelekh, 54
May 1945, 224
Mayn Mame Hot Gevolt Zayn Af Mayn Khasene, 50
Mein Vater wird gesucht, 9
Minutn Fun Bitokhin, 78

Mir Lebn Ebig, 114
M'khol Masada, 122
Moments of Confidence, 78
Motele from the Warsaw Ghetto, 71
Motele Fun Varshaver Geto, 71
Motýl, 222
My Father, He Was Tracked, 9
My Mother Wanted So to See My Wedding Day, 50
My Name is Lisa Kalvelage, 272

Neither Raisins Nor Almonds, 56
Never Say, 108
Neyn, Neyn, Neyn, 106
Nit Leyn Rozhinkes, Nit Keyn Mandlen, 56
No, No, No, 106
Novaks From Prague, The, 200
Now Close Your Little Eyes, 54

Oh, Masada, 122
Oh, Once I Had a Home, 44
Oh, the Fog, 166
Oi, Tumany Moyi, 166
O mis Hermanos, 238
O My Brothers, 238
On My Shoulder, Spade and Hoe, 168
Our Courage Is Unbroken, 111

Parpar, 118
Partigiani in Montagna, 170
Partisans in the Mountain, 170
Passport Relates, The, 196
Peat-Bog Soldiers, The, 3
People Call Me Ziamele, 100
Pesnia Belystokskikh Partizanov, 158
Przed Ostatnią Podróżą, 152

Rain Falls Down in Amsterdam, 282
Resistance Fighter, The, 131
Rivkele, di Shabesdike, 83
Rivkele, the Sabbath-Widow, 83

Sacred War, The, 162
Say, Why Was the Sky?, 68
Scarpe Rotte, 176
S'Dremlin Feygl, 102
Shlof, Mayn Kind, 70
Shtil, Di Nakht, 96
Si Me Quieres Escribir, 36
Skharkhoret, 120
Sleep, My Child, 70
So, One, Two, Three!, 62
So Long, Dear, 172
Song of Songs, 245
Song of the Bialystok Partisans, 158
Song of the International Brigades, 28
Song of the Partisans, The, 128
Song of the River Bug, 52
Song of the Vilna Ghetto, 93
Standing near the Old Oak Tree, 164

Still, the Night, 96
Street Singer of the Warsaw Ghetto, The, 74
Svyanshchennaya Voina, 162

Tattoo, 166
Thaelmann Column, The, 30
Theresienstadt, 182
Theresienstadt, die schönste Stadt der Welt, 184
Theresienstadt, the Best Town in the World, 184
Theresienstädter Fragen, 190
Theresienstadt Questions, 190
These Emigrants!, 210
This Have We, 148
Transport, 207
Treblinka, 80
Treblinke, 80
Tsi Darf Es Azoy Zayn?, 58
Tsigaynerlid, 65
Tsu Eyns, Tsvey, Dray!, 62

Und die Musik spielt dazu, 212
Under the Ruins of Poland, 88
Under the Yellow Patch, 258
Undzer Mut Iz Nit Gebrokhen, 111
United Front Song, The, 6
Unter Der Gelber Late, 258
Unter Di Khurves Fun Poyln, 88

Varshe, 76
Venga Jaleo, 39
Vilner Geto Lid, 93
Viva la Quince Brigada, 34
Vu Ahin Zol Ikh Geyn ?, 46

Warsaw, 76
Warszawo Ma, 156
Waterlooplein, 232
Waterloo Square, 232
We Are Here, 280
We Didn't Know, 277
We Live Forever, 114
Wenn ein Paketchen kommt, 146
We're Singing a Song, 140
Westerbork Serenade, The, 142
We Zingen Een Lied, 140
What Is the Meaning?, 125
When a Small Package Comes, 146
Where, O Where Shall I Go?, 46
Wir Singen Ein Schlager, 140
Women's Camp, 139
Worn-Out Shoes, 176

Yeder Ruft Mikh Ziamele, 100
Yet Soon for Us Will Come the Time, 216
Youth Hymn, 104
Yugnt-Himn, 104

Zog Nit Keynmol, 108
Żywe Kamiene, 136

Index of First Lines

English first lines are in roman type; all other languages are in italic.

After a battle with the elements now, 207
A gut morgn libe mentshn, 74
A law was passed in Nuremberg town, 23
Ami, entends tu, 128
A mol iz geven a mayse, 228
And it's Eichmann and Himmler, 261
Ani ma-amin, 116
An jedem Übel, wie bekannt, 210
Apple trees and pear trees, 160
Arise, arise, oh land of might, 162
Aroys iz in Vilne a nayer bafel, 90
Àsó, kapa vállamon, 168

Battered by woe, 152
Because a man is human, 6
Blow hard, you winds, 178
Butterfly, butterfly, living flow'r, 118
By lice we are bitten, 132
Byl Máj, 224

¡Como se fueron, 238

Dagene rinner, 148
Days have gone bye-bye, 148
Der yid vert geyogt un geplagt, 46
Di zelbe gasn, 59
Do you know the Novaks, 200

El diez y ocho día de julio, 39
Én még most kicsi vagyok, 230
Es hot undz di lebn gerufn, 62
Es iz geven a zumer tog, 93
Es loyfn un klapen di mashinen, 52
E sta matina, 173
Ev'rything is made of two sides, 184

Far and wide as the eye can wander, 3
Far vos iz der himl, 68
Finster di nakht, 65
For ev'ry evil it is known, 210
From our far-off fatherland we've come here, 28

Gehat hob ikh a heym, 44
Good morning, oh, my dear people, 74

Hallo, we zijn niet helemal in orde, 142
Hello, the situation seems to worsen, 142
Her new name was tattooed, 266
Hey, go 'round and 'round again, 120
Hey sekhor, sekhor vasof, 120
High on the yellow wagon, 216
Hoch auf dem gelben Wagen, 216
How many have passed away, 292
How they did perish, 238

I am still a little child, 230

I can't believe that it could be, 48
Ich glaub ich war noch nie ein Kind, 11
Ich hab' kein Heimatland, 13
Ich kenn ein kleines Städtchen, 194
Ich komm grad herein vom Land, 190
Ich liebe infernalisch, 212
If you want to write to me, 36
I have my gun upon my shoulder, 179
I have no native land, 13
I just arrived here from town, 190
I know a little city, 194
Ikh vil nit nemen gor in akht, 48
Ikh zits mir in kriuvke, 86
I know the whole neighborhood, 84
I'll tell you all a story, 228
I love it with a passion, 212
I missed out on childhood, it seems, 11
I'm sitting in my hideaway, 86
In a poylisher shtot, 80
In a time of cowardice, 275
In a village in Poland, 80
In di shmale geselekh fun geto, 71
In Madrid's outlying trenches, 26
In Nürnberg machten sie ein Gesetz, 23
In the Alps, 170
In the city of Warsaw, 256
In the narrow streets throughout the ghetto, 71
In Vilna was issued a brand-new decree, 90
I see a long train coming, 280
I tak kak vsye my liudi, 8
It happened on July the eighteenth, 39
It was a lovely summer day, 93

Jak ton cy okret, 152
Je connais tous le quartier, 204
Jedes Ding es ist zwei Zeiten, 184
Jeste my jak zywe kamiene, 136
Jews, you should be happy, 78

Kad u borbu, 178
Kak u duba starovo, 164

Lager, Lager, Frauenlager, 139
Lager, Lager, women's *Lager,* 139
Last train to Nuremberg, 270
Les All'mands étaient chez moi, 131
Liudi mira, 249
Loin dans l'infini s'étendent, 5
Long live the Fifteenth Brigade, 34
Los cuatro generales, 41

Má drahá poslal jsem vám list, 220
Mah ko mashma lon le camp, 125
Makh tsu du eygelekh, 54
Marie Theres, die Kaiserin, 182
Marie Theresa, empress fair, 182

Mayn mame hot gevolt zayn af mayn khasene, 50
Mein Vater war ein Polizeibeamter, 196
Mein Vater wird gesucht, 9
Me to doufeki mouston omo, 179
Mir lebn eybig, 114
M'khol Masada, 122
My father he was tracked, 9
My father was a hard-working policeman, 194
My grandpa was a scholar, 252
My mother wanted so to see my wedding day, 50
My name is Lisa Kalvelage, 272
My Warsaw dear, 156

Nach harten Kampfe mit den Elementen, 207
Ne dis jamais que tu prends ton dernier chemin, 110
Never say that you are on your final road, 108
Neyn, neyn, neyn, neyn, 106
Nit keyn rozhinkes un nit keyn mandlen, 56
No, no, no, no, 45
Now close your little eyes, 106
Nye skazhi chto ty idyosh' v poslyednyi put', 110

Off somewhere in hiding, 98
Oh friend, can you hear, 128
Oh, Masada, 122
Oh, my dear, I sent you a note, 220
Oh, once I had a home, 44
Oh, so beautiful, 245
Oh, the fog, 166
Oi, tumany moi, 166
On my shoulder, spade and hoe, 168
On the branches birds are dozing, 102
Our courage is unbroken, 111
Our song is full of sorrow, 104

Pardon, eh ich's vergesse, 187
Pardon, I must confess now, 187
Parpar, parpar, perakh khai, 118
People call me Ziamele, 100
People of the world, 249
Pitch-black the night, 65

Raisins, almonds we do not have any, 56
Rastsvetali yabloni I grushi, 160
Rivkele, di shabesdike, 83
Rivkele, the Sabbath widow, 83

Sage nimmermehr, du gehst den letzten Weg, 110
Say, why was the sky, 68
S'dremlin feygl oyf di tzveygn, 102
S'farshvindt di nakht, 76
Sharp barbed wire with death is laden, 18, 21
Shlof, mayn kind, 70
Shtil, di nakht iz oygeshternt, 96
Sie kennen die Novaks, 200
Si me quieres escribir, 36
Sleep, my child, 70
S'ligt ergets fartayert, 98
Spaniens Himmel breitet seine Sterne, 30
Spanish heavens spread their brilliant starlight, 30
Stacheldraht mit Tod geladen, 18, 21
Standing near the old oak tree, 164
Still, the night and decked with starlight, 98
Su in montagna, 170

Ten poslední, 222
The box cars they rattle as we ride them, 52
The four insurgent gen'rals, 41
The Jew, plagued and driven each day, 46
The life that we lived called to greet us, 62
The night lasts and lasts, 76
The rain falls down in Amsterdam, 282
The same old streets, 59
The war rages on, 158
There's a valley in Spain called Jarama, 32
This very morning, 173
Ti ore a pou, 245
Tous unis avec courage, 111
Tu es un ouvrier—oui!, 8
'Twas May, 224
'Twas the last one, 222

Under the ruins of Poland, 88
Under the yellow patch now, 258
Und weil der Mensch ein Mensch ist, 6
Undzer lid iz ful mit troyer, 104
Undzer mut vet nit gebrokhen, 111
Unter der gelbe late, 258
Unter di khurves fun Poyln, 88
Urla il vento, 176

Vifl zaynen shoyn nito, 292
Viva la Quince Brigada, 34
Voennye grozy, 158
Von Läusen zerfressen, 132
Vor Madrid im Schützengraben, 26
Vstavai, strana ogromnaya, 162

Warszawo ma, 156
Waterlooplein, waterlooplein, 232
Waterloo Square, Waterloo Square, 232
We are the living stone people, 136
"We didn't know, 227
We live forever, 114
Wenn der Tag erwacht, 16
Wenn ein Paketchen kommt, 146
We're here, our seeds are planted, 288
We're singing a pop song, 140
What's the meaning of the camp, 125
When a small package comes, 146
When the daylight breaks, 16
When the German army came, 131
When to battle, 178
Where the Vistula and Sola, 133
Wir, im fernen Vaterland geboren, 28
Wir sind die lebende sterne, 136
Wir singen ein Schlager, 140
Wohin auch das Auge blicket, 3

Y como ser humano, 8
Yeder ruft mikh Ziamele, 100
Yes, I do believe, 116
Yidn zol zayn freylekh, 78

Zog nit keynmol az du geyst dem letstn veg, 108
Zwischen Weichsel und der Sola, 133

Judaic Traditions in Literature, Music, and Art
Ken Frieden and Harold Bloom, eds.

Contemporary Jewish American Writers and the Multicultural Dilemma. The Return of the Exiled. Andrew Furman

The Dybbuk and the Yiddish Imagination: A Haunted Reader. Joachim Neugroschel, trans. & ed.

Enlarging America: The Cultural Work of Jewish Literary Scholars, 1930–1990. Susanne Klingenstein

Facing the Fires: Conversations with A.B. Yehoshua. Bernard Horn

The Holocaust in American Film. Second Edition. Judith E. Doneson

Hurban: Responses to Catastrophe in Hebrew Literature. Alan Mintz

The Image of the Shtetl and Other Studies of Modern Jewish Literary Imagination. Dan Miron

The Jewish Book of Fables. Eliezer Shtaynbarg; Curt Leviant, trans. & ed.

Jewish Instrumental Folk Music: The Collection and Writings of Moshe Beregovski. Mark Slobin, Robert A. Rothstein, and Michael Alpert, eds.

Jews in the American Academy, 1900-1940: The Dynamics of Intellectual Assimilation. Susanne Klingenstein

The Musical Tradition of the Eastern European Synagogue. Volume I: History and Definition. Sholom Kalib

The New Country: Stories from the Yiddish about Life in America. Henry Goodman, trans. & ed.

Nineteen to the Dozen: Monologues and Bits and Bobs of Other Things. Sholem Aleichem; Ted Gorelick, trans.; Ken Frieden, ed.

Old Jewish Folk Music: The Collections and Writings of Moshe Beregovski. Mark Slobin, trans. & ed.

Rock 'n' Roll Jews, Michael Billig

A Room of His Own: In Search of the Feminine in the Novels of Saul Bellow. Gloria Cronin

Songs from Bialik: Selected Poems of Hayim Mahman Bialik. Atar Hadari, trans.

The Stories of David Bergelson: Yiddish Short Fiction from Russia. Gold Werman, trans. & ed.

Translating Israel: Contemporary Hebrew Literature and Its Reception in America. Alan L. Mintz

A Traveler Disguised: The Rise of Modern Yiddish Fiction in the Nineteenth Century. Dan Miron

Vagabond Stars: A World of Yiddish Theater. Nahma Sandrow

www.ingramcontent.com/pod-product-compliance
Lightning Source LLC
Chambersburg PA
CBHW040750020526
44116CB00037B/2981